Microservices from Day One

Build robust and scalable software from the start

Cloves Carneiro Jr.

Tim Schmelmer

Apress®

Microservices from Day One: Build robust and scalable software from the start

Cloves Carneiro Jr.
Hollywood, Florida, USA

Tim Schmelmer
Broomfield, Colorado, USA

ISBN-13 (pbk): 978-1-4842-1936-2
DOI 10.1007/978-1-4842-1937-9

ISBN-13 (electronic): 978-1-4842-1937-9

Library of Congress Control Number: 2016961230

Managing Director: Welmoed Spahr
Acquisitions Editor: Louise Corrigan
Development Editor: Chris Nelson
Technical Reviewer: Tom Copeland
Editorial Board: Steve Anglin, Pramila Balan, Laura Berendson, Aaron Black, Louise Corrigan,
    Jonathan Gennick, Todd Green, Robert Hutchinson, Celestin Suresh John, Nikhil Karkal,
    James Markham, Susan McDermott, Matthew Moodie, Natalie Pao, Gwenan Spearing
Coordinating Editor: Nancy Chen
Copy Editor: James A. Compton
Compositor: SPi Global
Indexer: SPi Global
Artist: SPi Global, image courtesy of Freepik

Distributed to the book trade worldwide by Springer Science+Business Media New York, 233 Spring Street, 6th Floor, New York, NY 10013. Phone 1-800-SPRINGER, fax (201) 348-4505, e-mail orders-ny@springer-sbm.com, or visit www.springer.com. Apress Media, LLC is a California LLC and the sole member (owner) is Springer Science + Business Media Finance Inc (SSBM Finance Inc). SSBM Finance Inc is a **Delaware** corporation.

For information on translations, please e-mail rights@apress.com, or visit www.apress.com.

Apress and friends of ED books may be purchased in bulk for academic, corporate, or promotional use. eBook versions and licenses are also available for most titles. For more information, reference our Special Bulk Sales–eBook Licensing web page at www.apress.com/bulk-sales.

Any source code or other supplementary materials referenced by the author in this text are available to readers at www.apress.com. For detailed information about how to locate your book's source code, go to www.apress.com/source-code/. Readers can also access source code at SpringerLink in the Supplementary Material section for each chapter.

Printed on acid-free paper

To my wife Safora, for all her love, and for her support during the hundreds of hours that I spent on this book while she ran the family.

—Tim Schmelmer

For my family, Jane, Noah, and Sofia.

—Cloves Carneiro Jr.

Contents at a Glance

Contents

About the Authors

Cloves Carneiro Jr. is a senior software engineer with over 15 years of experience creating software for companies in many fields. In recent years, Cloves was first introduced to the idea of distributed services at Amazon.com, where he was exposed to services with challenging scalability requirements for the Kindle and AWS teams. In 2001, he joined the amazing Engineering team at LivingSocial, and has focused on building microservices as scalable pieces of software to help improve the reliability and availability of the systems at the company. In his free time, Cloves enjoys spending time with his family in sunny South Florida, and is an avid—yet slow—triathlete. Cloves has also previously written for Apress, authoring *Beginning Rails*, *Beginning Rails 3*, and *Beginning Rails 4*.

After abandoning his childhood dream of becoming a firefighter, **Tim Schmelmer** did the next best thing and became a software developer. He has spent the past 19.75 years extinguishing fires while working for technology consulting companies, telecommunications equipment manufacturers, building control systems for research telescopes, and selling things to people via a web browser and mobile apps. Tim found his love for building microservices systems while working at Amazon.com, and he has most recently been working on a team that does surprisingly little firefighting while building and maintaining LivingSocial.com's core services platform. When he is not hacking away on his keyboard, or trying to be a good husband, father of two girls, and tamer of an overly energetic puppy, Tim loves to run, bike, and hike in the mountains near beautiful Boulder, Colorado.

About the Technical Reviewer

Tom Copeland is a Rails developer at LivingSocial.com. He has programmed in Ruby since 2004, consulted at InfoEther on Ruby on Rails applications since 2007, and received a "Ruby Hero" award in 2008. Before focusing on Ruby, he wrote two books about Java programming (*PMD Applied* and *Generating Parsers with JavaCC*, both from Centennial Books) and was named Oracle's "Open Source Developer of the Year" in 2003.

Acknowledgments

Writing a book is never solely the accomplishment of the authors listed on its cover, and that is particularly true for the one you are holding in your hands right now. We would like to acknowledge that by expressing our gratitude to the people and companies that made this book possible.

First of all, we would like to thank the team at Apress Media LLC for helping us through this process. It all started with Ben Renow-Clark reaching out to us and planting the idea of writing another book in our heads. We are unsure how many times Nancy Chen, our coordinating editor, who did an amazing job getting all ducks in a row and chasing us for our content when chapter deadlines came approaching fast, must have cursed Ben for signing us on, though. We believe that the only person at Apress who might have had to show even more patience with us than Nancy must have been our development editor Chris Nelson, whom we owe many thanks for countless corrections, suggestions, requests for clarifications, and for pretending not to mind that neither of the authors is a native speaker of the English language.

If you find that reading this book has some positive bearing on your job in the field of software, then chances are that our technical reviewer Tom Copeland is largely responsible for that. Other than being a Ruby Hero (https://rubyheroes.com/heroes/2008), book author (https://pragprog.com/book/cbdepra/deploying-rails), as well as generally an exceptional engineer with oodles of experience, Tom gave invaluable feedback and practical tips on how to improve this book so that it matters for practitioners.

Thank you also to Toby Clemson at ThoughtWorks for letting us use some of his excellent diagrams illustrating testing strategies in a microservices environment. His excellent article on this topic, published on Martin Fowler's site, was the inspiration for much of the content in Chapter 9.

Cloves and Tim share very formative years of work experience at two corporations that have implemented microservices architectures: Amazon.com and LivingSocial. Both of us consider Amazon.com to be simultaneously the maverick and the gold standard for the architectural style that is now most commonly referred to as microservices. We had the privilege of working with some of the most talented engineers in the world in an environment that formed our understanding of how massively distributed services can be tamed and how they can provide value. If nothing else, then the rules of engagement we formulate in Chapter 2 are a direct result of our time at the world's number one e-commerce store. We consider ourselves very fortunate to have had the opportunity to contribute to Amazon's internal tech community.

Although both of us overlapped briefly during our time as Amazonians, the first time we met in person was when we both started at LivingSocial in late 2011. We have since worked together for the best part of five years, helping in LivingSocial's move from a monolithic Ruby on Rails application to a microservices setup, breaking some world records on the way (http://www.guinnessworldrecords.com/world-records/most-online-vouchers-sold-in-24-hours). Not only have we learned many lessons during this—sometimes painful—transition, but we also have LivingSocial to thank for being supportive by allowing us to describe some of their systems in this book. Also, we would never have met the amazing Tom Copeland if it had not been for our time on the LivingSocial engineering team.

Another very gracious contribution to this book was LivingSocial's sponsorship of Cloves' and Tim's attendance at AbrilPro Ruby (http://tropicalrb.com/2014/en/) and Rocky Mountain Ruby (http://rockymtnruby2014.busyconf.com/schedule) in 2014. The materials for, and feedback from, the workshops we held at both conferences laid the foundation for the ideas mentioned in this book. We will never possess the stamina, grit, and organizational talent it takes to arrange internationally renowned software development conferences, so we tip our heads to the organizers of such events.

Last but not least, both Cloves and Tim are family men with multiple children below the age of ten. We cannot imagine how any book project would ever see the light of day without the unwavering support of the authors' families. Tim would like to thank Safora, his wife and friend of more than 10 years, for keeping the ship that is their family afloat while he was often physically, and even more often mentally, unavailable and preoccupied with finishing this book. Cloves would also like to thank his family, Jane, Noah and Sofia, who were always present and understanding of the effort required to write another book.

Introduction

As you have surely deduced from its title, *Microservices from Day One* touches on many aspects of adopting microservices as the underlying principle of structuring your application.

Your choice to read a book on microservices may have any of several different motivations. If you have heard the buzzwords and general hype surrounding the budding trend in the industry to move toward this architectural style, and now you want to find out more about what really hides behind the curtains, then this book is certainly for you.

If you are working on a team where the decision has already been made, or if you are exploring the option, to decompose your application in a fine-grained manner with many small, interdependent services to help with ease of scaling and maintainability, and you are looking for practical advice and best practices for how to get started, then this book will also deliver what you need. It is meant to serve as a guide for developers who have a desire to build robust and scalable online applications in smaller, more focused and manageable chunks, but do not know how to get started.

As the book's title also indicates, you will get most the leverage out of this publication if you are in a situation where you are at liberty to design your business around microservices from the beginning. *Microservices from Day One* explains what microservices architecture are about, their advantages, how to avoid stumbling blocks along the way of implementing them, and the reasons why developers should think about using them when starting a new project.

It is complex, expensive, and at times frustrating to move a large, monolithic system to a microservices-oriented approach when the monolith has reached a sizable code base and traffic load, or has become business-critical in its mission. We know this to be true from multiple years of professional experience dealing with such a metamorphosis. It is not unusual that companies have to declare technological bankruptcy on their existing monolith, and then engage in re-architecture projects that involve 95% of their software development teams simply to break such large systems apart into applications of more manageable size. One of the main arguments of this book is that employing microservices from an early stage of development not only helps you avoid such a scenario, but is also feasible, convenient, and cost-effective if you follow the advice and recipes laid out herein.

But even though this book does not specifically focus on questions of transitioning from a monolith to microservices, a reader who is faced with exactly that predicament might still find a large number of the concepts described in this book helpful and relevant.

Another property of this book is its emphasis on practicality. While some parts certainly explain concepts in theory, priority is placed on showing these concepts in practice. This means that we will discuss sample code in the book, most of which is written in the Ruby programming language. This sample code is largely taken from an accompanying set of service and front-end applications that we developed while writing this book, simply to illustrate and put into practice most the theory discussed herein. These services together make up an imaginary bookstore business "_Books.com_".

From a content perspective, the book's 14 chapters are organized into 4 parts.

The first part discusses the basics of microservices architectures. Chapter 1 tries to answer the question of what microservices are, doing so by digging into the history of this style of building applications and looking at how they are implemented at companies that should count as early adopters. By Chapter 2, we are becoming much more opinionated when we are laying out a set of six fundamental rules that we see as necessary properties for any successful architecture based on microservices.

Part II describes how microservices adoption will allow you to view your business as a set of APIs.

Chapter 3 helps with the task of decomposing a problem domain into very basic services and also provides patterns for reaggregating information from these core microservices into secondary, more special-purpose services and applications. We show this using the practical example of our bookstore example, developing decomposition and aggregation patterns as we go.

Chapter 4 starts discussing the APIs as the interfaces exposed by the services in your business, with a special focus on explaining what all the properties are that together make up a high-quality design of your APIs. Here again we go into detail by show an example API from our bookstore application, and how it was designed.

Chapter 5 is a deep dive into how to use automated tools and IDLs to define, generate, explore and consume the APIs you build inside your business. We will again place high importance on showing real-life examples of how this can be done, using the fictional bookstore we designed for this book.

The main topics addressed in Chapter 6 are practical tips surrounding the dos and don'ts for designing and building client libraries for the services in a microservices environment. We list the concerns we believe need to be part of any decent client-side code that accesses any of your service resources.

After the API basics that were discussed in Chapter 4 through 6, we close out Part II by presenting an in-depth exploration of API optimization strategies in Chapter 7. In this context, optimization should not be understood as restricted to performance aspects, but also taking into account client convenience, maintainability, extensibility and immediacy of change notification.

In Part III the focus is on the particularities of setting up development environments and deployment processes in a microservices infrastructure. In Chapter 8 we define a wish list of 12 items to be successful in a microservices environment, and we show which tools can be used to check off every one of them. Chapter 9 identifies and explains five separate layers at which testing can and should be done to make sure your microservices architecture is sound, and we show concrete examples and code for automated test scenarios that exercise one of the services for our fictitious bookstore business. Chapter 10 is dedicated to all aspects of automated delivery, deployment, and releasing of microservice units, and we show practical examples of tools and strategies to achieve continuous integration and delivery in a safe and reversible manner. Along the way, we define seven tenets for deployment and all the currently available options for assigning computing resources to the various services in your infrastructure.

The fourth and final part of this book serves as a potpourri of practical techniques for making it easier to run microservices in production. Chapter 11 discusses the benefits and potential stumbling stones of adopting a heterogeneous technology stack using a hands-on scenario, and then Chapter 12 describes in detail one of the consumer-facing applications in our bookstore example. In Chapter 13 we move on to describe which parts of your microservices architecture deserve monitoring and alarming treatment, explaining some of the available tools. The book concludes with Chapter 14 on how to breed excellence in operational support in a self-learning organization that is structured around ownership of microservices.

Our aim was to have this book's topics be relevant, its structure conducive to your learning, its pace and scope appropriate, and—most of all—its focus on practical examples immediately useful to your career and business.

Last but not least, we hope that you enjoy reading the book as much as we loved writing it, which means that you will have a blast!

PART I

Service Oriented Architectures

CHAPTER 1

Microservices: The What and the Why

This first part of the book discusses what we mean when we talk about service-oriented architectures in general, and microservices in particular. We will spend some time explaining the benefits, as well as touching on potential pitfalls to be avoided, involved in adopting this architectural style.

In this chapter, we begin by showing the relevance of taking the microservices approach. After defining some general terms like *service*, *service-oriented architecture*, and *microservices*, we list examples of companies that successfully use them in the wild, and we discuss some of the reasons why these companies have adopted this architectural pattern. Next, we will look at some of the stumbling blocks that you encounter when utilizing microservices. We conclude the chapter by discussing the advantages of starting out with a service orientation compared to beginning with a single, monolithic application.

All Successful Software Undergoes Change

If your goal is to have a software application that is successful, there will be a point in the life of your application where it will have to undergo change.

Taking just web applications as an example, one change that comes to mind is that you might need to add an interface for administrators of your application data. What if you decide to add a mobile version of your site (or native mobile apps) after its initial launch? What will you do when you need to add more business intelligence into the mix and run regular business (or even continuous, real-time) metrics reports? What about the point in time when your customers request public API access to your application?

In short, it's not a question of *if* you will need to invest in changing your application, but *when* to make the change and how expensive it will be. Investing in building your application to be based on microservices from the beginning is your best chance at making changes expedient, safe, and inexpensive.

Remember Service-Oriented Architectures?

In order to understand what microservices are all about, it seems necessary to discuss how they relate to their older cousin: an architectural style commonly referred to as *service-oriented architecture (SOA)*.

© Cloves Carneiro Jr. and Tim Schmelmer 2016
C. Carneiro Jr. and T. Schmelmer, *Microservices From Day One*, DOI 10.1007/978-1-4842-1937-9_1

Although SOAs were all the rage in the early 2000s, there are a lot of often -conflicting ideas out there around what an SOA is really all about. Martin Fowler raises this point in a 2005 blog post,[1] and his attempt to classify the prevailing opinions can be summarized this way:

- An SOA is designed to expose software through web services, usually involving a common backbone—usually using HTTP—for an organization's applications to work with.

- It is meant to make the monolithic applications disappear, and to replace them with a set of core services that expose business functionality and data. Data and logic provided by the core services will be aggregated in separate user interfaces.

- For many, an SOA necessarily involves an asynchronous message bus technology, which communicates business events via "documents" (sometimes called *messages*) between the systems involved.

For the purpose of this book, let's define SOA as an architectural principle in which there is a bias to build systems through separately implemented, deployed, evolving, and maintained services.

In a set-up like that, any client-facing "front-end" applications then solely rely on a set of (back-end) services which expose the functionalities that the front-end applications consume in order to do their jobs.

What Is a Service?

To us, the definition of a software service is very close to the *Oxford American Dictionary* (nontechnical) definition of any service, in that it is "*a system supplying a public need.*"

Software services should serve the needs of one or more internal *or* external client applications. The interface of such services should therefore be designed from a client perspective, optimizing for maximum usefulness for its API consumer(s).

While ideally every service is different as it optimizes for its clients' use cases, it can generally be said that a service consists of a piece of *functionality* and its associated *set of data*.

If the service is also the authoritative and definitive source for the current state of the data it holds and vends, then we call such a service a *system of record*. An examples of services where this system-of-record test does not pass could be a service that aggregates data and functionality from other services, which in turn could themselves be the systems of record for this data (for example, in an attempt to improve the usability or performance of the entire system).

What Are Microservices?

It is hard to determine exactly who first used the term *microservice* and when. While it seems most likely that although the term first appeared on the scene around 2011, some companies adopted this style much earlier.

One example is Amazon, which broke apart its previously monolithic Obidos application into many smaller services. In a 2006 interview with Microsoft Fellow Jim Gray for *ACM Queue,*[2] Amazon CTO Werner Vogels describes as a general "service orientation" what comes very close to our definition of microservices:

> "*For us service orientation means encapsulating the data with the business logic that operates on the data, with the only access through a published service interface. No direct database access is allowed from outside the service, and there's no data sharing among the services.*"

---

[1]Martin Fowler, "ServiceOrientedAmbiguity," July 1, 2005. http://martinfowler.com/bliki/ServiceOrientedAmbiguity.html

[2]Werner Vogels, "A Conversation with Werner Vogels: Learning from the Amazon technology platform," interview by Jim Gray. *ACM Queue*, Volume 4, Issue 4. June 30, 2006. https://queue.acm.org/detail.cfm?id=1142065.

Former eBay and Google executive Randy Shoup summarizes[3] microservice characteristics as having three main features:

- They have a very focused scope that concentrates on a very few functionalities (at times a single one), expressed by a small and also well-defined API.

- They are all very modular, and independently deployable, essentially elevating the rules of software encapsulation and modularity from the program to the deployment unit level.

- Finally, microservices have isolated persistence, meaning that they do not share persistent storage, such as a common database.

Given the similarities to the earlier description of an SOA, how are microservices really different? Is the term just a more modern, trendier name for the same service-oriented architecture?

The main difference we have found is that microservices have the common trait of decomposing a large application into a set of small, focused, versioned, and loosely-coupled services, which are very inexpensive to spin up and maintain.

An excellent definition of microservices is that of Fowler and Lewis,[4] as an architectural style that

> "... is an approach to developing a single application as a suite of small services, each running in its own process and communicating with lightweight mechanisms, often an HTTP resource API. These services are built around business capabilities and independently deployable by fully automated deployment machinery. There is a bare minimum of centralized management of these services, which may be written in different programming languages and use different data storage technologies."

This approach is a significant departure from old-school SOA implementations, which ended up being much more accurately described as a set of medium-size to large monolithic applications, stitched together via expensive, and often complex, enterprise service bus (ESB) solutions. This often led to much more tightly coupled systems, where many of the interapplication contracts were not explicit, but rather implicit and hidden inside the ESB "glue layer."

By contrast, microservice architectures tend to work with very explicitly published, small and rather simple contracts between the single service applications. Most successful microservice implementations apply Postel's Law of being "conservative in what you do, be liberal in what you accept from others" to all services that make up the entire system.

Microservices Are *Not* "CORBA over HTTP"

Another difference between traditional SOAs and microservice architectures is that the latter approach seems to have thus far avoided the pitfalls of advocating distributed objects.

The idea of distributed objects, which was very popular during the time when SOAs were first developed, is to try to hide the difference between objects that live in the *same process* as the client code, or remotely in a *different* process—whether that is running on the same CPU or on an altogether separate machine. Technologies such as CORBA or Microsoft's DCOM would go to great lengths to hide these differences.

---

[3]Randy Shoup, "From the Monolith to Microservices: Lessons from Google and eBay", April 24th, 2015, Craft Con 2015, http://www.ustream.tv/recorded/61479577
[4]Martin Fowler and James Lewis, "Microservices: a definition of this new architectural term." March 25, 2014. http://martinfowler.com/articles/microservices.html.

The problem with distributed objects is that they are based on a fallacy that invalidates the entire approach: the boundary between in-process and out-of-process may be hidden to the developer, but it still always exists. The implications of a remote call simply cannot be removed. Out-of-process calls are *always* slower than in-process calls, and their likelihood and ways of failing need to be addressed by a distributed system's architecture.

Well-designed microservice contracts tend to reflect this fact by not pretending to be "Remote Method Invocation over HTTP." Whereas CORBA and similar RMI technologies tried hard to enable client applications to allow for very fine-grained calls, RESTful microservice APIs often favor coarse-grained, or even batch, endpoints to reduce the impact of the unavoidable latency introduced by out-of-process and HTTP calls, or the transfer of documents via lightweight ESBs.

Industry Adoption of Microservices

While more and more companies are starting to migrate their monolith application infrastructure to a set of smaller, more manageable services, or are continuing to do so, some prominent earlier adopters stick out.

Most likely the earliest large-scale adoption of what would now be called a microservices architecture was started at Amazon.com during the very early part of the third millennium.

In the 2006 interview cited earlier, Amazon's CTO Werner Vogels explains their evolution from a monolithic web application called *Obidos* to a large-scale service-oriented architecture. Obidos, which held "all the business logic, all the display logic, and all the functionality" for Amazon's web shop, had undergone years of extensions and performance tuning, until Amazon came to the conclusion in 2001 that its monolith-based architecture would simply not scale anymore. The same held true not just for their actual web application, but also for their efforts to optimize and scale their backing database resources.

To quote Vogels,

> *"the parts that needed to scale independently were tied into sharing resources with other unknown code paths. There was no isolation and, as a result, no clear ownership."*

Vogels goes on to disclose more details about the way and scale at which services are implemented at Amazon, mentioning that when a consumer hits Amazon.com, more than a hundred services contribute data to the page rendered.

It is also worth mentioning that Amazon.com does not necessarily expose the same APIs to its external customers as it exposes internally. While most internal services are streamlined to conform to an optimized version of WSDL (called Amazon Service Definition Language, or *ASDL*), externally exposed Amazon web services usually offer both RESTful, as well as WSDL-based, APIs in order to maximize customer convenience.

Amazon's process for developing and launching new features relies heavily on the use of small, isolated services. Amazon has built an infrastructure in which services are so commoditized that they can be easily spun up, soft-launched, measured, and iterated upon, until the problem domain and the new feature's business impact are well understood.

Another key component of Amazon's service-oriented architecture is the company's approach to operational support. Vogels describes this as: "you build it, you run it," in stark contrast to a more traditional approach that erects organizational walls between software development and technical operations departments. This not only exposes developers to the operational aspects of their product, it also incentivizes them to build robust systems.

According to Randy Shoup, former employee of both Google and eBay, both companies have also shifted significantly toward using microservices in the past years. In his talk at the 2015 CRAFT Conference cited earlier, Randy describes in great detail how quite a few large companies have migrated in three to five steps from a monolithic architecture to a current state that encompasses hundreds to sometimes thousands of microservices. The interplay between these services is not organized in a strict tier-based hierarchy. It is rather best represented in the shape of an ad-hoc direct graph, where the edges of communication evolve over time, based on the entire system's changing requirements and use cases.

Randy observes that in this graph, companies like Google, eBay, Twitter, Amazon and others who have been successful in adopting microservices have concentrated on standardizing the "edges, rather than the nodes" of their directed services graph. They unified communication (like network protocols, data formats, and specifying APIs in a unified way) and infrastructure support (for source control, configuration management, and monitoring and altering), rather than any particular programming language, application framework, or persistence mechanism. While it is essential that these communication and infrastructure choices are internally supported by excellent, automated tooling, there is usually no top-down mandate to use a particular tool chain. The result of what is actually in use is more like the outcome of a healthy competition for the most useful and expedient results.

According to Randy, another essential part of a microservices architecture is that it has no up-front master plan or architecture it aims to implement. In his experience, the architecture is constantly in flux and evolves over time, adapting to the pressures of usefulness: if a service no longer proves to be useful to any client, it is retired due to lack of use.

Similar to Vogels' points earlier, Shoup mentions that Google and eBay also place great importance on service ownership from cradle to grave. While teams there generally have a high degree of autonomy over their technology choices, they also carry responsibility for the functionality, quality, performance, reliability, and maintainability of what they produce. Their work on a service is not done until the service is unused and fully retired.

An interesting difference he brings up between Google and eBay compared to Amazon is that the former two tech juggernauts appear to have something like an internal marketplace for services, where clients are charged (mostly in a fictional, internal currency) for their usage of other teams' service resources. This often serves as an incentive to be more mindful of potential performance issues that a client's usage can cause, leading to greater cross-company efficiency.

Another well-known company to bet on microservices early is Netflix. Adrian Cockcroft, in his London QCon talk,[5] offers many insights into Netflix' migration to microservices in the public cloud. Netflix is one of Amazon Web Services' largest customers, and much of the tooling they developed in-house has been open-sourced under the moniker of NetflixOSS.

Much as Shoup reports from eBay and Google, Cockcroft describes that a service at Netflix is not done once the code is ready and deployed, but rather when the service is finished being useful, and hence can be retired.

He also delivers other valuable organizational insights about the Netflix internal structure. For example, he explains that at Netflix, decisions are made first about what a particular service architecture should look like, and only then are team structures built out to best match an ownership structure around this architectural layout.

Cockcroft calls this approach the "Inverse of Conway's Law." He adds that much of why the resulting teams work at a very high level of efficiency and creativity stems from the "high trust, low process" environment in which developers can operate. Efficiency there is greatly helped by the fact that all hardware is commoditized to such a degree that Netflix owns no data centers but relies entirely on cloud offerings of Amazon and (more recently) Google. This even holds true for its development-stage environments, so that developers will never have to run more service applications than the one they are currently working on modifying.

---

[5]Adrian Cockcroft, "Migrating to Microservices," QCon London. March 6, 2014. www.infoq.com/presentations/migration-cloud-native.

The trust invested in developers also comes with a price: much like Amazon, Netflix lets its software engineers "run what they wrote." Every developer has production service root-level access privileges, but they also all participate in operational support and carry pagers for being on call, in case any operational issues arise.

Cockcroft's talk also addresses some practical design choices that appear to have crystallized over the course of Netflix' experience with implementing a microservices architecture. There appears to be no actual limit imposed on the number of services they run. They instead use rule-of-thumb guidelines to decide when to spin up a new service. One such guideline is that more mature code should be kept separate from innovative or unproven features.

Another rule about service granularity appears to be that each "verb" (functionality) should be factored into a separate service. Cockcroft quotes the example of a service whose sole purpose it is to use a given customer ID and movie ID as inputs to return a list of other movie IDs that should be recommended to the customer based on these inputs.

The Netflix approach to service versioning is to run several instances of the same service simultaneously, but with distinct versions. Instances of older versions will only be shut down once all clients have been convinced that they need to migrate off such an existing, older version.

Other defaults chosen at Netflix are to make service interactions non-blocking, using an Observable Set / Reactive model for communications. Netflix even open-sources its internal tool for this purpose, called RxJava (`https://github.com/ReactiveX/RxJava`). Use of a message bus at Netflix seems to be restricted to "fire-and-forget" messaging, where no response is needed for the sending client. Cockcroft cites the example of a "delete this from all caches" message that one service can send on a reliable message bus topic, for other applications to consume and act on appropriately.

Regarding decisions about data storage implications of the CAP theorem, the guidelines at Netflix appear to favor "available when partitioned" over consistency, unless having data availability downtime has explicitly been mentioned as an acceptable trade-off in a service's nonfunctional requirements.

In a May 2015 blog post,[6] Martin Fowler coined the term *microservices premium* to describe the measures that an organization needs to take to address the added complexity introduced by distributing functionality across multiple services.

Netflix has certainly paid this premium by building, and additionally open-sourcing, many of its internal tools for automating and simplifying the additional overhead incurred by employing a large service-oriented architecture. Netflix uses Karyon as a basis for all services to be developed, and Zuul as an edge service component that fronts all of its applications. Edda serves as a change-tracking tool for Netflix' AWS server configurations, and Eureka is a load-balancing AWS service registry. To further enable reliability and resilience, Netflix also developed Hystrix, a Java library to help placing circuit breakers[7] around a service's points of remote system access. For a full list of Netflix' open-source tools, see `https://netflix.github.io/`.

The engineering team at SoundCloud (`https://soundcloud.com/`) made a similar move from a monolithic Ruby on Rails application to microservices written in Clojure, Scala, and Ruby. Phil Calçado, formerly director of engineering for SoundCloud's core team, described their experiences in another August 2015 QCon talk.[8]

The first feature that was pulled out of the monolith was search, but even at this very early stage they started wondering whether they were ready for the paradigm shift to microservices, which he calls a "microservices explosion," where a huge amount of new services were added within a matter of weeks.

One way they prepared was to hone their provisioning process. SoundCloud runs its own data-centers, but started mimicking the structure of Heroku (`https://www.heroku.com/`), using the same toolchain that Heroku is built on. As a result of running on a physical data center, SoundCloud encountered issues resulting from the nonoptimal resource sharing of co-hosted applications, paired with "naive scheduling."

---

[6]Martin Fowler, "Microservice Premium." May 13, 2015. `http://martinfowler.com/bliki/MicroservicePremium.html`.
[7]Martin Fowler, "CircuitBreaker" March 6, 2014 . `http://martinfowler.com/bliki/CircuitBreaker.html`.
[8]Phil Calçado, "No Free Lunch, Indeed: Three Years of Microservices at SoundCloud," QCon. August 2015. `www.infoq.com/presentations/soundcloud-microservices`.

Other choices they made during the migration to an SOA were to move applications written in Ruby, Node.js, and Go over to JVM-based languages like Clojure, Scala, and JRuby.

SoundCloud started employing Tumblr's Collins tool (`https://tumblr.github.io/collins/`) for automating their rapid provisioning process, packaging all their microservices into Docker (`https://www.docker.com/`) containers.

SoundCloud's telemetry approach was also home-built, and resulted in a tool called Prometheus (`http://prometheus.io/`), which had integrated alarm facilities via PagerDuty (`https://www.pagerduty.com/`). For operational support, SoundCloud made sure that all applications have uniformity of administration endpoint URL schemes, so that on-call engineers have an easy time determining, or modifying, application status.

SoundCloud also made sure to integrate request tracing into their API infrastructure, so that the complete graph of service dependencies can be determined and visualized more easily.

To automate deployment, SoundCloud adopted a continuous integration approach, combined with continuous deployment directly to Docker containers that are pushed to production servers in SoundCloud's data centers. SoundCloud's main challenge was to iteratively adopt an SOA and its necessary preconditions.

Why Use Microservices?

The list of reasons for employing microservices is long, and before summarizing the main advantages from our own viewpoint, we will first summarize the reasons each of the companies and consultants mentioned earlier have given.

Advantages as Seen by Industry Experts

Martin Fowler's "Microservice Trade-Offs" article[9] distils his view of the advantages down to three points:

- *Strong Module Boundaries*: In his view, designing and implementing any piece of software can benefit from applying a modular structure. Divvying up your business' IT architecture into microservices reinforces such modular structures, which become increasingly important as a company's development team grows. Organizations can form tight-knit teams around the ownership structure of a set of small services, which leads to clearer interfaces with stronger boundaries, not just between the teams, but as a consequence also between the software (sub) systems these teams are building. Decoupling subsystems in a monolith is of course also possible, but it is rarely done, and even less often upheld for any length of time, because it is all too easy to violate such module boundaries in a monolith. In Fowler's words, violating subsystems boundaries "… can be a useful tactical shortcut to getting features built quickly, but done widely they undermine the modular structure and trash the team's productivity. Putting the modules into separate services makes the boundaries firmer, making it much harder to find these cancerous workarounds." Another advantageous side effect of erecting service-based boundaries is that, if done right, the data storage and access should also be decentralized and become entirely opaque. All access to data will be at the "service model" layer, where the actual persistence structure is hidden behind the services' exposed APIs.

---

[9]Martin Fowler, "Microservice Trade-Offs," July 1, 2015. `http://martinfowler.com/articles/microservice-trade-offs.html`.

- *Independent Deployment*: Fowler praises the benefits of a Continuous Delivery approach to software development.[10] Where releasing software used to be a "once a quarter," or—at best—a monthly event, many teams using microservices have trimmed down their release cycles to happen several times per day. The main competitive advantage that results from the ability to deploy at a high frequency comes from the increased speed of responding to the market, or offering a new feature faster than your competitors. Deploying large monoliths makes such a deployment frequency very hard to maintain, as any botched change to such large code bases can mean that the entire deployment will fail. If, on the other hand, microservices are designed to be autonomous, and hence independently deployable, components, then the risk of a complete system failure due to a deployment of any of its (mircroservice-encapsulated) parts is greatly reduced.

- *Technology diversity*: In Fowler's view, the main advantages of this point are not only the more obvious greater ease to "choose an appropriate tool for the job": it is evident that, in a microservices environment, you can more easily introduce, and experiment with, more diversity in programming languages, frameworks, and data stores. Another often overlooked advantage is the ability to take a more fine-grained, less all-or-nothing approach to upgrading libraries and other common dependencies. As Fowler puts it: "Dealing with library versioning issues is one of those problems that gets exponentially harder as the code base gets bigger."

Werner Vogels' arguments for why Amazon switched to what today would be called a microservices architecture are as follows:

- Developers have a deeper feeling of software ownership and control, which leads to more innovation and focus on system stability and performance than was possible when all code lived in a single monolith.

- A fine-grained, service-oriented architecture gives Amazon a "level of isolation" between each of its pieces of software that allows the company to build its components independently, and hence more quickly than before.

- New ideas can more easily be implemented, launched, tried out, and potentially discarded, both at a developer level and in operational support.

- While the number and (lack of) structure of microservices employed at Amazon may appear chaotic when viewed from close up, they make sense at a larger scale. They are simply an acknowledgement of the fact that large-scale distributed systems possess "many organic and emerging," and hence nondeterministic, properties. These nondeterministic properties are not seen as problematic at Amazon, but rather as a fact of life that helps their innovation cycles.

- Amazon now considers it a competitive and strategic advantage to be able to build large, complex applications via composition of "primitive" services. Vogels claims that Amazon can scale its "operation independently, maintain unparalleled system availability, and introduce new services quickly without the need for massive reconfiguration."

---

[10]Martin Fowler, "Continuous Delivery," May 31, 2013. http://martinfowler.com/bliki/ContinuousDelivery.html.

- Using a microservices architecture also provides organizational advantages. Teams at Amazon are created to form around a set of services they build and own cradle to grave, making the owners "completely responsible for the service—from scoping out the functionality, to architecting it, to building it, and operating it." Amazon employs a "you build it, you run it" approach to software development, exposing developers to the needs of production support for all the software they launch, as well as to the customers (be they internal to Amazon or external) that rely on the functionalities provided by the respective service. The resulting customer feedback loop is a key element for improving the service's "quality of the service."

Randy Shoup quotes many points that he sees as disadvantages of running a business on top of a monolith:

- As a company's software development team grows, coordination of the developers becomes increasingly challenging. Developers will start to step onto each other's feet, and become much less productive as build-times grow with the size of the application.

- While it's not impossible, it is much harder to enforce well-modularized software design in a monolith, where all code eventually has direct access to all resources without having to pass through a layer of abstraction. On the other hand, dividing a system into separate services with well-defined interfaces and resources that are owned exclusively by such services is a very potent facilitator for enforcing modularity.

- Monoliths leave very little room for adaptable scaling strategies. If all code lives in a single, large application, then the only way to add performance is via vertically scaling the resources providing the application. While it is again possible, breaking up a single, underlying data store into well-modularized units takes much more discipline in a monolithic system. The database easily becomes a point of strong coupling between the various parts of the application, and tuning a database for all the different use cases quickly becomes impossible.

- Having a single unit of deployment for your system makes every change, however minute, carry an enormous risk for your business, as the entire application can stop functioning because of a single botched code change. Additionally, times for deploying, and potentially reverting, code to the production environment have the potential to grow to a point where they become a burden and productivity impediment for the entire business.

- Shoup similarly and inversely lists the advantages of adopting microservices as follows:

- Each single service making up the application is a much smaller piece of the entire system to understand, and to reason about.

- Services become independently deployable, thereby reducing risk and speed of deployments. Additionally, each of the services becomes testable in isolation.

- Scaling services individually allows for more options to choose from when the need to performance-tune the application arises.

- Large-scale organizations like Google and Amazon, which are trying very hard to optimize for development velocity, have many projects moving in parallel, with little to no coordination overhead. Organizing their teams and business capabilities around small services enables this desire to move faster than many of their competitors of a similar scale.

Adrian Cockcroft has three main arguments for microservices:

- The removal of much friction from product development cycles increases the speed of the business as a whole.

- As a staunch proponent of cloud-based microservices architectures, Cockcroft points out that adding horizontal scaling resources can be completed extremely quickly; when done right, scaling up in the cloud can be done within a matter of minutes.

- Speed and availability of the overall system are improved, while at the same time cost, size, and risk of software development to the business are reduced. One enabler is the much shortened feedback loop for code that is deployed via small, isolated services, which means the overall rate of change to the system can be increased relatively safely. As Cockcroft puts it, the "Observe, Orient, Develop, Act" loop is shortened.

According to Phil Calçado's blog-post about SoundCloud's move to microservices, its motivation "had to do much more with productivity than pure technical matters."

While implementing the "Next SoundCloud" project on top of an existing Ruby on Rails monolith (lovingly dubbed "the mothership"), they found themselves mostly in scaling issues in which their team processes posed the largest bottleneck to their velocity. Changes to their monolithic code base were so risky, and had caused so many large-scale outages, that they introduced a process of mandatory, intensive code reviews for pull requests. Reviewing such changes took an expert in the existing code base often several hours of their time. In Calçado's words: "Larger changes required a lot of time to be reviewed and, due to the spaghetti nature of our Rails code, were very risky. People avoided these big Pull Requests like the plague."

And even after such intensive reviews, there remained a significant risk of causing unforeseen negative side effects. To quote Calçado again: "Turns out that the monolithic code base we had was so massive and so broad no one knew all of it. People had developed their own areas of expertise and custodianship around submodules of the application."

SoundCloud found that their switch to smaller, independent deployment units, organized as services with specific focus on a small set of functionalities, helped them overcome their process scaling issues, as well. They built teams with true system ownership around these smaller services: "These teams were explicitly told that they had full ownership over the modules they owned. This meant that they would be on call for any outages related to those, but would also have the freedom to evolve these in any shape they thought reasonable. If they decided to keep something in the monolith, it would be their call. They were the ones maintaining that code anyway."

Our Reasons to Adopt a Microservices Architecture

Our personal experiences with the advantages of microservices are very close to what many of the experts we've seen cite as reasons to employ them.

When done right, services have much smaller code bases than monolithic applications. They are therefore easier to maintain, as they are easier to read, reason about, and to independently maintain, upgrade, and evolve.

Using services can be compared to employing the "single responsibility principle" of object-oriented design on an application design level. Services implement a self-contained, well-defined and documented set of functionalities, which they expose only via versioned APIs.

They can more easily be designed to be a true system of record for all data they access from a data store (such as an underlying database). No other service or application has direct read or write access to the underlying data store. This enforces true decoupling, while at the same time achieving a high level of transparency of the implementation details of data storage from information access.

In most cases, the use of services also makes it easier to scale your application. For one, you can hone the design of your services to be scaled by their traffic pattern: read-intensive API endpoints can be cached independently from write-intensive functionality. You can also more naturally separate cache expiry based on the tolerance for staleness of information based on your individual endpoints, or even by particular clients requesting information (for example, information about the descriptive text on any given inventory item should in most cases have a higher tolerance for staleness than the quantity of the item left to be purchased.)

In Chapters 6 and 7 of this book, we will show how to implement such caching strategies client-side, as well as taking advantage of the HTTP protocol's conditional GET facilities service-side. You will see how this can be paired with the use of reverse proxies, precalculating results service-side, as well as employing dedicated database read-only replicas for resource-intensive queries.

Potential Pitfalls and How to Avoid Them

It would be irresponsible and almost reckless to pretend that microservices are a silver bullet without any potential challenges or trade-offs. This section will try to summarize the trade-offs and concerns mentioned by the experts we have previously quoted, and it will conclude with our own views on impediments to introducing microservices.

Martin Fowler is the expert who has been most explicit in discussing some of the trade-offs[a] that come with the use of microservices:

- *Distribution*: Distributed systems are harder to program, since remote calls are slow and are always at risk of failure.

- *Eventual Consistency*: Maintaining strong consistency is extremely difficult for a distributed system, which means everyone has to manage eventual consistency.

- *Operational Complexity*: You need a mature operations team to manage lots of services, which are being redeployed regularly.

In addition to these technological considerations, Fowler and his colleague James Lewis agree that there are also many political factors in a company's surrounding culture and environment that can affect the chances of a successful microservices adoption. We will later explain our own experience and the cultural landscape that is needed for such an approach to thrive.

Phil Calçado agrees with Fowler and Lewis on many points. In his August 2015 QCon talk, cited in the preceding section, he emphasizes the need for any organization using microservices to have rapid resource-provisioning, basic monitoring and telemetry, and rapid deployment in place.

Particularly important to him is the monitoring and alarming component. In his words: "Tracking down issues in a monolith is easier … it's in some component of the monolith." When trying to find the root cause of an issue in a distributed environment, it is much harder for any operational support personnel to figure out where in the entire system a problem that has arisen is rooted. Calçado suggests that this be addressed by unifying dashboards for the monitoring data of all services and apps involved, to more easily identify which services were acting up.

Another hurdle is to aid application developers during their implementation and test efforts. Development becomes challenging and cumbersome in an environment where the application you work on is never run by itself, because it has dependencies on many other services. SoundCloud decided to address this by having all applications ship as Docker images that could be installed on a single server, or even a developer's laptop.

---

[a]Martin Fowler, "Microservice Trade-Offs", July 1, 2015, http://martinfowler.com/articles/microservice-trade-offs.html.

In his "Microservice Prerequisites" article,[11] Fowler also lists ways in which a mature organization can address the potential drawbacks via good planning. He sees three main conditions that need to exist in any successful implementation of a microservices architecture:

- *Rapid provisioning*: while he thinks that companies can gradually approach a full automation of such expedited server provisioning, he is convinced that any organization that is serious about microservices adoption will need to get to a state where new servers can be fired up in a matter of hours. Hosting such servers in a (private or public) cloud environment will make this more natural in his view, but he says that this can also be achieved without a full switch to cloud computing.

- *Basic Monitoring*: Because fully simulating or testing an environment where often hundreds of independent service components interact is very difficult, he considers it "essential" to have monitoring and alarming in place to quickly be notified about any issues that impact the production environment. Such monitoring should not be restricted to technical problems (like errors or drops in availability or performance), but should extend to business metrics (such as order drops, revenue decrease, or click-through rates).

- *Rapid application deployment*: when the number of services in an organization increases significantly, the need for very short deployment (and rollback) cycles arises, both for the test, as well as for the production stages. This usually involves automated, or even continuous, deployments that can change the code running in any particular stage in less than an hour. Again, Fowler concedes that some initial adoption phases can tolerate manual processes for application deployments, but he also says that full automation should be a near-term goal.

Fowler makes the point that especially monitoring and fast deployments go hand in hand:

"This collaboration is needed to ensure that provisioning and deployment can be done rapidly, it's also important to ensure you can react quickly when your monitoring indicates a problem. In particular any incident management needs to involve the development team and operations, both in fixing the immediate problem and the root-cause analysis to ensure the underlying problems are fixed. ... There's also the shift to product centered teams that needs to be started. You'll need to organize your development environment so developers can easily swap between multiple repositories, libraries, and languages."

Randy Shoup's talk mentions a good list of pitfalls of microservices, and he also adds occasional tips on how to avoid them.

Much like Fowler, he explains that while each small service itself becomes simpler and more intuitive to understand, coordinating the simple parts becomes complex, and understanding the whole distributed system and its information flows becomes more complex than in a monolith. Additionally, the introduction of network latencies between the services needs to be considered, and addressed by the development processes and standards employed in an organization.

A switch to microservices also often results in the active use of hundreds of code repositories. That number is large enough to justify spending time on devising a strategy for managing them in a unified way; for example, to address refactoring concerns across such a large number of repositories.

---

[11]Martin Fowler, "Microservice Prerequisites," August 29, 2014. `http://martinfowler.com/bliki/MicroservicePrerequisites.html`.

As the many successful examples of microservices adoption prove, the problems we've just seen can certainly be managed, but companies will need more sophisticated tooling to address the challenges than was previously needed in a monolithic environment.

Shoup continues by defining what he calls "microservices anti-patterns":

- *The Mega-Service*: This is an instance of failure to adopt the right granularity for a service extraction. An example of this anti-pattern is a service application that hosts too much functionality, or too many areas of responsibility, to maintain the advantage of a code base that can be easily understood. But a service that has too many up- or downstream dependencies can also be seen as an instance of this anti-pattern, as it counteracts the advantage of greater stability and availability of the overall system architecture.

- *Shared Persistence*: Having several services or applications share the same data store "under the hood" breaks the isolation advantages that switching to a loosely coupled collaboration of small services promises to bring. Even if the external interfaces of these coupled services are distinct, tying them back together at the database level leads to near-invisible coupling.

- *Leaky Abstraction Service*: In a well-designed service, its interface needs to reflect the *client's* needs, so the API model exposed should cater to its customers' needs. Implementations of the leaky abstraction service anti-pattern, on the other hand, expose an API design "from the internals outward," thereby leaking the underlying persistence model of the API *provider's* constraints instead.

Another concern Shoup raises is that in his experience, companies that have not reached sufficient size will not benefit from a microservices architecture. In his view, there are certain "stable points" in the size of companies as they evolve. The first stable point is when all employees still "fit around a conference table." The next stable size point is twenty to twenty-five people on the payroll, and the step after that will be when the number of employees reaches around 100 people. Shoup's advice is to switch to microservices when the second stage (of 20–25 people) is reached.

Shoup lays out his rationale for this advice in an interview with InfoQ:

> *"Google and Amazon are very intentionally trying to optimize for velocity of large-scale organizations, which means lots of things moving in parallel with little coordination. They behave like 1,000 tiny companies rather than one monster company and that is why those companies versus a bunch of even larger organizations, move fast and the other one do not. But in the case of smaller organizations, if you are all one team, do not subdivide."*

Adrian Cockcroft's "Migrating to Microservices" QCon talk does not reveal much information about his concerns regarding any potential pitfalls with microservices adoption. The main take-away from his talk appears to be that he whole-heartedly supports commoditization of server resources in the cloud, as opposed to owning and maintaining your own data centers. To summarize his advice in his own catch phrase: "Don't be a server hugger!"

Werner Vogels' interview also only touches on a very few points that lay out the challenges of adopting a large-scale SOA:

- *Unified service access*: Vogels makes the case for a single, commonly adopted service access protocol. It is Amazon.com's experience that such a mechanism is a precondition to easily aggregate services, and to enable monitoring, request tracking, and other more advanced "infrastructure techniques." Amazon implements this in its home-grown *ASDL* standard.

- *Developer productivity*: A fair amount of up-front thought should be invested to ensure efficiency of feature development in a large SOA architecture. Amazon addresses this by making sure that developers only ever need to run locally the code bases for the particular services they are currently trying to modify or extend. All other system dependencies run in a development-stage server fabric, which is also maintained and supported 24/7.

- *Quality assurance*: integration testing in a widely distributed environment becomes a large-scale challenge for an organization's quality assurance measures. To quote Vogels:

"If you have this decentralized organization where everybody is developing things in parallel, how can you make sure that all the pieces work together as intended, now and in the future? An important part of that is, for example, testing. How do you test in an environment like Amazon? Do we build another Amazon.test somewhere, which has the same number of machines, the same number of data centers, the same number of customers, and the same data sets? These are very hard questions, and we have no simple answers. Testing in a very large-scale distributed setting is a major challenge."

> Our own experience from working at Amazon.com in the years after Vogels' interview was that the company has heavily invested in doing just what Vogels alludes to above: production-like server fabrics have been spun up and populated with realistic test data, which a sizeable QA team uses to verify (automatically, as well as manually) larger software changes before they are deployed to the production stage.

Our own views on pitfalls to avoid, and what measures to implement to counteract them, overlap with many of the experts quoted in this chapter. Martin Fowler's and Phil Calçado's points about the need for monitoring and alarming approaches are particularly necessary, based on our own extensive experience in working in SOA environments.

It is also important to realize that working in a truly distributed environment introduces a large number of new failure modes, which include but are not limited to handling dependency timeouts or downtime. The need to avoid cascading failures of any system, which can be easily caused by any of the dependencies being unavailable or slow, must be engrained into every developer's workflow and thinking.

Another absolutely essential point for us was touched on by Werner Vogels: the need to unburden the individual developer of the complexity and inefficiency involved in running the *entire* system locally. Most changes are to be made only to a small portion (usually, a single service component) at any given time, so requiring any developer to set up, provision, or run any more than just the component(s) under change means continual grief and friction during the development cycle.

We do, however, explicitly disagree with Randy Shoup and others in that we do *not* think that microservices requires a certain level of company or development team size; after all, this book is dedicated to adopting the approach that it is not just possible, but actually preferable, to start out with a microservices architecture.

Randy's description of "microservices anti-patterns" hits the nail on the head, though. In our own experience, the most harmful of these is the "*Shared Persistence*" anti-pattern. Applying this defeats the entire purpose of splitting large applications into smaller decoupled parts, precisely because the resulting parts are no longer truly decoupled: they are tied together by having to adhere to the same underlying database schemas and—potentially even worse—shared data access model logic.

The second most dangerous anti-pattern to employ is Shoup's "*mega-service*." Service repositories of that kind are often born out of an irrational fear (or lazyness) of being potentially "slowed down" by spinning up separate code repositories and deployment units. This approach defeats the fundamental advantages of applying a "single responsibility principle" at a service application level, robbing the implementers of the chance to build a self-contained, easy-to-understand, and inexpensive-to-maintain service code base.

The rest of this book will present practical tips and examples for handling these measures.

When Should I Start with a Microservices Architecture?

You should not be surprised to find that we strongly recommend employing microservices from a very early stage in your application: after all, you have bought a book entitled *Microservices from Day One*.

If you are looking for more information about why other practitioners advocate the approach of starting a project with a monolith before deciding whether to switch to microservices, we recommend Martin Fowler's "Monolith First" blog post.[12]

Also posted on Fowler's treasure trove of a site is an article by Stefan Tilkov that takes the exact opposite stance, titled "Don't start with a monolith."[13] The following points from this article very accurately summarize our own experiences and the reasons we recommend a "services first" approach:

- Tilkov states that the point at which you start building a new system is also exactly the point in time when good design practices demand that you think about "carving it up into pieces," in order to build them as decoupled from each other as is possible. Postponing such system modularization to any time later in the lifecycle of a system should be strongly discouraged, because "you make it hard—or at least harder—to do the wrong thing: Namely, connecting parts that shouldn't be connected, and coupling those that need to be connected too tightly."

- Tilkov's experience that it is a challenging task , and sometimes well-nigh impossible, to divvy up an existing monolith into coherent modules entirely matches our own experience. When you begin developing in a monolith, each part will access shared domain logic and shared data access model, and assume that database transactions are always a possibility. This leads to very tight coupling inside the application. He mentions that owners of a monolith are "tempted to assume there are a number of nicely separated microservices hiding in your monolith, just waiting to be extracted. In reality, though, it's extremely hard to avoid creating lots of connections, planned and unplanned. In fact the whole point of the microservices approach is to make it hard to create something like this."

- He concedes the "monolith-first" camp's argument that one needs to know the problem domain very well before being able to correctly break it down into subdomains small enough constitute functionalities for microservices. The main reason is the difficulty of making significant changes in the system composition. As he puts it: "Refactoring in the small becomes easier, refactoring in the large becomes much harder."

- To him, "the ideal scenario is one where you're building a second version of an existing system." This observation also coincides with our own experience: we recommend building a proof-of-concept first to understand the business domain well enough. But, as any proof-of-concept, such a prototype needs to be entirely considered a throw away effort, and not "production-worthy." The second system can, and should, be built with services in mind.

---

[12]Martin Fowler, "MonolithFirst," June 2, 2015. `http://martinfowler.com/bliki/MonolithFirst.html`.
[13]Stefan Tilkov, "Don't start with a monolith," June 9, 2015. `http://martinfowler.com/articles/dont-start-monolith.html`.

- Tilkov also argues the counter-intuitive point that developing in more than one code base actually increases efficiency and the speed of tangible results. His point is that microservices are an enabler for parallel development, because they establish "a hard-to-cross boundary between different parts of your system," and hence are a forcing function for developers to discuss interfaces up-front. The parts that are being developed in parallel can also be delivered independently from each other, so that the feedback loop is shortened.

- Moreover, Tilkov states that concentrating on a microservices-based approach, where each subsystem "with its own development, deployment, and delivery cycle, and (the possibility of) its own internal architecture, is a very powerful concept that can help you to deliver a system in the first place."

The main point of this book is to show that adopting a microservices-based approach from the beginning does not have to be much more expensive than just going the ordinary (monolithic) "one app to rule them all" way.

In our view, the investment is very comparable to the "write tests or not?" question: investing in repeatable, automated pre-launch testing will pay off almost immediately by sparing companies the cost of addressing bugs found post-release.

Similarly, starting out with small, more focused services in the early phases of your applications life cycle will prevent you from involving very large parts of your engineering resources in ripping apart and rewriting your platform in a year from now, or so.

Another advantage to starting out with microservices is that an organization will be forced very early in a system's lifecycle to address the infrastructure concerns that are prerequisites to succeeding with such an architecture. Making an investment in development, testing, continuous integration and deployment, as well as monitoring and alarming strategies in the early phases will make the total amount of time and resources invested smaller, and the organization will reap the efficiency benefits of these measures much earlier.

Summary

In this chapter we laid out what services are and what a service-oriented architecture (SOA) is. We discussed what microservices are, and also what specifically they are *not*. We looked at four technology industry juggernauts (Amazon, Netflix, Google, and eBay), and discussed their respective reasons for relying on microservices, as well as the advantages such adoption brings in our view.

We moved on to describing some of the potential pitfalls that result from distributing systems at a large scale, and suggested remedies, again based on what industry leaders suggest, and what our experience tells us. We closed the chapter with an appeal to start using microservices from the earliest stages of your application development, having mid- to long-term efficiency and effectiveness in mind.

The next chapter will introduce some ground rules and best practices that are going to make it easier for you to get to such an architectural style once you are ready to adopt it.

Then, in part II of this book, we will look at ways and guidelines around decomposing your business application into microservices, and how to design, define, consume, and finally optimize your services' APIs.

The third and final part of this book will focus on the development environment, deployment infrastructure, testing strategies and monitoring & alarming aspects of running a microservices architecture.

All parts will be tied together by a set of example services implementing a fictitious online bookstore.

CHAPTER 2

Rules of Engagement

In this chapter, we'll go over what we call our "Rules of Engagement," which is a set of principles and best practices we find valuable to follow to ensure an efficient microservices environment. It would be correct to state that this entire book is a collection of what we consider best practices; but the principles we outline in this chapter are a foundation of many of the tools and design ideas we will discuss throughout the book. We have six Rules of Engagement for successfully building applications in a microservices environment. Those rules are based on our years of experience, and are phrased from a developer's point-of-view.

As with most rules, there may be cases where you will have a very good reason to move away from them, which is completely acceptable; however, make sure the set of principles that **you**—and your organization—believe in are easily accessible to your technical team when questions about software architecture arise. We believe that guiding principles like these help your development team spend less time thinking about high-level architecture, and more time writing business-related code and providing value to stakeholders. Our rules of engagement follow in order of importance, with the most important ones coming first.

Customer-Facing Applications Cannot Directly Touch Any Data Store

"Consumer-facing applications" are interfaces used by an organization's customers. They are usually but not always web sites, administrative interfaces, and native mobile applications; there could even be public-facing APIs that you expose. Consumer-facing applications will be a mere mashup of data retrieved from authoritative systems-of-record, and will never have a database or any other mechanism that persists state. Such systems-of-record will always be service applications with well-defined, versionable interfaces. Apart from the fact that some nasty security issues will be easier to address this way (SQL injection should be a thing of the past), different consumer-facing apps that work on the same information exposed by the owning service will be able to evolve independently, regardless of changes in the underlying data schemas of your data store.

An important side effect of this rule is that all the features in consumer-facing applications are implemented via service calls to microservices.

This is a rule that if ever broken will take you on a slippery slope you will regret for a really long time. We've seen many features being implemented with direct database access "because it's quicker," but quickly become a nightmare to evolve because of tight coupling from one client. Do not believe it when someone—possibly you—says that "this will be extracted it into a service later"; you may have good intentions, but shifting business needs may mean that you will not be able to follow up on fixing your application's design later.

© Cloves Carneiro Jr. and Tim Schmelmer 2016

C. Carneiro Jr. and T. Schmelmer, *Microservices From Day One*, DOI 10.1007/978-1-4842-1937-9_2

No Service Accesses Another Service's Data Store

In 2002, Jeff Bezos sent out an email at Amazon saying that "all teams will henceforth expose their data and functionality through service interfaces" and "there will be no other form of inter-process communication allowed," and that's how Amazon adopted and built an extremely efficient service-oriented architecture. This principle is mainly about implementation encapsulation; however, we mention data stores in our version because that's where we've quite often seen this rule being broken, causing all sorts of implementation leakage that ends up slowing down service evolution.

Similarly, all inter-service interactions should happen *only* through well defined, versioned APIs. While a service has ownership of the data for which it is itself the system-of-record (including direct read and write access), it can only access other information via its dependent authoritative services.

Invest in Making Spinning Up New Services Trivial

This point, combined with the preceding rule, is very important; it's essential to have both your developers and your TechOps teams embrace the "SOA way" inside your company. Driven, smart people tend not to tolerate being seemingly held back, and from a business viewpoint, they are too expensive an asset to be slowed down.

Make everyone happy by having a small accepted list of technologies to support. Invest in creating templates for service code. And, last but not least, introduce rules and guidelines for your interfaces: consider the use of an Interface Definition Language to define APIs, and think about the structure of your RESTful interfaces (what consistent error status codes will you expose, what is in the headers and what is in URI parameters, how will authentication / authorization work? and similar questions).

These rules stem from more than a decade of combined personal experience (both from the ground up, as well as via refactoring existing monoliths). With a growing number of deployable units (that is, services); it's important to be serious about automation (DevOps) —of all aspects of your infrastructure. In a perfect scenario, most code changes would kick off a build that runs a suite of automated tests. When a successful build happens, the change should be deployed to a shared development environment, and then later deployed to production without manual intervention in each step of the way.

When a developer—or development team—decides that a new service is required, a lot of steps are needed to get that new service live. Some of those steps are:

- Defining the language stack to be used based on requirements
- Creating a repository
- Defining a data-store
- Setting up continuous integration,
- Defining deployment
- deploying To development/staging/production
- Setting up monitoring and logging

... and so on. If your company has an environment where most of those steps are automated, then creating one—or multiple—services doesn't incur any sort of time penalty from the point of view of development, and you help your team keep code that needs to be separated in different services. By the same token, if spinning up a new service requires "asking for permission" and takes a few weeks, then it's likely that your development team will bunch APIs into existing services to avoid those delays in getting services up and running.

When a developer shoehorns new APIs into an existing service just because it's less friction than starting a new service, he or she ends up breaking the single-responsibility concern that should be applied to microservices, which can lead to confusion and disrupt a focused system into becoming a set of seemingly unrelated APIs. The famous "broken windows theory" well fits this situation. It becomes hard to keep proper separation of concern when one API that is a bad fit goes into a service; it will undoubtedly invite similar behavior from other developers.

Build Services in a Consistent Way

All services you build should behave consistently in many aspects. In the perfect scenarios, all your services will:

- Communicate using the same protocol and format—for example, JSON over HTTP

- Define APIs in a consistent manner

- Log request access using a standard log format

- Be monitored with the same tools

- ...

The keyword of this rule is "consistency; surprises are evil and slow everyone down. This rule doesn't mean that you put the brakes on innovation and don't try new languages or libraries. You should always be assessing new technologies and practices, but in an organized way. It's well known that, in the software development lifecycle, software spends most of its time in the operations and maintenance phase, and you really want to avoid snowflake services that require very specific knowledge for maintenance because some technologies were tested with no process for either applying those technologies broadly or retiring them.

Define API Contracts in Code

An API is generally defined by its inputs and outputs, which should ideally be described using an artifact that computers and people—other developers—can parse. We really mean, at any point in time, the API definition must be clearly defined, and clients of that API can validate and test it unambiguously. In practice, a mechanism known to achieve this is an IDL, Interface Definition Language, a term for a language that allows developers to define the characteristics of an interface—in our case API endpoints. Using IDLs, developers can programmatically define accepted input and output parameters—including data types—for an interface.

All your services will expose and consume data via APIs; so documenting them is a necessity. At every point in time, there should be a clear way of describing your endpoints in detail. You need to find out the expected inputs and outputs of each endpoint, and having those items in code that is exercised often is a way of making sure that you really know what is being exposed. In this book's sample project, we will be using Swagger, a specification used to define RESTful APIs, and you will see some of the benefits of using an IDL, including the usage of tools built around standards, which help to increase developer productivity.

We'll go into a lot of detail about API development in Part II.

Every Service Has at Least a Development and a Production Instance

When developing in SOA, you cannot expect your development and QA teams to run all the various environments for all the services to be deployed, on their local development machines, and on any host for that matter. Not only will this slow down their computers (and hence negatively impact their velocity), but nobody should be expected to update potentially several dozen service applications (and their test data) locally on a regular basis.

No developer should ever need to run, on their personal development environment, any system other than the one(s) that need modification in the context of their task. Dependent services should have standard, well-known URIs for server instances to which all consuming applications point by default. Ideally, you should use a service-discovery service to take away a lot of the pain involved in knowing how to connect to each service in your entire environment. We will show some techniques to achieve this in Part III.

Existing Code Bases

Most of the content of this book is geared toward green-field development, and it may sound too opinionated and hard to apply to existing code bases. Even if you work on an existing code base that doesn't follow those principles, however, you may still be able to apply them selectively, in order to improve your existing architecture.

The rule of thumb for applying those principles to a suboptimal code base is to optimize your ROI. For example, if you have a couple of services that share the same database, it will probably be a very large effort to split tables into two separate databases; your existing code could even make it impossible because of joins and reliance on too many tables; so, you'd be better served by properly documenting your existing APIs. On a similar note, if you have a talented DevOps team, then your best improvement may be to invest in making it easy to spin up your next service. We recommend you analyze and use common sense to start making progress toward a more sane microservices environment.

Summary

In this chapter, we outlined our six rules of engagement for using microservices:

- Customer-facing applications cannot directly touch any data store.

- No service accesses another service's data store.

- Invest in making spinning up new services trivial.

- Build services in a consistent way.

- Define API contracts in code.

- Every service has at least a development and a production instance.

We hope all of these Rules of Engagement make sense at this point. They may seem quite opinionated and complex to follow now. If some of the rules seem blurry to you, that's almost to be expected at this point. We will refer to them often in the rest of the book, and hope they will make more sense as we go deeper into each subject.

In Chapter 3, we will dive into how you can decompose your business model into services. We'll define some easy-to-follow rules for defining how to split parts of an application into services, and will use our sample project as an example to put those rules into practice.

PART II

APIs

CHAPTER 3

Partitioning Your Business into Services

This chapter presents some guidelines for composing a larger business application out of a set of microservices. We start by explaining some general criteria by which to partition a software system into a set of core services. We then explain how these core services can be composed into one or more layers of higher-level services, which eventually are the building blocks for the entire application. Finally, we will apply some of these generic principles to begin building our example bookstore application.

General Approaches for Application Decomposition and Aggregation

This section offers some general guidelines for breaking down an entire application into services components. Many of the principles laid out in here are based on the excellent book *Service-Oriented Design with Ruby and Rails* by Paul Dix (Addison-Wesley Professional 2010), which uses a social feed reader application as an example for demonstrating these principles. In that application, users can subscribe to feeds, comment on articles in the feed, as well as vote them up or down, and follow other users' feed commenting and voting activities.

Application Decomposition

The first set of methods for breaking apart an application domain into a list of services has in common that they decompose the larger scope of the entire application into small, low-level services.

Decomposing by Functionality

The first, and possibly most natural, principle to apply when splitting up a problem domain to be addressed with a larger software application is to analyze the functionalities it is meant to provide. Once you have identified the individual pieces of functionality the whole system is to provide, start by grouping them together into bundles that fit together logically.

Some such general candidates for functionalities to factor out into a separate service can be email processing (sending or receiving), application resource monitoring, or connecting to and consuming external data sources (for example, scraping external sites for data, or collecting data via other site's APIs).

© Cloves Carneiro Jr. and Tim Schmelmer 2016
C. Carneiro Jr. and T. Schmelmer, *Microservices From Day One*, DOI 10.1007/978-1-4842-1937-9_3

Dix's book example of a social feed reader application shows that the logic function of "updating feeds" sticks out as a separable functionally, as its "only purpose is to download XML files, parse them, and insert [them] … into the data store." Another example he quotes is the feed and feed entry storage functionality: The users in his sample scenarios share feed and article data, and they subscribe to feeds. But these feeds and article in and of themselves do not exhibit an ownership relationship with the subscribing users. These are good characteristics for factoring the feed functionalities into their own service component.

As mentioned in Chapter 1, Netflix also takes a functionality-driven approach to divvying up its system into services. In fact, one could argue that Netflix is following this approach quite to the extreme, in that they have a guideline to have a single functionality per service, such as recommending a list of movies based on a given user and her past ratings for different movies.

More low-level functionalities that could be candidates for splitting out into separate services could be a system's messaging component, or even a key-value–based data store. Amazon's Web Services business unit capitalizes on this approach by offering its Simple Storage Service and Simple Queue Service.

Going the other way, it is also possible to find service candidates at a much higher level. More than just partitioning out data and business logic into a service, we can also isolate UI components rendered in a larger application. Many projects have been successful in splitting out components at the presentation logic layer. Paul Dix gives the example of bundling typical Ruby on Rails framework-based views and controllers into separate services that render consistent HTML (like a "*comment service*" that renders HTML snippets of a comment section on multifarious pages). To give the look of a single web-application, the controller-and-view based applications can be stitched together via Edge-Side Includes (ESI). The same effect could even be achieved via a fronting Ruby-On-Rails or Rack application instead, where this application's goal is just to combine the routes of all the backing HTML-component rendering applications into includes as modules.

When German etailer OTTO (`https://www.otto.de/`) re-engineered the second generation of its entire online presence in 2013 and 2014 as a "from-scratch" service-oriented system,[1] the engineering department followed an approach of what they coined "*vertical decomposition*."

They split their system according to business subdomains. As part of this process, they divided the online shop into 11 different verticals; for example, their back office, product, and ordering verticals, to name just three. Each of these verticals is serving its own web UI. Other verticals' web UIs are referenced by explicitly linking to them via HTML links. The goal of integrating the verticals into a coherent, single web application from the end user's viewpoint is achieved via ESI includes, which a fronting varnish proxy server resolves and pulls from all respective verticals into a single, top-level HTML view.

Decomposing by Maturity

Another method of identifying parts of a prospective application that are good candidates for successfully combining into a service is to look for parts that have reached a similar level of maturity.

A company's business organization typically has had several iterations of defining goals and specifications, and these are reflected in the functionalities and behaviors of parts of the application in question. Parts whose functional and nonfunctional requirements are well understood should be bundled together, while things that are less stable and subject to more and faster iterations might move into other separate, versioned services (or not split out into separate services at all, initially).

Dix's example for a core, and fairly static, part of his sample social feed reader application is the storing and updating the feeds, as it "will exist regardless of other iterations." On the other hand, the services for users, comments, and votes components will be iterated upon more frequently, so they should not be part of the same service as the feed-handling.

---

[1]Guido Steinaker, "On Monoliths and Monoliths and Microservices," September 30, 2015. `http://dev.otto.de/2015/09/30/on-monoliths-and-microservices/`

The online marketplace LivingSocial has moved to this approach whenever pilot efforts for new business initiatives are being explored. A recent example is the Restaurants Plus initiative (`https://www.livingsocial.com/restaurants-plus-rewards/`), which was launched early to a set of LivingSocial employees and early-adopters to gather feedback and refine the product before a wider launch. Given the need for speedy and frequent iterations on the nascent business model while at the same time avoiding impact to the existing business, the decision was made to implement all new functionalities in dedicated applications and services.

Decomposing by Data-Access Pattern

The next method of partitioning an application into service components focuses on data retrieval and persistence efficiency. The advice here is to analyze expected storage access for the various functionalities and classify them into "read intensive," "write intensive," and "balanced read and write" buckets.

The advantage of this approach is that a service's schemas, access queries, or even the data store engine (whether RDBMS, key-value store, document-based, or other method) can be optimized for either read- or write-intensive access in isolation. Similarly, different data caching strategies can be applied for each of the services. One might, for example, decide not to introduce the complexity involved with caching and cache invalidation at all if a service deals mainly with write-intensive data.

Sometimes, partitioning an application by the data-access pattern leads to different results than trying to decompose along lines of related functionality. To illustrate this, let's again consider Dix's social-feed reader example: user profile data and a user's reading list are functionally closely related, but the profile data is often read, while the reading list is much more often updated than it is accessed for displaying.

Special care needs to be taken with "balanced read and write" data. Dix's example is the voting data in the feed reader, which is updated about as often as it is read. Modularizing this functionality into a dedicated service enables the service owners to experiment with different optimization strategies to optimize performance for vending voting aggregates at both the user and the feed entry level. Another way to optimize this particular scenario would be to store voting statistics with the users and the feed entries themselves. While this could certainly result in performance improvements, that strategy does *not* come for free: one will have to live with the implications of only eventually achieving consistency of vote aggregate data duplicated in this way.

Decomposing by Context

Sometimes it makes sense to implement multiple services that seem to focus on exactly the same entity. This is appropriate if they represent different distinct meanings in separate *bounded contexts*, one of the key concepts of an architectural design approach called *domain-driven design*.

Martin Fowler's article on the matter of bounded context[2] explains that, for example, a customer can be *polysemic*. A customer can mean two different things in different business contexts; the attributes and business logic associated with a customer will differ greatly for the customer support unit of an organization from the attributes and associations in the sales unit's business context.

Such a separation of concerns could go so far that the only shared data between such customer-focused services would be a common, unique customer identifier (best in the form of a universally unique identifier, or UUID). Both such domain-specific customer services could also cross-reference a third, lower-level customer-service for shared data (such as the customer's address or other contact information).

LivingSocial's infrastructure serves information about cities in which the company runs voucher-based offers out of a service called city-service. This core data includes information about the city's location, its relative size, its name, and so on.

---

[2]Martin Fowler, "BoundedContext," January 15, 2014. `http://martinfowler.com/bliki/BoundedContext.html`

In addition, there are at least two other services that map such city entities one-to-one to model objects in different contexts: a market-area-service that is used in the context of sending user-subscribed promotional emails, as well as another service that attaches information to cities that is needed only in the context of a new business initiative.

Both services refer back to the original, core city entities via a shared city ID.

In his December 2015 talk at GOTO Berlin, "DDD & Microservices: At Last, Some Boundaries!"[3], Eric Evans—the inventor of domain-driven design —confirms that bounded contexts and microservices play well together. In his words, microservices "are a good vehicle for domain-driven design," because they provide "real isolation for the work within these different teams," where teams can work in different bounded contexts. In his mind, employing microservices to implement the bounded contexts makes it easier to erect context boundaries and to subsequently enforce them.

Application Aggregation

The opposite of the previously mentioned approach, which arrived at service components to make up an entire application system via decomposition, is to reaggregate smaller, lower-level services into new larger services. The following sections attempt to classify the set of motivations that can make such aggregations desirable.

Aggregation for a Derived Functionality

One motivation for such an approach could be that a desired functionality can best be provided as a mash-up of other existing, more basic core services. An example of such derived functionality could be a `recommendation` service for an e-commerce website. Such a service could be used to vend a set of personalized product recommendations for a given user. The data upon which the `recommendation` engine bases its suggestions can come from several, more basic services. One example of a more elementary service that provides input to the `recommendation` service might be a `purchases` service, which exposes data about a user's previous purchases. Another input for data to be mashed up inside the `recommendation` engine can be a `product` service, which categorizes products and potentially relates them to complementary products. Combined, those two basic services' APIs can be combined to recommend other "up-sell" products that are either in the same category as the user's previous purchases or complement such previous purchase activities.

This approach is often taken when new features of an application are conceived in the later stages of the application's lifecycle. Encapsulating such features into their own service enables the business to receive quick feedback, while the engineering team is able to launch the changes in relative isolation.

Going this route, and again using the previous example of a recommendation service, the business can more easily test the effectiveness of new recommendation algorithms, for example, adding in data about purchases of other users that have bought similar products as the user for whom a recommendation is to be made.

Aggregation for Business Intelligence

Another good reason to aggregate a set of services into a secondary layer of services is to provide organizations with tools to gather and evaluate business metrics.

Many companies aggregate data from other core sources in extremely large data stores, such as Apache Hadoop. Systems often called "data warehouses" are built as a service-layer on top of this data, providing "Extract, Transform, and Load" (ETL) functions for use by business analysts.

---

[3]A recording of the talk can be found at `https://www.youtube.com/watch?v=yPvef9R3k-M`

A popular use case for such a system is financial reporting and forecasting, and other monitoring of business-related key performance indicators. Another common use case for this type of data analysis and data mining approach is to build fraud detection services on top of the large data sets available in such aggregated data stores. Similarly, the tasks of personalizing functionalities to the granularity of a single consumer of an e-commerce site often rely on post-processing large amounts of other data, from disparate sources.

Typically, most of the business intelligence capabilities relying on such large data are not updated in real time. While a service that provides this data could be called as part of an HTTP request cycle from a consumer's browser, the underlying logic often is based on precalculated data.

Aggregation for Client Convenience

Another common motivation for composing services is to make life for client applications as easy as feasibly possible.

Designing service APIs with the maximum level of utility to the prospective clients in mind can significantly contribute to an application's success. Tailoring the service endpoints such that they present a coherent design and only expose data and functionality that a client truly needs is crucial.

Hiding implementation details of the underlying data design of the service's internals helps not only with usability, but also with security aspects, especially for publicly accessible APIs.

Often this service aggregation pattern is also applied to provide a more coherent, or generally just more useful, presentation layer of data that a client application needs to perform *its* own duties. One example of this use case could be a "mobile façade service."

Native mobile applications (such as iOS or Android apps) often have a lifetime that spans multiple years, and there usually is no good way to force all client devices to upgrade to newer versions of the application. This means that the service APIs used by such native mobile apps are publicly exposed, and hence need to be virtually frozen once any app version uses them. Unless you want to run the risk of causing breakages in the installed base of already shipped clients, those APIs should not be changed. Newer versions of the mobile apps, which want to take advantage of new features or changes in the APIs that break existing API contracts, will need to use an entirely new version of the previously exposed API. Over time as the number of supported features and mobile app versions grows, so does the number of APIs that need supporting separately and almost eternally.

LivingSocial has such a mobile façade service at the edge between the public network and the application provider's internal network. One reason for this choice was to shield native clients from the complexities and potential inconsistencies in other downstream services' API contracts. This way, it is possible to introduce coherence and provide guarantees about data formats: not having to support the many different possible data formats for calendar dates, times, or currency value can greatly reduce the complexity of client applications. This edge service also performs validations of data it vends to native applications (for example, via enforcing that currency data conform to a schema complying with ISO 4217, dates that conform to ISO 8601), so that publicly shipped native applications can be more stable themselves. It also is a central point of dealing with the above-mentioned need for long-term support for publicly exposed APIs.

Aggregation to Aid System Performance

A final purpose for service aggregation is to use it to improve response times or availability of the overall application.

Some out-of-the box solutions exist for such efforts, for example caching proxy-services like Varnish (`https://www.varnish-cache.org/`). Architecturally, Varnish can be introduced as a caching layer to front one or more HTTP-based services, exposing those services' endpoints directly to clients that otherwise would have directly produced traffic to the back-end services. Varnish is lightning-fast, and it has highly configurable caching and data aggregation capabilities, which include support for ESI and HTTP conditional `GET` header processing.

Besides serving as a proxy that can aggregate and cache service-exposed data for performance improvements, Varnish can also be configured to aid system availability, as it can continue to serve data from its caches even if the back-end services fronted by varnish are currently unavailable.

Another example of aggregation for performance tuning is the case of services that expose aggregated data in different data representations, or are optimized to provide search APIs.

One example from our work experience at LivingSocial is an internal service for the company's overall product catalog. While each of the different product types is owned by a dedicated "systems-of-record" service, this `catalog-service` aggregates data about all product types. This data is stored in a denormalized fashion, and special database indexes are built to allow for very fast search and retrieval of product data by a configurable set of criteria.

Yet another service at LivingSocial whose main raison d'être is to improve overall performance is called `inventory-service`. It is a service that serves almost the exact same information as `catalog-service`, but which is specifically optimized for fast geo-location based product searches.

Additionally, the service provides a way to define special purpose representations of the product data, which can be tailored to the respective client's needs. This way, the payload received about a set of products can be greatly reduced, so that network transmission time and latency, as well as service-side data serialization and client-side deserialization, can be kept to an absolute minimum.

Paul Dix's book about service-oriented design also speaks about improving efficiency by aggregating data that is often accessed together to provide information for service clients. He calls this "partitioning by join-frequency," as this information is often generated by joining data from several database tables.

While joining database tables can often be costly, combining data procured by multiple, potentially sequential, service calls across process and network boundaries can become even more prohibitive to meeting performance requirements. While this realization is surely easy to understand, the problem is much harder to avoid: all nontrivial applications usually expose functionalities that require almost all data to be joined. Dix formulates a few guidelines to impact performance as little as possible:

- Analyze the functionalities of your application up-front, and consider the expected frequency of joining the various data objects. Looking at the results, you can make decisions about placing data and logic that is most frequently joined inside the same service and data store.

- If the previous approach impedes the rest of your application design too much, you can denormalize the joined data, and then push it (for example, via a messaging bus) to all the services that want to join against it. This will give you the best performance improvements if the joined data is often accessed. Otherwise, the cost and complexity involved with broadcasting to, and storing it in, all joining services might not be justifiable.

When to Use Decomposition versus Aggregation?

After spending a significant amount of time trying to research, we have failed to come up with hard-and-fast rules or checklists for which of the above strategies to use under given conditions. Many of these design decisions are made weighing the pros and cons of the given characteristics of each of the approaches laid out above.

The best general rule of thumb we have been able to identify during a decade building and maintaining services is that favoring decomposition techniques over aggregation techniques appears to be a cyclic decision. We have found that decomposition of a domain into small services is often how a business should start out, while aggregating services appears to be more needed and helpful to address the issues that arise later in the lifecycle of an application. Once a business is established and wants to diversify, that situation often triggers another phase of breaking down new ideas into additional small core services, which will then again be composed (often, together with other existing services) to form larger, aggregated services.

While we realize that these observations and considerations appear rather general, we hope that the example business case discussed next might help to provide additional guidance.

Decomposing and Aggregating a Sample Application

To illustrate many of the concepts laid out in this book, we have decided to put them into practice in a sample application that is partitioned into several small services.

The following section first lays out the main features of this application, and then explains decisions about how the application could be structured into a set of microservices, based on the previous section's guidelines.

Welcome to Our Bookstore!

The sample domain chosen to accompany this book is that of an online bookstore. Throughout the rest of this book, we will use this fictitious bookstore to illustrate the concepts laid out in this book. These illustrations include partially implementing some of the services and applications that together could make up the entire system that supports this sample domain, discussing the resulting code samples, and deploying them to a cloud infrastructure.

Here is a list of features that we see as needed for our bookstore business:

- Visitors to the bookstore's site will be able to *view*, *read reviews* about, and *search* for, books (by category, title, author, or topic), and place them in a personal *shopping cart*.

- Once *registered* on the site, such visitors become users, who can also *buy existing books* for themselves, or as *gifts* for others, and *preorder books* soon to be released.

- Users can also sign up for *promotional email newsletters* and *notifications* about events regarding *order status* or *activities of other users* (see the social component described shortly). Users can also choose to receive *personalized recommendations* based on previous reading or shopping activity, category or author preferences, and recommendations by users they follow.

- Site-wide and category-specific *bestseller lists* will be maintained and displayed in the store.

- The bookstore is aiming to serve all of North America, and therefore not only is obliged to follow Canada's *bilingual* regulations, but also Quebec's strict rules about the use of the French and English languages.

- Books can exist in *different formats*: a *physical* book in paperback or library binding, as well as *e-books* in PDF, Mobi, or epub formats. Physical books can be bought, using a range of *different payment instruments*. Physical books are *shipped to a set of user-associated addresses*, and *book returns* are permitted within 7 work days after delivery. Electronic books are *delivered electronically* (via a download link on the user's account summary page) and cannot be returned once purchased and delivered.

- The bookstore will also have several *social features*: users can have *reading lists* and *wish lists* for books. They can *write comments and reviews* of books on the site, *up- or down-vote books* they have read, and *follow other users'* reading lists, commenting, and reviewing activity.

- A *fraud detection* system integrated in the online bookstore *monitors purchasing, review, and voting activities* on the site. The system *can flag suspicious activities* to site administrators, as well as *autonomously take action* regarding user, vote and review activation statuses.

- Writing reviews about books and voting on them, are ways for a user to *receive in-store credits*, which can be used to purchase more books on the site.

- *An internal web interface* to the bookstore will allow bookstore personnel access to various *administrative tasks*, based on the *fine-grained access control* restrictions. Examples of such tasks are adding, removing, or altering data about the books (for example, descriptions, pricing, category, keyword, or author-related data), and administering user-related data (like email and physical addresses, in-store credits, resetting user passwords, changing a user's registered payment instruments, and toggling the user's activation status) or curating comments and reviews on the site.

- Additionally, *business intelligence reports* can be run on all data entities that are part of the application, for example, about users and their activities, book sales and review performance, current and projected financials.

- Last but not least, most of the consumer-facing functionalities are also exposed in *native mobile applications* running on iOS and Android devices. Other mobile devices are supported by a *mobile web interface*.

Partitioning the Bookstore

Let us start out with a few words of warning: as should be clear from the first section of this chapter about guidelines, decisions about the exact set of services to make up the entire system are very often design trade-offs to be made by the team(s) involved. There really are no black-or-white answers to this task, or anything like a "correct" partitioning, and even less so one that is optimal under all circumstances now and for the entire lifecycle of the bookstore.

Also, the bookstore business we'll describe next has a rather large feature set and complexity; much more than anything we are intending to implement in the accompanying example code. Do not be overwhelmed by the number of services proposed in this section. While we advocate having a rather large number of services for any application (very often larger than the number of developers working on them), it should be clear by now that we do *not* recommend rushing into a microservices architecture approach head-long or naively; adopting strong supporting development, deployment, and monitoring tools prior to engaging in such an architecture remains a necessary prerequisite.

With that said, we mentioned in the first section of this chapter that decomposing the bookstore business along lines of functionality is probably the most natural way to start.

Decomposing into Core Services

Key and core functionalities are most obviously the data and logic directly related to the books that are sold on the site, so envisioning the existence of a `books-service` seems very appropriate. It seems very prudent to spin up an authoritative service for all attributes and direct functionalities directly associated with the products to be sold, commented and voted on, and reviewed on the site. The various versions of a book, in their respective formats (paperback, library binding, epub, and so on) will be called "book variants."

To help performance, the `books-service` will vend product information in several different formats, or representations, each of which has a different subset of the entire set of book attributes. As an example, the bestseller list displayed in the web application will request a representation called a *tile*, which contains only a book's title, author, a default price, and thumbnail URL for the cover image. In contrast to the page that lists bestsellers, a book's detail page will request the "full" representation, which also contains the number of up- and down-votes, a full descriptive text, a summary, pricing and other details for all different variants of the book, and more.

It is important to note that books (much like any other entity in the store) are never truly deleted from the data store. They might be marked as "out of stock" or "out of print" or otherwise unavailable for purchase, but they will always be available in the data store via their direct resource UUID. This ensures that things like a user's purchase history will be able to refer to them.

Another key entity is surely the user on the site; so for similar reasons as for books, implementing a `users-service` seems a strategy in line with partitioning the application domain by functionality, as well.

A user service necessarily handles the core data attributes that are associated with a user (for example, her name, email address, user handle, unique UUID, activation status, and potentially her salted and encrypted password) and the core logic to create, change, or read some or all of these attributes. In addition, it is also often tasked with authenticating a site user. This most likely means that a session cookie containing an encrypted user ID is generated and vended at an authentication endpoint used by browsers. For inter-service authentication, which mostly serves to authenticate the acting user for sessionless API requests, such a `users-service` often employs OAuth 2.0[4] tokens.

In other contexts, it might seem more prudent to separate the authentication functionality out of the core user service into a separate service. Sometimes, such an authentication service even lives outside the actual application domain. OAuth authentication via providers like Google, Facebook, Amazon, LinkedIn, or Twitter, to name but a few, is quite commonplace in today's online applications.

Looking at the fact that administrative tasks also need to be performed on the site by authenticated personnel, a `users-service` might not just be responsible for consumer customers, but also for handling company employees. Depending on how fine-grained access control will be to various administrative options on the site, a simple, Boolean `admin` flag to identify administrative personnel might not be sufficient. In this case, many sites apply more or less sophisticated systems for role-based access control (RBAC). Such a service could either be integrated into a `users-service`, or developed as a dedicated authorization service.

Given the scenario for our fictitious bookstore described earlier, we are making the decision to combine the core user data and authentication functionalities into a single `users-service`, while isolating the RBAC functionality into a separate service. The main reason for this decision is the expected access pattern for these separate functionalities. The store will have a consumer-facing set of applications, which will be kept separate from the ones to be used by administrative staff. Both the consumer applications and the administrative interfaces will need to create, alter, and read core user data, as well as authenticate users. RBAC, however, mainly applies in the realm of the administrative context; consumer-facing applications are not envisioned to have much use for fine-grained access control. We only want to prevent consumers from modifying other consumers' information or viewing other users' sensitive information.

Related to users is another entity: addresses. We have decided to also dedicate a separate `addresses-service` to these core data objects. Among the main reasons for this decision are data sensitivity and compliance concerns; billing and shipping addresses, for example, are personally identifiable information (PII), and therefore protected by specific laws in many jurisdictions. Many companies therefore decide to keep such data in separate, specifically protected environments, so that any potential security breaches to less restrictive environments do not lead to loss of personal information.

---

[4]Internet Engineering Task Force (IETF), Request For Comment 6749, "The OAuth 2.0 Authorization Framework," October 2012. `https://tools.ietf.org/html/rfc6749`

Applications and Aggregated Services

There will be three major applications that are directly at the edges of the bookstore business, catering to external customers, and hence are exposed to the public network:

- The application that renders HTML for desktop web users (let's call it desktop-web),

- One application that serves HTML to mobile web clients (called mobile-web)

- A mobile façade service exposing public APIs for access by the iOS and Android mobile applications (named mobile-service)

Administrative applications for company personal, including the reporting tools for running business intelligence queries against the data warehouse, will only be exposed inside the company's firewall.

Important to note here is that none of these "pixel-rendering" edge applications will have access to any authoritative data store. While they might use some local caching technologies, they will rely solely on data that they retrieve from other non-edge service applications. This holds true even for the mobile API façade service, and—if there will ever be such an extension to the bookstore—for any other publicly facing APIs for external customers' apps to consume.

The introduction of the "one-stop shop" mobile-service is done following the previously mentioned pattern to aggregate services further downstream for the convenience of the Android and iOS apps. Localizations are done in this service, and attention is paid that all data is transformed into formats that can be easily and efficiently processed by the native mobile apps. As there is no way to ever truly force mobile devices to upgrade the bookstore apps, this mobile façade will need to implement strict versioning for the exposed APIs, with multi-year support for each of the versions introduced.

For maximum stability of the native apps, all data formats vended by the service will be specified using JSON Schema (http://json-schema.org/), and the service's integration test suite will verify that all the versioned APIs conform to the schema specifications.

Additionally, mobile-service will serve as an aggregator to help overall system performance, adding HTTP conditional GET and caching headers like ETags and Cache Control max-age.[5] This is a very effective and unobtrusive way to help native mobile applications improve performance, as the most used iOS and Android HTTP libraries support honoring and inserting the respective headers without any additional configuration or coding efforts.

Supporting Platform Services

Given that the bookstore will operate in Canada, translations in at least the Canadian English and Canadian French locales will be required. In order not to duplicate the responsibility for correct localization of any given string across all edge applications mentioned above (for example, desktop-web, mobile-web, and mobile-service), a central translations-service will be developed. Translators and other company personnel will use an internal web UI to define strings via unique keys, and provide translations into all needed locales. The translations-service will store this data and might decide to expose it via RESTful APIs. The main way to communicate these translations internally to the bookstore infrastructure will be by publishing any changes or new translations on a system-wide message bus topic. Because of its message delivery guarantees and replay options, we will opt for using Apache Kafka.

Any (existing and future) edge application that needs to render localized text will consume the translation's topic in a dedicated consumption process, and then update an internal storage engine (for which we will use a simple, file-based Berkeley database) to have the latest translations available inside the edge application.

Purchasing books will also be handled by a separate service, called purchase-service, which encapsulates this functionality. It plays together very directly with two other services: cart-service and payments-service.

---

[5]See https://www.w3.org/Protocols/rfc2616/rfc2616-sec13.html

A user can populate her cart with a number of book variants in various quantities. The `cart-service` will therefore have a dependency on the `books-service`, as it will reference the book variants by the UUID identifying each book option.

The `payments-service` encapsulates the various accepted payment instruments a user can register with her account on the site. The bookstore will initially accept the major credit cards, but encapsulating this functionality into its own service will make it much easier to accommodate foreseeable extensions like the desire to also support PayPal payments, or maybe even in-store credits a user could accrue (for example, in return for reviewing many books). To simplify PCI compliance requirements, the service acts as a gateway an for external charging service (such as Braintree), never actually storing more than an inconspicuous payment instrument foreign key (as opposed to actual credit card numbers, or the like).

The steps that happen during purchase as part of the checkout process are as follows:

- The book variants' prices are retrieved from the `books-service`, multiplied by the selected quantities, and summed up to retrieve the totals of the cart's value.

- An attempt is made to charge the payment instrument chosen for the cart's value using `payments-service`.

- The cart data, cart total, and payment instrument ID are denormalized and then sent as inputs to `purchase-service` to create a record of the sale.

- A message about such a successful sale is placed on the appropriate Kafka message topic to inform dependent systems (like a service vending best-seller lists based on sales numbers) of this purchase event.

To allow for customer refunds, we implement a `refund-service`. It relies on historical purchase data, and the fact that a `purchase-service` record entirely describes the sale transaction (including the pricing information that was current at the time of purchase, as well as the payment instrument to which to refund the sale total). Refunds are also events that are published to a Kafka topic, so that other systems (for example, a data warehouse used for financial reporting queries, or again the best-seller list service) can update their own internal states accordingly.

The `fraud-service`, which detects suspicious or clearly fraudulent consumer behavior, has no directly callable endpoints. It autonomously monitors purchasing and other user activities, and subsequently notifies administrative personnel. Depending on the severity of the fraud suspicion and impact, the service can deactivate users, votes, or reviews without prior human approval.

Feature-Focused Services

The `bestsellers-service` exposes only a single search endpoint that responds to the HTTP GET method to vend the various bestseller lists based on criteria like a book category, an author, the book format, the language a book was written in, or the year it was published. This service's backing data store can be optimized based on its purely read-intensive data access pattern to use a key-value store, or a search-optimized back end like Elasticsearch (`https://www.elastic.co/products/elasticsearch`). Updates to this data store will happen in a separate message-consuming process that listens to the topics published `purchase-service` and `refund-service`, while querying other data sources (like `books-service`) for additional data, like a book option's title, author, category, format, language, and so on.

The social features mentioned in the bookstore scenario will also mostly be implemented using dedicated services. When partitioning these features into service components, we are placing special care on the data-access patterns and data join frequencies, in order to ensure that these features function efficiently at scale.

Separate services for comments, voting, and reviews functionalities are justified by their separate functionalities and potential maturity and iteration speeds.

A decision that is harder to make is this: which service should own the information about the set of users any given customer follows? From a functionality-driven perspective, the most natural place to store and retrieve such "user A follows users B, C, and D" data would be inside the `users-service`. But, given that we also have a requirement to notify all users of commenting, voting, and review activities by the users they follow, an `activity-notifications-service` (which will be in charge of notifying all following users) would have to constantly make service calls to the `users-service` to retrieve the current list of users to notify. Therefore, instead of keeping the "follows" relationship inside the `users-service`, we decide to keep this information inside the `activity-notifications-service` data store, so main cross-service data joins can be avoided.

The `recommendations-service` vends personalized recommendations and is a good example of a service that exposes a functionality that is mostly a mash-up of other, more basic service information. Recommendations will be based on purchase history data retrieved from the `purchase-service` application, combined with current `cart-service` information, and joined against `books-service` information about categories and authors.

A `promotions-service` is an example of an entirely out-of-request-cycle service, which exposes no synchronous API endpoints. It operates entirely as a background process that sends promotional emails and push notifications to users based on data from the `recommendations-service`, as well as a `users-service`, once every week, or during holidays specials.

Summary

This chapter has focused on ways to break down a business domain and its related features into a set of smaller web applications and microservices. We looked at the two general approaches of application decomposition and application aggregation, and identified a set of patterns for them.

We examined and explained the following decomposition approaches:

- Decomposing by functionality
- Decomposing by maturity
- Decomposing by data access pattern
- Decomposing by context

We discussed the following aggregation patterns and the effects of their properties:

- Aggregation for a derived functionality
- Aggregation for business intelligence
- Aggregation for client convenience
- Aggregation to aid system performance

We concluded the chapter by outlining a fictitious online bookstore business application and its desired features. We then applied some of the patterns and techniques discussed in this chapter to partition the bookstore into a set of core services, supporting services, and user-facing applications.

Chapter 4 will focus on the design aspects involved in exposing specific service APIs, both internal to a company and externally to the public, and we will describe a set of characteristics that we think make up a good API.

Designing Your APIs

In this chapter we will start explaining in detail how APIs should be designed. We will define what APIs are and will describe a set of characteristics that we think make up a good API, using what you now recognize as our opinionated approach.

We'll then explain how you should design your own APIs by describing a set of APIs from our bookstore sample application, listing each use case and describing our thought process when defining inputs and outputs for each API.

Introducing APIs

To answer the question of what we understand by the term *API*, let's look at some quotes from standard web resources that we think capture our understanding well and clearly.

> *API (application program interface) is a set of routines, protocols, and tools for building software applications. The API specifies how software components should interact and APIs are used when programming graphical user interface (GUI) components.*

—Webopedia[1]

> *An API expresses a software component in terms of its operations, inputs, outputs, and underlying types, defining functionalities that are independent of their respective implementations, which allows definitions and implementations to vary without compromising the interface. A good API makes it easier to develop a program by providing all the building blocks, which are then put together by the programmer.*

—Wikipedia[2]

One aspect often overlooked when describing any API is its nonfunctional requirements. You will see why it is generally important to understand those requirements early on in the design process, and to include them in each individual API description.

The use of APIs is not exclusive to microservices or even other web-based applications. Many different kinds of computer systems employ them to enable software developers to build applications for these systems based on published programming interface specifications. As an example, a programmer who develops apps for Android will use Android APIs to interact with the system to build screens and access phone capabilities and hardware, like the front camera of an Android-based device.

---

[1]"API—application program interface", Webopedia (August 24, 2016). http://www.webopedia.com/TERM/A/API.html
[2]"Application programming interface", Wikipedia, referenced on May 5, 2016. https://en.wikipedia.org/wiki/Application_programming_interface

© Cloves Carneiro Jr. and Tim Schmelmer 2016
C. Carneiro Jr. and T. Schmelmer, *Microservices From Day One*, DOI 10.1007/978-1-4842-1937-9_4

APIs are especially important in the realm of microservices because most communication between applications happens via API calls. Each of your microservices will expose its functionalities via a set of endpoints that have a well-defined set of inputs and outputs, and that perform the task(s) the service is responsible for.

The Significance of API Design

API Design is easy ... Good API Design is HARD

—David Carver[3]

Depending on your line of business, your API may be the actual product you sell and expose to your customer; if so, you have to take as much time as you need before you expose that service to your clients. If possible, come up with a process that helps you start developing and exposing your APIs early to a small subset of your users, so that you start to validate those APIs iteratively.

When you decide to use an external API, you acknowledge that it takes a certain amount of time for your development team to learn that API and understand its interaction points. One needs to read documentation and write code, sometimes using trial and error, to take advantage of an API's functionalities. With that in mind, you should strive for providing an API that is well documented, behaves in a consistent manner, and performs well. Creating APIs that are inconsistent across different endpoints or perform poorly will frustrate the developers that have decided to invest in your API, so you really want to get that right the first time.

At Amazon Web Services, new services are usually extracted from known internal services at Amazon that are already successfully used by a set of developers. Once a service is identified as a possible external product, then getting a first beta of the to-be-public API to a very small set of Amazon customers is the next step in the product development cycle, because that allows some validation of that API. After the service team is happy that internal customers have successfully deployed solutions with the beta API, then a small set of external (to Amazon) customers are selected to be private beta users of the new service, to further validate the service API. Of course, at the scale of AWS, it's probably impossible to fix a bad API after it goes live; so, they have a validation process to make sure that their APIs will be useful in the designed state before they become public.

Why is Designing a Good API Important?

Once customers started building their applications and systems using our APIs, changing those APIs becomes impossible, as we would be impacting our customer's business operations if we would do so. We knew that designing APIs was a very important task as we'd only have one chance to get it right.

—Werner Vogels[4]

Our goal as API designers is to deliver a product that is easy to learn and use, easy to maintain and extend, and perform its functions correctly and according to the client's nonfunctional requirements.

---

[3]"API Design is easy ... Good API Design is HARD", David Carver (October 20, 2009). https://intellectual-cramps.wordpress.com/2009/10/20/api-design-is-easy-good-api-design-is-hard/
[4]Werner Vogels, "10 Lessons from 10 Years of Amazon Web Services," March 11, 2016. http://www.allthingsdistributed.com/2016/03/10-lessons-from-10-years-of-aws.html

Joshua Bloch, formerly the lead designer of many APIs and features of the Java platform at Sun Microsystems makes the following key point about placing high importance on API design:

Thinking in terms of API Design improves code quality

—Joshua Bloch[5]

On the opposite side of the equation, bad API design will cause you a lot of issues that will require you to make—often big—changes to your API design, which in turn will potentially break the code of your clients who are using the initial poorly defined API. There's nothing worse than asking your clients to rewrite code for no good reason. Another reason to avoid rushing your API designs is that you will probably still have to support the old versions of an API for clients who cannot upgrade to your new version when you want them to, so you may end up having to support both versions for a long time.

What Makes an API Good?

Now that we understand why API design is very important for microservices, we will talk about a set of properties and best practices that we think make a good API.

General Characteristics

Any API designer should pay special attention to the big picture of the interfaces that the system under design exposes. In our experience, the following properties have proven particularly important to the success of APIs. Please note that we see all these characteristics as equally essential, so we do not rank or prioritize any one over others in this list.

Clear Naming

Every API should have an obvious name that makes sense to its users. It's known that naming is one of the hardest problems in software engineering, but it's especially important when you're creating an endpoint that other developers will call to make it very easy to remember. If you manage to give your API a name that developers can guess just based on its functionality, then you've nailed it.

Focus

APIs should do one thing and do it well; the purpose of each API has to be clear to all its clients. If you make the reason for an API easy to understand, remember, and use, then you achieve this goal.

Completeness

An API needs to be able to fulfil its *raison d'être*; the functionality you advertise has to be properly implemented. This may sounds contrary to the previous characteristic, but is actually complementary.

---

[5]Joshua Bloch, "How to Design a Good API and Why it Matters", JavaPolis 2005, Antwerp, Belgium. https://www.infoq.com/presentations/effective-api-design

Intuitiveness

The best APIs are the ones you can call without having to think a lot about them. If an API consumer can guess what your API does by glancing at your documentation, then you've achieved this goal.

Consistency

Within your company, it's imperative that you have a set of consistent rules around API development. When you adopt consistent naming conventions for how you call your APIs, and how inputs/outputs are expected in the same way across your APIs, using them will become easy and intuitive.

Hypermedia Type

In the name of consistency, you need a set of rules that any team working on APIs should follow. In our experience, organizations that let each developer and/or development team build APIs as they see fit will end up with a ton of inconsistencies in inputs, outputs, error treatment, and response envelopes. Over time, those inconsistencies will cause headaches and slow down your development effort overall. We've seen cases of APIs that were very inconsistent within the same service. This causes a lot of frustration for API clients who can't reliably reuse code to handle basic things like error-handling, because those endpoints don't follow a standard.

Mike Amundsen, author of the 2011 O'Reilly book *Building Hypermedia APIs with HTML5 and Node*, makes an important point in an article called "Hypermedia Types" about the characteristics of hypermedia types and their relationship of the flow of an application using them:

> *Hypermedia Types are MIME media types that contain native hyper-linking semantics that induce application flow. For example, HTML is a hypermedia type; XML is not.* [6]
>
> —Mike Amundsen

We think it's vital that your organization picks one hypermedia type option as a standard for API communication, and sticks with it on all your APIs, and it will be the answer to questions that could cause inconsistencies. Some options are:

- *HAL* (https://tools.ietf.org/html/draft-kelly-json-hal-06)
- *JSON API* (http://jsonapi.org/)
- *JSON-LD* (http://json-ld.org/)
- *Siren* (https://github.com/kevinswiber/siren)
- *Collections+JSON* (http://amundsen.com/media-types/collection/examples/)

Each of these hypermedia types has its rules that describe the exact format that requests and responses should conform to, with varying degrees of robustness, verbosity, and strictness. We have decided to use JSON API in this book because it's a complete solution for describing what our APIs are supposed to look like, and it provides the consistency we're looking for. It could be that your preferred programming language has better support for other hypermedia types, and we recommend you do some research to pick the tool that helps you be most efficient.

---

[6]"Hypermedia Types", Mike Amundsen (2010). http://amundsen.com/hypermedia/

Some hypermedia types have fairly long and strict specifications, and some leave a lot of room for developers to maneuver around their definitions. We prefer hypermedia types that leave no room for guessing how APIs should behave and recommend ones that take all of the following into consideration:

- Request/response envelopes

- Authentication

- Response code

- Error codes/messages

- Pagination parameters

- Sorting/ordering responses

- Versioning

While we will not discuss the pros and cons of each of the hypermedia type options noted earlier, there are some very good articles that go over many of the characteristics of each type, and we recommend you experiment to find a specification you're happy with.[7] The important part is that you make it obvious what hypermedia type you are using and make sure that it's respected by all teams in your company. By doing that, you won't have surprises when calling services, making your developers happier. As a general rule, we highly recommend making sure to research the tool chain that exists for the hypermedia types you choose with regard to the languages and the rest of your technology stack.

We realize that choosing a common hypermedia type across team borders is often a challenge, and that the preferred choice can and will vary over time. In such scenarios it will often be necessary to introduce breaking changes to existing APIs, and we will present a process to address such evolution later in this chapter.

API Design Guide

After you have selected a hypermedia type to standardize on, we recommend you create an API Design Guide document (often also referred to as a *Style Guide*) that describes your organization's best practices regarding API design/development. You should aim for a document that is easy to read, searchable, concise, and explains your practices well. Make sure to update your API Design Guide as you improve your design practices based on what you've learned, and provide guidance about prioritizing potentially conflicting goals.

A good API Design Guide should touch on all of these:

- Hypermedia type to adopt

- Request formats

- Response envelopes

- Consistent attribute names

- Exposed IDs

- Other concerns commons across your services

---

[7]Chapter 7, which focuses on optimizing APIs, will show the use and virtues of a few hypermedia types in more detail.

You've probably noticed that hypermedia types may dictate some of the things that go into your Design Guide; selecting a complete hypermedia type will make your API Design Guide simpler to write, as a lot of concerns are already covered in the hypermedia type specification.

A great example to follow—and find inspiration in—is Heroku's *HTTP API Design Guide* (`https://geemus.gitbooks.io/http-api-design/content/en/index.html`). It's a very easy to read document that describes Heroku's set of HTTP+JSON API design practices. You will see that it answers quite a few questions about how APIs are expected to behave, and again, removes the need for developers to guess about many aspects of API development, making APIs consistent across the company.

Nonfunctional Requirements

Often, most of the discussion around APIs navigates toward the inputs, outputs, and side effects of API calls. In our experience, the nonfunctional requirements for API calls—which usually relate to availability, performance, scalability, capacity, recoverability, and reliability—can end up being ignored or not seen as crucial. We, of course, disagree with that emphasis and think it's essential to be explicit about those requirements when exposing and consuming APIs. We'll discuss some of the most important nonfunctional requirements of APIs in this section.

Service-Level Agreements

Make sure that you have service-level agreements—SLAs—as part of your service API contracts. For example, you can have service-level availability agreements that apply to all the endpoints exposed by your service, and can go into detail about specific endpoints that have more fine-grained requirements.

Availability

Availability is probably the most important nonfunctional requirement a service owner needs to guarantee, because an unavailable service is not very useful; so your SLA should have an availability clause that explicitly states your service's availability guarantee. The simple fact of thinking about availability will make you think about the various scenarios that can impact availability, and necessary steps to guarantee that your service can be back online in a short time. It may be that, because of their responsibilities, specific services can be unavailable for extended periods of time without affecting a business; if so, make sure that is documented as well.

For a public-facing commercial service, a sample availability clause in a SLA could read:

> *AmazingAPICo will use commercially reasonable efforts to make sure its API is available 99.95% of the time. In the event AmazingAPICo does not meet the goal of 99.95% API availability, you will be eligible to receive a service credit.*

For an internal service within a corporation, the clause could be as simple as this:

> *ServiceA should be available 99.5% of the time. In the event ServiceA is continually unavailable for more than 5 minutes, please page TeamA.*

By being explicit about your nonfunctional requirements, you make sure that your clients are aware of the type of service they will receive, they can plan for fallback measures during outages, and you have measuring sticks for your monitoring and alarming setups. Also, SLAs for internal-only APIs can be used to estimate resources and justify operational expenditures (for example, for fail-over hardware if a given uptime requirement cannot otherwise be met).

Performance

Performance is another extremely important nonfunctional requirement, and it can affect the actual implementation of your service; therefore, you don't want to start thinking about performance only when your service is about to go live, because you may need to make substantial changes if its performance is not acceptable for its clients.

We go into a lot more detail about performance monitoring and alarming in Chapter 13, but the important aspect here is to make sure performance is not an afterthought. Your SLA should state some metrics that you want to respect during the operation of your service; this could be an average or p90[8] response time for all endpoints in your service, or an endpoint-specific performance metric for endpoints that have stricter performance requirements.

Scalability, Capacity, Recoverability, and Reliability

We will not go into detail about every aspect of your nonfunctional requirements, as those may vary widely. Our recommendation is to make sure you give them the attention they deserve and spend some time thinking about how to answer most of the following questions:

- How do we scale the service? How do we measure scalability on day 1?

- How many requests can the service support while maintaining its performance? How do we add extra capacity?

- How fast can we recover from known failures?

- How reliable is the service? Do we have specific reliability concerns? Is eventual consistency acceptable?

Ideally, you should have a template SLA that can easily be adopted by your services with little adaptation, to avoid making "adding an SLA" feel like a complex task that requires weeks of analysis.

Implementing APIs the Right Way

Now that you know what an API is, it's time to dive into how APIs should be implemented. We'll outline a fairly simple set of steps to follow when you sit down to think about a problem you're solving by implementing one—or many—endpoints. After we describe those steps, we will move to a set of examples based on our sample project that will illustrate our thought process in building some APIs.

Gather Requirements

The first thing you need describe when thinking about writing a new API is a use case that describes the functionality required. We use the term *use case* informally; we really want to come up with a nontechnical description of the business functionality required, ideally with no hints at implementation or technical constraint.

A sample use case can be as simple as this: "As a User, I want to be able to save a file to storage for later retrieval." This description of the functionality tells us who the main actor/participant is (User), the action he wants to take (save a file), and the input to the function (the file).

---

[8]The p90 value is the number of milliseconds latency in which 90% of the requests reaching the API are serviced. In other words, no more than 10% of all requests take longer for the service to process and respond to.

The approach just described is known as a *contract-first* design style, which means we completely ignored all aspects of implementation and focused on what the API should do at a conceptual level and what inputs and outputs it requires. After you understand the requirements of your API, follow these steps to deliver it:

- Pick one use case you understand well.

- Define one API that fulfills an aspect of that use case by describing what it does, its inputs and outputs, and its error cases.

- Publish the API using a known protocol to your team members, and to the team that will consume your APIs. Your design approval process can vary from formal to informal based on the characteristics of the teams involved in the process.

- Once the API documentation is vetted, it is ready to be implemented, and then verified via client integration.

Using this process, you will have involved multiple teams/individuals in helping you design your API, and you can start implementation knowing that you didn't miss obvious inputs/outputs, speeding up your overall development effort.

Maximize Information Hiding

In software development, a leaky abstraction is an abstraction that exposes to its users details and limitations of its underlying implementation that should ideally be hidden away.

—Wikipedia[9]

One of the main advantages of exposing functionality via APIs is that you provide a public interface to a functionality—described by the API name and its parameters list, and are able to make changes to your implementation without having to disrupt your API's clients; therefore, APIs are an "information hiding mechanism" for the code you are sharing via APIs. With that in mind, it becomes very important that you only expose enough attributes to make your response fulfil its goal, and nothing more.

Some frameworks make it easy to generate API responses by serializing all attributes of a model in a JSON response by default; this seems to save the developer time deciding what attributes should be exposed, but it turns out to be an anti-pattern. In the long run, those easy-to-generate responses end up restricting the API developer when changes to the API implementation require database schema tweaks, which could break the actual API. Make sure that your APIs expose only attributes that are obviously useful to your clients, and make an effort not to expose artifacts that are too tied to your implementation, which creates what we call "leaky abstractions." Another drawback is that clients will come to rely on implementation details you didn't need—or mean—to expose; you will have a hard time requesting clients to stop using those attributes, or will have to support them forever.

The rule of thumb for API design is to "hide" as much information as possible, and only expose data that is needed by clients, by using a vocabulary that is a level above the one you use in your implementation. Using our bookstore, a very simple example of this is a feature of the book detail API called has_errata?, which initially has the following Ruby implementation:

```ruby
def has_errata?
  confirmed_errata.any?
end
```

---

[9]"Leaky abstraction," Wikipedia, referenced on May 2, 2016. https://en.wikipedia.org/wiki/Leaky_abstraction

In this case, we could have taken a shortcut and exposed an `errata` array with all the data we had and let the API users figure out whether a book has any errata, which would have exposed our implementation to outside clients; to avoid this, stick to exposing an attribute called `has_errata?` which helps clients extract the same information without exposing too much information. If you were to expose your raw data—the `errata` array— then in the future, when you want your errata entries to have a status that could be one of "submitted," "verified," "invalid," or "corrected," this would cause issues with clients that rely on any record in `errata` to mean that a book had errors; so, exposing your `errata` array broadly is a design mistake that you should avoid.

By this point, you're starting to understand that consistency is a key aspect of good API design. Here are some aspects of your API where consistency means that there will be no surprises, and the development team will be able to make progress without guessing how each API behaves.

When we talk about RESTful APIs, we already picture "JSON over HTTP" described with a verb and a resource. One thing that REST does not describe is how to standardize requests and responses, which will cause developers to be inconsistent across different services and endpoints, causing confusion in day-to-day development when, for example, the set of parameters required to query service A differ from those for service B, or one service returns an array while another returns a hash with an element called `data`.

APIs Change

The one aspect of API design that is a constant is that APIs will change over time, and often during your development process. Like any other piece of software, APIs are never considered "complete" until the day they are retired.

Acknowledge and Accept Changes

The Agile Manifesto[10]—like its practices—is widely accepted in our industry; it has the following principle that also applies well to APIs:

> *Welcome changing requirements, even late in development. Agile processes harness change for the customer's competitive advantage.*

All code bases go through many evolution steps during development, even when requirements are not a moving target. As soon as one accepts the fact that some code changes will happen over time, and in many layers, then changing an API just becomes part of the job of owning a service. As we mentioned before, APIs describe a contract that has to be followed for data exchange. Changes may sometimes break that contract in incompatible ways. Those are the cases where an API change needs to be thought out extremely well because not only is a service changing, but it's also requiring its clients to make changes.

Nonbreaking changes are API changes that, when deployed, will not break the expected behavior for existing clients. Nonbreaking changes happen, for example, when one or more data attributes are added to an API response. If your API uses JSON to describe its responses, then adding attributes to clients that are not expecting them will have no effect on how your clients are accessing your API.

Breaking changes are API changes that, when deployed, cause failures for existing clients. Some of the reasons that can cause breaking changes are:

- Change in the endpoint URL, which will cause clients to get 404 errors

- Change in the list of required input, which will cause client requests to fail for the lack of that attribute

---

[10]"Principles behind the Agile Manifesto,". http://agilemanifesto.org/principles.html

- Change in the format of the response, which will cause client requests to fail because the previously expected data structure is no longer available

Depending on the size of your development team and the scope of your breaking changes, you can possibly update all clients in a short time, and not cause a lot of disruption; however, by the same token, you could require changes in applications that belong to other busy teams, and it may take months until your new API is used by all its intended audience.

The Development and Communication Process for Breaking Changes

When possible, breaking changes should be avoided because they cause disruption of existing client calls, which may require a nontrivial amount of time to be updated across possibly many clients. When breaking changes cannot be avoided, it's crucial that you have a process to communicate that those changes are coming to your clients. Assuming that your clients can still use the current version of your API, a simple process to track API changes should include these:

- Documentation about the change, explaining exactly what has changed, how important it is that your clients move to the updated API, and when you'd expect all clients to migrate.

- Timelines for when the new version of the API will be available for testing and in other environments, such as staging and production.

- Ideally, some sample code that communicates how the change in the API can be consumed. This is especially valuable in an organization that standardizes in a specific technology, where all API clients will benefit from seeing code changes.

In small companies, it's possible that developers who are making breaking changes are expected to also change the code of the clients that consume those APIs. This is efficient when you have a small team; so, if your environment allows you to do so, it may be part of your process for introducing breaking changes.

Add a New API

When a breaking change alters some of the fundamentals of how your existing API behaves, it may make sense to explain—and expose—your API change as a new API altogether. This can be seen when large companies release new versions of the APIs/libraries that completely break backward-compatibility with the existing version. As software evolves, some large refactoring may be unavoidable, making the new version of the API look like a new API, and you should consider doing that in cases where it's likely that you will need to make changes in various endpoints because of design decisions taken in early stages of development. Of course, creating a new API—or set of APIs—is a very disrupting type of breaking change, and should be avoided when possible.

Version Your APIs

As we've said before, change happens! Over time, new requirements for your service will arise. Causing breakages in existing client applications—whether internal or external—can and should be avoided completely. In the vast majority of cases, upgrading your service and all its clients in lock-step is simply not possible.

This situation is best addressed by versioning your APIs. Put very simply, you can bump the version number of existing API endpoints that change. If you continue supporting the previous version of such API endpoints ("API V1"), then current clients will continue to function unchanged, while new clients can choose to call the updated API endpoints at the new version, API V2.

Negotiating the API Version

Clients need to communicate to the service which version of an API resource they would like to receive, while the service needs to indicate which version it serves up. There are many options for specifying a version for the API. Let's look at the most common approaches we have seen used.

Using HTTP Headers

In this approach, the negotiations happen based on HTTP headers. The most HTTP standard-compliant way to do this is to use the Accept and Content-Type headers to request, and respond with, a specific version of an API resource.

The requesting client will specify the acceptable content type and version in an Accept header, for example:

```
Accept: application/vnd.books.com; version=2
GET /books
```

The service will then include an appropriate version of the result in its response, indicating the type and version in the Content-Type response header, as shown here:

```
HTTP/1.1 200 Success
      Date: Wed, 26 Aug 2016 06:25:24 GMT
      ...
      Content-Type: application/vnd.books.com; version=2
```

A variation of this versioning strategy is to accept a nonstandard, application-specific header in place of the Accept header in requests destined for your service. One example for accepting (and including in service responses) is to support a header like, for example, X-BookStore-API-Version:

```
X-BookStore-API-Version: 2
GET /books
```

The service response could then look like this:

```
HTTP/1.1 200 Success
      Date: Wed, 26 Aug 2016 06:25:24 GMT
      ...
      X-BookStore-API-Version: 2
      Content-Type: application/json
```

Using HTTP headers for versioning is the way most REST "purists" will probably choose. The argument for this is that the version of a resource should not be part of the resource's URI, as it is in essence still the same resource that is addressed. A disadvantage of this approach is the loss of convenience in quickly testing an API endpoint from a browser, as most browsers need additional plugins or extensions to allow for specifying HTTP request headers.

Using the Request Path

Some APIs accept the version specification as part of their endpoint's URLs, usually as a prefix before specifying the resource in the path. When translated to our bookstore example, the request to the list of all books in version 2 would look like this:

```
GET /v2/books
```

While it's not uncontroversial, many API designers usually use this approach because of its simplicity, compatibility with browsers, and intuitiveness for handling of versions. If your web application framework's request routing mechanism supports it, we suggest that you at least consider allowing for specifying the resource version as part of the request path, in addition to relying on HTTP headers as discussed earlier.

Using a Query Parameter

Another approach to specify the requested version is to accept it as a query parameter, as shown here:

```
GET /books?version=2
```

Some API designers choose this approach, but we do not recommend it. We have found that this strategy seems the least intuitive of the approaches described here. Using a query parameter for the version of a resource muddies the waters around other query parameters that are better placed there, such as representations, search terms, and the like.

Determining What Numbering Scheme to Use

For the concrete values that signify a list of versions, most implementations we have observed use either consecutive integers (v1, v2, v3, …), or dates (v20160424, v20150811, …). Another popular software versioning scheme is *semantic versioning* (http://semver.org/), but we have rarely seen it in use for web-based APIs.

While the details can certainly cater to personal preferences, we encourage using something that allows for easy and efficient analysis by the server to evaluate which API is the later version. In other words, we discourage using schemes like v_new, v_old, vXmasEdition, or even v08112015 (as using dates in the ISO 8601 format yields larger integers for later date values).

Supporting and Deprecating API Versions

Any published API can potentially live for longer than its designer. This point is especially true when exposing an API publicly, where third-party entities decide how long they will attempt to use it. But even for private, company-internal APIs, time and thought invested in considering support and deprecation policies prior to launch pays off.

A very important step is to make sure that there is a way to identify your clients for any given version of your API. One approach we have taken to help with this is to require an API key parameter (preferably as a special header) for every API call.[11] If you do so, make sure to log such client information. You will find numerous opportunities to use it while your service is in production, even if it is just to perform usage pattern analysis.[12]

---

[11]For internal APIs, the security and authentication features surrounding the authenticity of this API key can be quite relaxed; that is, clients can usually be trusted to reliably self-identify. More stringent rules for authentication, authorization, expiry, and encryption need to apply for externally accessible API keys.

[12]We will discuss aspects of monitoring your services in more detail in Chapter 13.

You should also think about how to contact and notify your clients about any updates to your APIs. Do you have email addresses or other reliable contact details for all owners of client applications? Internal to your company you could use a simple mailing list for communicating changes, bug fixes, and so on, that are part of a new API version.

Also, be sure to publish your API's deprecation and support policy alongside any API release. That way, clients can plan ahead, and you are in a better position to tell them to get off a version for which you are about to drop support. Teams that strive to support no more than two versions of the same API, where an outdated version is only available for a small number of weeks after the updated version has been released, can focus more time and resources on development tasks.[13]

For internal APIs, be sure to set expectations regarding which team is responsible for upgrading the client applications when new (potentially breaking) API changes occur. Is the client application team responsible for acting on it, or will the service-owning team be on the hook?[14]

Designing / Splitting Up by Example

In this section, we will take a practical approach to API design. We'll talk about two major interaction points of our bookstore project, and will describe some of the features of a couple of its pages, to help us identify the attributes that each page requires to be properly rendered. We'll then group those attributes and talk about the services and endpoints we should hit in each case, and we'll design a few request/response examples that will hopefully help drive home some of the concepts we touched on in this chapter.

For all examples in our sample project, we decided to adopt the JSON API hypermedia type, so some of the characteristics of our responses and requests are defined by that specification.

The Bookstore Home Page

The bookstore home page has a fairly complex set of features distributed across some of our services (see Figure 4-1). In this section, we will describe those features and talk about the API calls needed to properly render the home page.

---

[13]Some companies, like Netflix, on the other hand opt to keep old versions of internal APIs around until no client can be identified as using them. See Chapter 1 for more details on the Netflix approach.

[14]We discuss this and other topics of operational support in a microservices environment at length in Chapter 14.

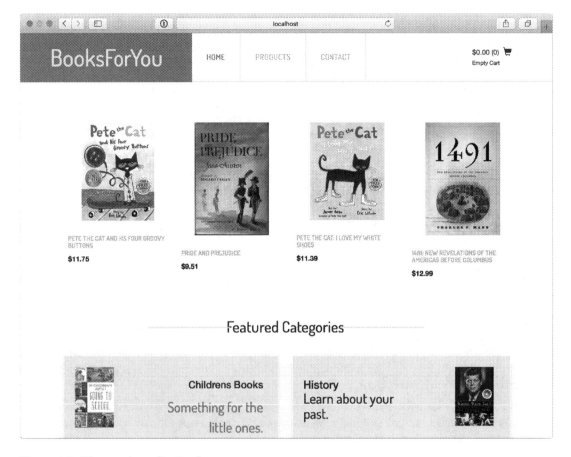

Figure 4-1. *The sample application home page*

Cart Information

The cart widget, which contains the price and number of elements added to the cart, appears in most pages of the web application. We have decided that carts are saved on a per-user basis, and therefore require the widget's clients to pass in a UUID representing the current user, who could be logged in or not. In order to retrieve the user_id, we will ask users-service for the ID of the current user, which can be extracted from a secure cookie holding the user's authentication token.

```
GET /users?token=6BbWOpxOOYENxn38HMUbcQ==
Accept: application/vnd.api+json
```

The response returns a match that lists some information about the user who matched the token we passed in as a parameter.

```json
{
  "links": {
    "self": "/users/d83d6c58-e05a-43a7-8d58-5995f68e1ba9"
  },
  "data": {
    "type": "users",
    "id": "d83d6c58-e05a-43a7-8d58-5995f68e1ba9",
    attributes: {
      "name": "Cloves Carneiro Jr",
      "email": "cloves.carneiro@example.org",
      ...
      "phone": "",
    }
  }
}
```

Now that we have a user ID handy, we can go back to `cart-service` and request the `carts` detail information, but we don't need all the details of the cart; we just want a really small subset of its attributes, the current total price, and number of products. The JSON API specification has a feature called *sparse fieldsets*, which states that an endpoint can return only specific fields in the response on a per-type basis by including a `fields[TYPE]` parameter:

```
GET /cart?user_id=d83d6c58-e05a-43a7-8d58-5995f68e1ba9&fields[carts]=total_price,products_count
Accept: application/vnd.api+json
```

The response returns just the data we requested, increasing efficiency both on the client and on the server.

```json
{
  "links": {
    "self": "/carts/178c3c65-16ee-46e8-8931-cdef1fb0568c"
  },
  "data": {
    "type": "carts",
    "id": "178c3c65-16ee-46e8-8931-cdef1fb0568c",
    attributes: {
      "total_price": 2259,
      "products_count": 1,
    }
  }
}
```

User Recommendations

It's common that e-commerce landing pages display a set of products that are recommended to the logged-in user. Our proposed `recommendations-service` takes as parameters the `user_id` of the currently logged-in user and the `cart_id`, so that it can look up recommendations based on the user's previous purchases and current items in cart. Although `recommendations-service` sounds complex, it knows how to do its job and requires only a simple API call with the parameters we mentioned. We also know that we only want to display four recommendations in our home page, so we pass in `page[size]` with a value of 4.

```
GET /recommendations?user_id=d83d6c58-e05a-43a7-8d58-5995f68e1ba9&cart_id=178c3c65-16ee-
46e8-8931-cdef1fb0568c&page[size]=4
Accept: application/vnd.api+json
```

```
{
  "links": {
    "self": "/recommendations?used_id=d83d6c58-e05a-43a7-8d58-5995f68e1ba9&cart_id=178c3c65-
    16ee-46e8-8931-cdef1fb0568c&page[size]=4"
    "next": "/recommendations?used_id=d83d6c58-e05a-43a7-8d58-5995f68e1ba9&cart_id=178c3c65-
    16ee-46e8-8931-cdef1fb0568c&page[size]=4&page[number]=2",
  },
  "data": {
    "type": "books",
    "id": "5ea3d5c2-13a7-4282-9d33-693ae38c48e0",
    attributes: {
      "title": "Beginning Rails 4 (Expert's Voice in Web Development)",
    },
    "relationships": [
      "main_author": {
        "links": {"self": "http://books-service.books.com/authors/ec84275e-0e8a-495c-9ba7-
        68e791b0fad7""}
        "data": {"type": "authors", "id": "ec84275e-0e8a-495c-9ba7-68e791b0fad7"}
        "attributes": {"name": "Cloves Carneiro Jr"}
      },
      "cover": {
        "links": {"self": "http://images-service.books.com/images/e54c65b6-2916-4573-a494-
        1e71188ae754"}
        "data": {"type": "images", "id": "e54c65b6-2916-4573-a494-1e71188ae754"}
        "attributes": {
          "file_name_url": "https://bucket.s3.amazonaws.com/book/5ea3d5c2/c421cdd8-865f-
          4bc6-8db5-107ccb1d4459.jpeg"
        }
      }
    ]
  }
}
```

The response served by recommendations-service provides books resources with a limited set of book attributes, only enough to display basic information about a book, which the user can then click on to get to a book detail page.

The Book Detail Page

Let's now think about the book detail page of our sample application. It has most of the features customers would expect from a bookstore website; some of the obvious pieces of information it needs to render are the actual book details, all images for a book, and book reviews (see Figure 4-2).

Figure 4-2. The sample application's book detail page

Book Details

In the context of the home page, `books-service` returned a list of books displaying a limited number of attributes for each book, because at that level, there wasn't a requirement for displaying much more than the book title, author, and image. In this case, the book detail page takes the opposite approach; its job is to display as much information as possible about a book to help customers make educated purchase decisions; thus, we can say that we will need all the book data available in that service.

We've used a feature we call *representations* to define a well-known set of attributes with a name that conveys the type of data that will be returned. In this case, we will be requesting the "full" representation view of a book detail API endpoint. It will provide the following attributes:

- Title
- ISBN
- Author(s)
- Excerpt
- Description

- Table of contents (TOC)

- Page count

- Language

- Publisher

- Edition

- Release date

- Dimensions

- Weight

- Price

- Original price (if the current price is promotional)

- Formats (paperback, hardcover, ebook)

- Top category

- Sub-category

- Tags

The book details endpoint will be a resource identified by the URI /books/{*isbn*}, where *isbn* will be the ISBN that uniquely identifies each book; so, when a client application needs to access the detail endpoint for a book, it will send the following HTTP request:

```
GET /books/978-1430260349?representation=full
Accept: application/vnd.api+json
```

It will receive a response that—using the JSON API hypermedia type—looks like this:

```
{
  "links": {
    "self": "http://example.com/books/978-1430260349"
  },
  "data": {
    "type": "books",
    "id": "5ea3d5c2-13a7-4282-9d33-693ae38c48e0",
    attributes: {
      "title": "Beginning Rails 4 (Expert's Voice in Web Development)",
      "page_count": 232,
      "excerpt": "",
      "description": "",
      ...
      "tags": []
    },
```

```
      "relationships": [
        "authors": [
          {
            "links": {"self": "http://example.com/authors/UUID"}
            "data": {"type": "author", "id": "UUID"}
            "attributes": {"name": "Cloves Carneiro Jr"}
          }
        ],
      ]
  }
}
```

You see that the top-level data element is what describes the book—the resource—we are interested in. It's a JSON API requirement that responses have a data element. It can include a hash, as in this case, or an array when the response describes multiple resources instead of one, which is the case with the reviews and image requests this page will make.

Some of the resources associated with the book are returned in that response—all under relationships, as is the case of the authors array, which returns us enough information to display a list of authors, and links to URLs where we can load more details about those authors when necessary.

Reviews

The same book details page wants to list a small number of highly relevant reviews associated with the book the customer is looking at. For that, it will request that data from the reviews-service by sending an HTTP request to:

```
GET /reviews/5ea3d5c2-13a7-4282-9d33-693ae38c48e0?page[size]=3
Accept: application/vnd.api+json
```

You can see that, in this request, we requested only the first three reviews associated with the book by using the page[size] parameter to limit the number of resources we want to see. We assume that the reviews-service will default to its most important sort order, and hence have not provided an explicit value for the sort parameter.

```
{
  "links": {
    "self": "/reviews/5ea3d5c2-13a7-4282-9d33-693ae38c48e0?page[size]=3",
    "next": "/reviews/5ea3d5c2-13a7-4282-9d33-693ae38c48e0?page[size]=3&page[number]=2",
  },
  "data": [
    {
      "type": "reviews",
      "id": "UUID",
      "attributes": {
        "title": "Everything you need as a Rails programmer",
        "rating": 5,
        "name": "Jane Doe",
        "content": "Lorem ipsum ..."
      }
    },
```

```
    {
      "type": "reviews",
      "id": "UUID",
      "attributes": {
        "title": "When learning is a pleasure",
        "rating": 5,
        "name": "Martin Z",
        "content": "Lorem ipsum ..."
      }
    },
  ],
  "meta": {
    "records": 22
  }
}
```

That is a response that packs a ton of information, and it displays some of the great features of the JSON API. In this response, we have:

- The list of reviews we requested, under `data`

- The location where to get the next page of reviews, in `links#next`

- The total number of review that match our request, in `meta#records`

For books that do not have any reviews, the only difference in the response would be an empty `data` array:

```
{
  "links": {
    "self": "/reviews/5ea3d5c2-13a7-4282-9d33-693ae38c48e0?page[size]=3",
  },
  "data": []
}
```

Images

The same book details page needs to display an image for each available version of the book the customer is looking at. For that, it will request that data from the `images-service` by sending an HTTP request to:

```
GET /images/5ea3d5c2-13a7-4282-9d33-693ae38c48e0
Accept: application/vnd.api+json
```

```
{
  "links": {
    "self": "/images/5ea3d5c2-13a7-4282-9d33-693ae38c48e0"
  },
```

```
  "data": [
    {
      "type": "images",
      "id": "UUID",
      attributes: {
        "file_name_url": "https://bucket.s3.amazonaws.com/book/5ea3d5c2/a1d4efb5-7908-4683-
        a1b9-20438c16eedb.jpeg",
      }
    },
    {
      "type": "images",
      "id": "UUID",
      attributes: {
        "file_name_url": "https://bucket.s3.amazonaws.com/book/5ea3d5c2/c421cdd8-865f-4bc6-
        8db5-107ccb1d4459.jpeg",
      }
    }
  ]
}
```

In this response, we can see that there are two images associated with the book, which we can display in the book detail page.

As you can see, we were able to load enough data to render all the details needed in the book detail page by calling three services, each responsible for a type of data associated with the book.

Summary

In this chapter, we covered a lot of ground related to designing APIs. We started by stating the importance of good API design, and listed a set of principles we think are important for your API process. We touched on the fact that you also need to think about your API's nonfunctional requirements and listed a set of properties to consider during your design process. Tips on how to deal with breaking changes and API version control were explained next. We ended the chapter with some hands-on examples of how we defined APIs in our sample book project, describing some of the pages that customers see and endpoints that are hit to render those pages.

In the next chapter, we will go into more detail about implementing APIs. We will introduce approaches and tools for describing your services' APIs in a machine-readable format, by introducing the Swagger specification and some of its toolset.

CHAPTER 5

Defining APIs

This chapter will introduce approaches and tools for describing your services' APIs in a machine-readable format. First we will introduce the concepts behind Interface Definition Languages (IDLs) and will briefly introduce a number of such languages. Next, we will introduce the Swagger IDL framework and its associated tool chain in more detail, and we will conclude the chapter by illustrating how to use Swagger to define the APIs of one of the services in our bookstore application.

Interface Definition Languages (IDLs)

An IDL is a language for specifying any software component's API in a format that is easy for computers to process. The size of the component described in an IDL can vary widely; some IDLs describe the APIs of a single object, whereas others aim at defining the APIs of an entire application.

There are many advantages in describing your APIs in such a manner. As shown in the previous chapter, an iterative definition process that involves early drafting, sharing, and soliciting and incorporating feedback helps to increase the chances that your API will be useful to its clients.

Another advantageous trait of IDLs is that they are usually platform- and language-independent; clients of the APIs do not need to be implemented on top of the same operating system, or even in the same programming language as the service providing the APIs.

The biggest selling point in our eyes for the use of a machine-readable IDL revolves about the possibilities for developing a supporting chain of tools. Automatic processing of API definitions means that tools for generating client and/or service stub code in many programming languages can be created. Additionally, code for the validation of client requests and service responses based on the IDL specifications can be introduced. Some IDLs also come with tools for generating documentation, or with automatically generated web sites that let you explore the APIs based on their definition.

The first implementations of Interface Defining Languages date back to the early to mid-1980s, when Sun Microsystems introduced the Remote Procedure Call protocol. Sun's first version of what is now called Open Network Computing RPC was specified in RFC 1057 and adopted in 1988. The style of defining interprocess communication in ONC RPC was firmly rooted in the Unix operating system and C programming language traditions. To exchange data between clients and services, ONC RPC used the External Data Representation (EDR) serialization protocol. This standardization strategy enabled even this very early IDL to develop a tool chain that included rpcgen for generating C language client libraries and service stubs, which were available across multiple operating systems (Unix derivatives and Microsoft Windows).

The list of IDLs used in the industry has grown large since these early beginnings. Some IDL frameworks (like Apache Thrift or Google's Protocol Buffers) introduce special binary formats for transmitting data over the wire, favoring terseness and the resulting speed of transmission and decoding. Other IDLs (for example, JSON-based approaches like Swagger or API Blueprint) favor text-based protocols because of their human-readable format, and despite their implicit inefficiencies the growing availability of mass storage and bandwidth has made such protocols gain large popularity.

© Cloves Carneiro Jr. and Tim Schmelmer 2016
C. Carneiro Jr. and T. Schmelmer, *Microservices From Day One*, DOI 10.1007/978-1-4842-1937-9_5

A Matter of Style: RPC versus REST

Most IDLs can be classified into two categories based on which architectural style of interprocess communications they most naturally support: Remote Procedure Calls (RPC) or REpresentational State Transfer (REST).

We will not go into detail about the specific differences between RPC and REST. For our purposes here, it is sufficient to say that we consider RPC a style that focuses mostly on traditional object-oriented method invocation and message passing. The approach is usually implemented via invoking a method on an object stub that exists in the local process address space of the client. Under the hood, this local invocation triggers a network call to a remote service, in whose process the actual object method is executed instead. The main point is to make the remote aspect of the procedure execution as transparent as feasibly possible.

In a RESTfully styled API, a set of particular constraints is imposed on the client and the service. Here, clients can retrieve information about, and perform a very limit set of actions (also known as verbs) on, a set of resources that are exposed by the service's APIs. Services provide clients with multiple representations of the API-defined resources, and the client can use the action verbs either to retrieve a particular new representation of a resource, or to manipulate the resources. Additionally, communication between clients and the service is stateless. In almost all practical implementations, RESTful APIs are implemented on top of the HTTP protocol, which itself can be seen as the prototypical implementation of the REST architectural style; its set of methods (GET, PUT, POST, PATCH, DELETE, and so on) can be seen as the verbs that are applied to resources, identified via Uniform Resource Identifiers (URIs).

RPC-Style Interface Definition Languages

The first IDLs available all followed the RPC style, focusing mostly on allowing for invoking methods on remote objects. In addition to the already-mentioned ONC RPC, another early RPC IDL was the Common Object Request Broker Architecture (CORBA). This architecture, standardized by the Object Management Group (OMG), was a big step forward from ONC RPC for usage of an IDL outside a LAN and in more polyglot environments that demanded language and OS interoperability. Later, technologies like XML-RPC and WSDL, and their close younger cousin JSON-RPC, implemented remote method calling mechanisms on top of the HTTP protocol. Today, technologies like Apache Thrift (originally developed by Facebook), Google's Protocol Buffers,[1] and Apache Avro[2] have entered the arena of RPC IDLs, and each is used in production by many large companies.

RESTful Interface Definition Languages

RESTful IDLs probably started when Sun Microsystems first drafted the Web Application Description Language (WADL) in late 2005. WADL lets you describe REST APIs using an XML-based language, and much like WSDL, which added REST support with its version 2.0, WADL is mainly used in the Java ecosystem, especially in the JAX-RS APIs and its Jersey reference implementation. Another XML-based API definition language that developed fairly recently is RESTful Service Definition Language (RSDL), which is trying to improve on some drawbacks that practitioners found with WADL (mainly the perceived tight coupling between the service and the client caused by insufficient support for hypermedia-driven design).

---

[1]https://developers.google.com/protocol-buffers/
[2]http://avro.apache.org/

Other, more modern and less Java ecosystem-centric IDLs seem to find the use of XML to express the API specifications too cumbersome and verbose. One such example is the RESTful API Modeling Language (RAML),[3] which expresses API specifications in YAML, and which has an increasingly large set of community-maintained tools surrounding it. API Blueprint[4] is a similarly active IDL project, which chose a Markdown dialect as the language in which to write down API descriptions.

Another notable modern format in which to describe your APIs is JSON, and a significant number of RESTful IDLs specify service endpoints using it. An important part of such API descriptions is the specification of returned and accepted data types, and JSON Schema[5] currently seems to be crystalizing as the common approach for this. The main advantage that JSON Schema appears to be providing is that there is a well-defined, community-supported specification format that has found wide adoption amongst RESTful IDLs.

Cloud application platform provider Heroku describes in a 2014 blog post their extensive open-source RESTful IDL tool chain, using JSON Schema as a central technology. Similar to what Heroku's API Design Guide[6] aims at, the JSON-API project tries to codify guidelines about sane choices for API design conventions. The aim is to foster consistency and similarity between APIs described using JSON Schema.

Probably the most mature JSON Schema-compatible IDL framework in existence today is Swagger. Swagger has recently been donated to a consortium called the OpenAPI Initiative[7] and has hence been renamed the OpenAPI Specification. Swagger sports an impressive tool chain, some of which we will be exploring in the next section of this chapter.

Our Stance

To conclude this section we would like to mention that we have taken sides and decided to design most of our service APIs in a RESTful manner. The REST approach seems more natural to the world of microservices, in which APIs are designed around resources, reachable via the (RESTful) HTTP protocol, and owned by systems of record and authority. This style also appears to make the undeniable fact more obvious that in-process object method invocations are different in many ways from remote, cross-network boundary service calls; external calls are much less reliable, have more failure scenarios, and expose very different performance characteristics, all of which should have an impact on API design.

Describing APIs using Swagger

As explained in the general section on IDLs, the main benefit is that once you have defined your API operations, a computer can automatically process the IDL definitions to produce tooling for you: it can generate documentation from that IDL, it can generate a complete test suite that exhaustively exercises your API endpoints, it can generate load testing scripts for the endpoints, and handle many similar tasks.

As mentioned in the previous section, Swagger is focused on specifying RESTful web services. The tool chain around Swagger has matured greatly in recent years, and the framework now helps not only with describing, but also with producing, consuming, visualizing, and testing RESTful web services in a multitude of programming languages.

While the main focus is surely on allowing computers to understand and discover the service APIs, the tooling also makes it easier for humans to comprehend and explore the described service.

---

[3]http://raml.org/
[4]https://apiblueprint.org/
[5]http://json-schema.org/
[6]https://github.com/interagent/http-api-design
[7]https://openapis.org/

Hosting Swagger Specification as JSON Schemas

Let's start by looking at the concrete example of the JSON Schema definitions of one of the sample services' APIs shown in Listing 5-1—the users-service hosts this specification itself at the /swagger/api path.

▓ **Note**   Although it is of course possible to produce and maintain these API definitions manually, we will show you tools later in this chapter that help you with JSON schema generation and upkeep.

Listing 5-1. Swagger API JSON specification of the users-service

```
tim$ curl http://localhost:5002/swagger/api | jsonpp
{
  "swagger": "2.0",
  "info": {
    "title": "Users-Service",
    "description": "Service that owns the concern of user accounts for the bookstore",
    "version": "1.0"
  },
  "host": "localhost:5002",
  "basePath": "/",
  "paths": {
    "/users": {
      "post": {
        "tags": [
          "Users API"
        ],
        "operationId": "Users API-create",
        "parameters": [
          {
            "name": "email",
            "description": "Email address for the new user, needs to be unique.",
            "required": true,
            "in": "query",
            "type": "string"
          },
          {
            "name": "name",
            "description": "Full name of the user.",
            "required": false,
            "in": "query",
            "type": "string"
          },
          {
            "name": "password",
            "description": "Password for the user.",
            "required": true,
```

```
          "in": "query",
          "type": "string"
        }
      ],
      "responses": {
        "default": {
          "description": "",
          "schema": {
            "$ref": "#/definitions/User"
          }
        },
        "422": {
          "description": "User data invalid"
        }
      },
      "description": "Creates a new user for the given data",
      "summary": "Creates a new user for the given data",
      "x-controller": "users",
      "x-action": "create"
    },
    "get": {
      "tags": [
        "Users API"
      ],
      "operationId": "Users API-index",
      "parameters": [],
      "responses": {
        "default": {
          "description": "",
          "schema": {
            "type": "array",
            "items": {
              "$ref": "#/definitions/User"
            }
          }
        }
      },
      "description": "Returns all users' data",
      "summary": "Returns all users' data",
      "x-controller": "users",
      "x-action": "index"
    }
  },
  "/users/{id}": {
    "get": {
      "tags": [
        "Users API"
      ],
```

```
        "operationId": "Users API-show",
        "parameters": [
          {
            "name": "id",
            "description": "Scope response to id",
            "required": true,
            "in": "path",
            "type": "string"
          }
        ],
        "responses": {
          "default": {
            "description": "",
            "schema": {
              "$ref": "#/definitions/User"
            }
          },
          "404": {
            "description": "User not found"
          }
        },
        "description": "Returns a user's data for a given user by uuid",
        "summary": "Returns a user's data for a given user by uuid",
        "x-controller": "users",
        "x-action": "show"
      }
    }
  },
  "definitions": {
    "User": {
      "type": "object",
      "properties": {
        "user_id": {
          "type": "string",
          "description": "UUID for the user's ID"
        },
        "name": {
          "type": "string",
          "description": "the name for user"
        },
        "email": {
          "type": "string",
          "description": "user's email address"
        }
      },
      "required": [
        "user_id",
        "email"
      ]
    }
  },
```

```
  "tags": [
    {
      "name": "Users API",
      "description": "This document describes the API for creating and reading user
      accounts."
    }
  ],
  "securityDefinitions": {}
}
```

After some initial declarations about the Swagger version used, and general information about the users service, the host and base path for reaching its APIs are declared.

What follows is the top-level `paths` key, where the value is another JSON hash in which each entry represents one of the resources exposed by the users service. This simple service only exposes two resources called `/users` (for the general list of all accounts for the bookstore application), as well as `/users/{id}` (which is a parameterized resource that refers to each single user account).

Before we dig deeper into the resources, let's look at the next top-level entry, called `definitions`. The `definitions` key holds a hash with an entry for each API model's schema definition. Here, the only API model to describe is the `User` model. As you can see, this model consists of two required string attributes (`email` and `user_id`), as well as an optional `name` string.

The Swagger JSON specifications of our users service hash are concluded by the `tags` entry, which is a list of `name` and `description` key-value-pairs for the APIs, as well as a `securityDefinitions` section that can specify authentication and authorization requirements for the APIs.

Getting back to the resource and paths definitions, we can see that they are organized by the HTTP action verbs they support: you can use an `HTTP POST` request with required input query parameters `email` and `password`, as well as an optional `name`. The results of this user account creation endpoint are captured in the `responses` section: the operation returns either the newly created `User` object, or an error response with a 422 status code when the user data passed in was insufficient.

After a short `description` and `summary` section, you can find `x-controller` and `x-action`. These entries are interesting in that they illustrate that the Swagger JSON-Schema is extensible. In this case, the x-prefixed fields are used by a LivingSocial internal tool to better identify the code sections in a Ruby on Rails application that implements the API endpoint to create a new user.

The next endpoint defined is the parameterless `GET /users`, which simply returns an array of all bookstore account holders as `User` API model objects and is tied to the Ruby on Rails `users#index` action of the users service.

Finally, the JSON schema defines the `GET /users/{id}` operation, which takes as an input from the URI's path the user's UUID as a string, and returns either the identified user's data as a `User` object, or an error that indicates that a user by that UUID cannot be found.

The Swagger User Interface

As mentioned earlier, one of the major selling points of Swagger over other RESTful IDL frameworks is the large list of tools surrounding it.

A real gem in this tool chain is the Swagger UI. Swagger UI is a purely HTML/CSS and JavaScript-based tool that helps to visualize the JSON specifications of an API, as well as to interactively explore the described APIs.

Our users service is hosting the Swagger UI at `http://localhost:5002/swagger/doc`, shown in Figure 5-1.

Users-Service

Service that owns the concern of user accounts for the bookstore

Users API : **This document describes the API for creating, and reading user accounts.**

| | | Show/Hide | List Operations | Expand Operations |

| GET | /users | | Returns all users' data |

| POST | /users | | Creates a new user for the given data |

Implementation Notes
Creates a new user for the given data

Response Class (Status default)
Model | Model Schema

User {
    user_id (string): UUID for the user's ID,
    name (string, *optional*): the name for user,
    email (string): user's email address
}

Response Content Type [application/json ▼]

Parameters

Parameter	Value	Description	Parameter Type	Data Type
email	[(required)]	Email address for the new user, needs to be unique.	query	string
name	[ ]	Full name of the user.	query	string
password	[(required)]	Password for the user.	query	string

Response Messages

HTTP Status Code	Reason	Response Model	Headers
422	User data invalid		

[Try it out!]

| GET | /users/{id} | | Returns a user's data for a given user by uuid |

[BASE URL: / , API VERSION: 1.0]

Figure 5-1. *Swagger UI for users-service*

As you can see in Figure 5-1, the UI provides access to and descriptions of all API endpoints, as well as API models, based entirely on the API specifications hosted locally at `http://localhost:5002/swagger/api.json`.

Additionally, the UI allows for specifying the APIs' input parameters in a web form, and exposes "Try it out!" buttons to send requests to the respective endpoint. Each request triggered this way results in displaying the response body, code, and headers in separate sections of the UI. Sample cURL statements and resulting request URLs can also be found on the Swagger UI page.

The schemas of API request and response models are shown right above the section where input parameters are described and can be entered before making requests. Boldface type indicates that the named parameter is required, and there are also definitions about the data type and request location (that is, whether in the request body, the URL path, or the URL query) for each parameter.

At the end of each entry describing an API endpoint is a list of declared response messages, detailing potential error codes and conditions, models, and headers.

Let's look at the results from calling the GET /users/{id} API endpoint via the Swagger UI (Figure 5-2).

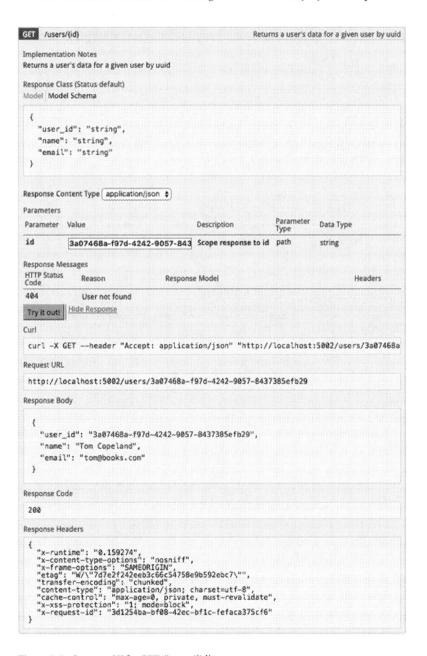

Figure 5-2. *Swagger UI for GET /iusers/{id}*

Once the request triggered by the "Try it out!" button completes, new sections appear. The "Curl" section details the exact Unix curl command-line statement equivalent to that made by the Swagger UI.

▨ **Note**   For simplicity of illustration, the API exposed here has no authentication or authorization built into it. Internal, inside-VPN-only facing APIs should probably at least make sure that an API key is required to authenticate and authorize access. Externally-facing APIs will need more protection; we recommend OAuth 2.0 via JSON Web Token (JWT). See https://tools.ietf.org/html/rfc7523 for more details.

This new section shows the request URL, a formatted version of the JSON response body, and the response code and headers returned from the service.

Swagger UI is just one of many tools surrounding the framework, and the official Swagger website lists a large number of core, as well as community supported tools. The list is still growing, and it is already too large to explain each one of them in this book. Therefore, we will just focus on two more categories of tools: automatic code generation from Swagger JSON specifications, and generating the JSON schema specification itself based on more human-readable DSLs.

Generating Code from Swagger Definitions

Starting out with code generation, we are using the swagger-codegen tool (https://github.com/swagger-api/swagger-codegen), which is included as a core project in the Swagger toolset. This tool allows automatic generation of client libraries to communicate with APIs based on the service's Swagger API specifications. Another option that the tool provides is to generate an actual service stub to vend the APIs based on a predefined JSON schema specification. Both client and service generation can be configured to generate code in around 35 languages and service frameworks.

Let's look at an example of how to use this tool to generate a Ruby language gem (Ruby's equivalent to other languages' libraries) for our users service:

```
swagger-codegen generate -i http://localhost:5002/swagger/api -l ruby -o /tmp/users-client/
```

The directory tree of the code generated by this command can be seen in Figure 5-3.

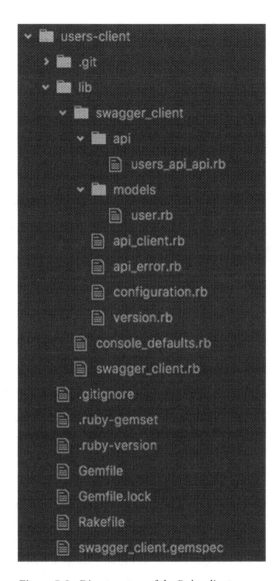

Figure 5-3. *Directory tree of the Ruby client gem*

Listing 5-2 demonstrates how this auto-generated client library can be used.

Listing 5-2. Using the generated Ruby client gem

```
users-client tim$ bundle exec rake console
irb -I lib -r swagger_client.rb -r console_defaults.rb
2.3.0 :001 > client = SwaggerClient::UsersAPIApi.new
 => #<SwaggerClient::UsersAPIApi:0x007fb0c4938b00 @api_client=#<SwaggerClient::ApiClient:0x
007fb0c4938ad8 ...>>
2.3.0 :002 > all_users = client.users_api_index
```

```
=> [#<SwaggerClient::User:0x007fb0c488b298 @user_id="3a07468a-f97d-4242-9057-8437385efb29",
@name="Tom Copeland", @email="tom@books.com">, #<SwaggerClient::User:0x007fb0c488ae10 @user_
id="943f3586-8f8e-4513-90ff-9da59e86f013", @email="cloves@books,com">, #<SwaggerClient::User
:0x007fb0c488aa00 @user_id="b635e0b4-14db-4737-9672-2b5c678156bb", @email="tim@books.com">]
2.3.0 :003 > tom = client.users_api_show(all_users.first.user_id)
=> #<SwaggerClient::User:0x007fb0c3a89230 @user_id="3a07468a-f97d-4242-9057-8437385efb29",
@name="Tom Copeland", @email="tom@books.com">
2.3.0 :004 > tom.to_hash
=> {:user_id=>"3a07468a-f97d-4242-9057-8437385efb29", :name=>"Tom Copeland", :email=>"tom@
books.com"}
```

If you're familiar with idiomatic Ruby code you can see here that using the client gem is rather easy and without surprises. After creating a client object, you call methods on that client that correspond to the API endpoints, accepting as arguments the parameters laid out in the Swagger JSON specification. The API call results also match auto-generated Ruby classes for the API models from the Swagger specification. We made the complete source of the generated Ruby client available at https://github.com/microservices-from-day-one/user-client.

If your language of choice is Clojure, the only tweak to generating a client library is the language for the -l option of the swagger-codegen command-line tool:

```
swagger-codegen generate -i http://localhost:5002/swagger/api -l clojure -o /tmp/users-
client-clj/
```

The code structure generated looks like Figure 5-4.

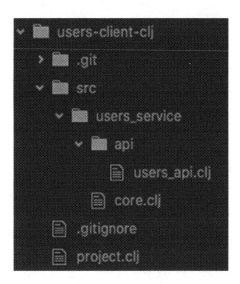

Figure 5-4. *Directory tree of the Clojure client library*

Using the client code from the Clojure REPL is also very idiomatic, as shown in see Listing 5-3.

Listing 5-3. Using the generated Clojure library

```
user-client-clj tim$ lein repl
nREPL server started on port 51209
REPL-y 0.1.10
Clojure 1.7.0
    Exit: Control+D or (exit) or (quit)
Commands: (user/help)
    Docs: (doc function-name-here)
          (find-doc "part-of-name-here")
  Source: (source function-name-here)
          (user/sourcery function-name-here)
 Javadoc: (javadoc java-object-or-class-here)
Examples from clojuredocs.org: [clojuredocs or cdoc]
          (user/clojuredocs name-here)
          (user/clojuredocs "ns-here" "name-here")
user=> (require '[users-service.api.users-api :as u])
nil
user=> (u/users-api-index)
({:user_id "3a07468a-f97d-4242-9057-8437385efb29", :name "Tom Copeland", :email "tom@
books.com"} {:user_id "943f3586-8f8e-4513-90ff-9da59e86f013", :name nil, :email "cloves@
books,com"} {:user_id "b635e0b4-14db-4737-9672-2b5c678156bb", :name nil, :email "tim@books.
com"})
user=> (u/users-api-show "3a07468a-f97d-4242-9057-8437385efb29")
{:user_id "3a07468a-f97d-4242-9057-8437385efb29", :name "Tom Copeland", :email "tom@books.
com"}
```

Again, all API endpoints are accessible via unsurprisingly named functions. The choice of data type for the User API model is a simple Clojure map, not a record structure, which is also available in the language. We made the complete source of the generated Clojure client available at https://github.com/microservices-from-day-one/users-client-clj.

Generating the Swagger JSON Specifications

The last category of tools we discuss aims at making it easier to generate the Swagger JSON specifications for an API from within the project that implements the service.

Given that our main language of choice for implementing the sample services is Ruby, we are showing two Ruby tools for this task.

Swagger-Blocks

The first tool we would like to demonstrate is swagger-blocks (https://github.com/fotinakis/swagger-blocks/). Including the swagger-blocks gem into your Ruby on Rails lets you specify your API endpoints using a DSL instead of JSON.

Listing 5-4 shows sample documentation that describes the UsersController in our users service, and which generates part of the JSON specification shown earlier in this chapter.

Listing 5-4. Swagger-blocks description of /users/{id}

```
class UsersController < ApplicationController
  include Swagger::Blocks
```

```
swagger_path '/users/{id}' do
  operation :get do
    key :description, "Returns a user's data for a given user by uuid"
    key :operationId, 'Users API-show'
    key :tags, [
      'Users API'
    ]
    key :summary, "Returns a user's data for a given user by uuid",
    key :'x-controller', "users"
    key :'x-action', "show"
    parameter do
      key :name, :id
      key :in, :path
      key :description, 'Scope response to id'
      key :required, true
      key :type, :string
    end
    response 404 do
      key :description, 'User not found'
    end
    response :default do
      key :description, ''
      schema do
        key :'$ref', :User
      end
    end
  end
end
# Here comes the actual code that implements the `users#show` API
def show
  # ...
end

#...
end
```

While the swagger-blocks tool has some very nice features and supports the latest Swagger version v2.0, we chose a different tool to specify our Rails APIs.

One reason we chose a different tool is that the structure of the swagger-blocks DSL very closely matches the structure of the JSON schema specifications. There doesn't appear to be a lot of simplification or lowering of the abstraction barrier as a result of choosing this tool.

Additionally, mixing the specification DSL Ruby code with the Ruby code that implements the actual API endpoints is confusing to read.

Swagger-YARD

The LivingSocial-maintained open-source tool swagger_yard (https://github.com/livingsocial/ swagger_yard/) approaches the documentation is a different way; the Swagger JSON schema is generated from comments in the code, rather than Ruby code itself. Under the hood, swagger_yard uses the YARD gem that serves as the Ruby community's standard tool for generating code documentation. YARD uses @-prefixed tag definitions to annotate regular Ruby code methods and classes.

Swagger_yard specializes the general YARD tags to provide tags like @resource, @path, @parameter, @response_type, @error_message, @model, and @property that describe the respective related Swagger specification entities.

In Listing 5-5 you can see the full JSON specification again describing the UsersController, but this time expressed using swagger_yard.

Listing 5-5. Swagger_yard description of the UserController

```
# @resource Users API
#
# This document describes the API for creating, and reading user accounts.
#
class UsersController < ApplicationController
  ##
  # Creates a new user for the given data
  #
  # @path [POST] /users
  # @parameter email(required)    [string]    Email address for the new user, needs to be
unique.
  # @parameter name               [string]    Full name of the user.
  # @parameter password(required) [string]    Password for the user.
  #
  # @response_type [User]
  #
  # @error_message 422 User data invalid
  def create
    ...
  end

  ##
  # Returns a user's data for a given user by uuid
  #
  # @path [GET] /users/{id}
  # @response_type [User]
  #
  # @error_message 404 User not found
  #
  def show
    ...
  end

  ##
  # Returns all users' data
  #
  # @path [GET] /users
  # @response_type [array<User>]
  #
  def index
    ...
  end
end
```

The User API model (see Listing 5-6)referenced in the API endpoint definitions just shown is described as a leading comment associated with another Ruby class (in this case the `ActiveRecord` model used to persist a user to the database).

Listing 5-6. Swagger_yard description of the User API model

```
# @model User
#
# @property user_id(required)    [string]   UUID for the user's ID
# @property name  [string]     the name for user
# @property email(required)   [string]    user's email address
#
class User < ActiveRecord::Base
  include ActiveUUID::UUID

  has_secure_password

  validates :email, presence: true, uniqueness: true
  validates :password, presence: true

  ...
end
```

Summary

We hope that this chapter helped to illustrate the advantages of defining your APIs in a computer-readable format. Adopting the use of an IDL and tools like Swagger very early on in your development process allows for soliciting feedback during the API design process. This enables a very iterative approach to API development.

In our daily work, we find ourselves defining API drafts almost every day using `swagger_yard` before implementing a single line of business logic.

We can then proceed very quickly and share the API drafts via the Swagger UI with the teams that will be consuming the APIs. The resulting feedback loop is very tight and fast, and we can iterate on change requests within minutes, speeding up the entire development cycle.

Additionally, involving the client teams early and defining APIs with their help leads to much more useful and robust APIs, as they are closely focused on the clients' needs and hence much more likely to contribute to your business goals.

We will focus on aspects that deserve more consideration when consuming such service APIs in the next chapter.

CHAPTER 6

Consuming Your APIs

The size of client-side libraries, and the features included in them, can vary widely. We will discuss the pros and cons of including various responsibilities, like exposing network errors, or making service calls, validating service responses, caching expensive API calls, handling errors, and alarming when things go wrong. Key topics in this chapter include

- How much code should live in a client library?

- Libraries should not have business logic, ever.

- Handling errors is a must, and depends on the nature of the endpoint being called.

What Are Client Libraries?

In a microservices environment, we call client libraries, the application code used to interact with a service. It's a set of code, that, when added to an application, will give developers access to the APIs of the service it was written for. We believe that client libraries should be a very thin service access layer that implements a convenient set of objects that mimic specific service APIs. For example, a client library for books-service should expose a Book class that has methods that correspond to the API response of the service, returning values of the correct type for each attribute, making it palatable and convenient to interact with the API.

In general, your client libraries will have a set of plumbing features that should be common to all client libraries, they provide functionality that is not associated with each underlying API, but is required in order to provide all the tools developers need to interact with services. We call the following plumbing features:

- **Network access.** The main characteristic of distributed systems is that APIs require a network access layer in order to be accessed. That network access layer is implemented in client libraries; so, that developers don't need to write network code in all their applications.

- **Object serialization/deserialization.** APIs use a serialization format to retrieve and expose data, which needs to be handled at the client library level. It's expected that client libraries will abstract the details of the serialization format to its users, making responses look like regular objects, as expected by users of the language in which the library is implemented.

- **Low level errors, like timeouts.** Client libraries have to handle expected errors, such as access to invalid resources, or network timeouts. Depending on the programming language, client libraries will handle those type of errors, and will raise exceptions, or set specific response codes to service calls, allowing its users to write error handling code according to each failure coming from a service.

© Cloves Carneiro Jr. and Tim Schmelmer 2016

C. Carneiro Jr. and T. Schmelmer, *Microservices From Day One*, DOI 10.1007/978-1-4842-1937-9_6

- **Expose application errors.** Client libraries can choose to translate some service response into code that is common in programming languages. For example, when a service returns a "404" to a request for a nonexistent resource, the client library may decide to expose that as a `ResourceNotFound` exception, which may make programming more natural, instead of forcing API users to check response codes.

- **Caching.** Client libraries may have code to cache service responses, thus increasing overall system performance. The caching layer in client libraries can have custom caching code, or it can just be HTTP-compliant to send and honor certain headers, performing tasks such as storing response based on ETags or expiry headers.

- **Service discovery.** A client library needs to know how to connect to the services it exposes, and allow its users to override its default configuration.

This may seems like a lot to implement in what is supposed to be a "thin" layer; however, if you decided to use an IDL and/or a Hypermedia type, as explained in Chapters 4 and 5, you'll probably be able to get a lot of this "for free" by using tools available for users of your IDL/Hypermedia type of choice. For example, in the sample project of this book, we decided to follow JSON API, and can use a wide array of libraries (`http://jsonapi.org/implementations/`) to help us building client libraries.

We'll go into more detail on some of the features we expect to see in most client libraries; however, we'll first take a quick detour to talk about the type of code you should never have in a client library.

What *Not* to Do

Here are a few suggestions, based on our experience, about things to absolutely avoid when designing client libraries in a microservices environment.

Don't wait eternally

In a microservices environment, a web page could make a large number of service requests for rendering each page, which will mean that slow response times from a single service could turn the user experience into something abysmal. It's imperative that, when you consume your own APIs, you define timeouts that, if reached, will not make your site unusable.

The one thing that will always happen in a microservices environment is seeing service requests time out. In a distributed application, there are a multitude of the reason for seeing such timeouts, be they general networking snafus, network congestion or just general latency increases along the full trajectory of a service request.

Don't make the clients smart

We recommend you never put any sort of business logic in a client library, be it some constant of default values, or any logic that may seem straightforward to code as you're working on your gem. For example, in our book store example, we will need to know whether or not a specific book is available for purchase at a specific moment in time. Following the initial, very simple requirements for out hypothetical bookstore logic, a book would be considered available if we have more than 0 copies in stock, which seems fairly obvious, however also naive.

If we decide to implement an `available?` method in our Ruby library, it would look like:

```
def available?
  stock>= 1
end
```

Someone, even yourself, could try to convince you that having that logic live in the client library is not harmful, and even more efficient than requiring the service to vend yet another attribute. Don't be fooled by that influence because every piece of business logic starts simple and gets more complex with time. Keeping the theme of our hypothetical future evolution, your book store may start selling books that can be considered as "always available" because they can be printed on-demand; so, you decide to make tweaks to your "in-library" code.

```
def available?
  type == 'on_demand' || stock >= 1
end
```

That wasn't that bad; however, you now need to release a new version of your library, and get all consumers of that data to migrate to it, which may not be that simple, and will cause, even if for a small amount of time, to have different clients using different versions of the library that have a different implementation of that method in production.

In another unsurprising turn of events, you find out that the bookstore has a new supplier that promises same day delivery of books to your warehouse; so, the business wants to not lose any sales of books that belong to that supplier; so, you need to tweak your implementation, you decide to add a new attribute to Book resource called `inventory_management`, which, when set to allow means that a book can be sold even when it is not in stock. Off you go to update your client library, which now reads:

```
def available?
  inventory_management == 'allow' || type == 'on_demand' || stock >= 1
end
```

The code is starting to look like spaghetti, we've seen how ugly it gets, don't do that. Once again, we will have the issue of possibly having clients using different versions of the library at some point in time. Also, in an ideal world, you'd never have to expose the `inventory_management` to certain clients, it's an implementation detail that should be kept inside the domain of the `books-service`; however, it had to be exposed to allow the logic in the library to be updated. We've been showing you the `available?` method implemented in Ruby, but, if your application happens to run in an environment where multiple languages are used, then, you would also have to implement that code in each one of those languages; so, trust us, business logic should never live in a client library. The general rule should be to keep your client libraries as dumb as possible, and move the business logic into service endpoints instead.

Service Orchestration

We can also offer an important positive recommendation: Try to understand how you can orchestrate the information retrieved, so you can optimize the workflow and cut down on load time.

In some cases, when working on user-facing applications, you may notice a specific pattern of service access that could be optimized. For example, suppose you know that on a book detail page, you need to access detailed book information from `books-service`, as well as a large amount of information from a set of other services, such as images, reviews, or categories. You may be tempted to add a class into your client library that could load data from those services in parallel, and return it in a faster fashion.

That type of connected service call is what is called *service orchestration*, and it is very helpful for increasing the efficiency from an end-user point of view. We'll discuss in Chapter 7 the way backend-for-frontend (BFF) services have started to be used for exactly that reason, and we recommend you take that approach—add orchestration to a BFF, and have a thin client library for that service, which will give you all the advantages of optimizing your workflow to improve performance, and will keep logic away from your client libraries.

Caching in the Client

In order to increase speed, caches are often used in distributed systems, and a layer that sometimes becomes responsible for caching is the client library. It seems like a decent choice for caching because, by handling caching in the client library, it makes caching transparent to its clients, which can be seen as an advantage, reducing system complexity.

In quite a few cases, service clients can often tolerate data that is slightly stale. A good way to exploit this fact is to cache service responses within the client application (which can of course be either a consumer-facing front-end application or some other service that depends on data from your service). If, for example, the client can tolerate service data being 5 minutes old, then it will incur the interapplication communication costs only once every 5 minutes. The general rule here is that the fastest service calls are the ones your applications never need to make.

Build Caching into Your Client Library

Often the team that builds a service will also be developing the libraries (such as Ruby client gems) to access that service. Some of these client libraries are built to offer the option to have a cache store object injected into them via a configuration option. A cache store injected that way can be used to store all response objects returned by the service. A prudent approach when allowing cache store injection in your client library is to require as little as feasibly possible about the cache object that is injected. That strategy provides the client applications with more flexibility in choosing which cache store to use.

Caching should be entirely a client application's responsibility. Some clients might not want to cache at all, so make sure to provide the ability to disable caching in your client. It is also the client application's responsibility to set cache expiration policies, cache size, and cache store back-end. As an example, Rails client applications could simply use `Rails.cache`; some others might prefer a `Dalli::Client` instance (backed by Memcached), an `ActiveSupport::Cache::MemoryStore` (backed by in-process RAM), or even something that is entirely "hand-rolled" by your clients, as long as it conforms to the protocol your gem code expects of the cache store.

We'll go into more detail about (mostly service-side) caching in Chapter 7, and just recommend that client libraries offset caching to standards—HTTP headers—or have a pluggable caching mechanism.

Error Handling

In a distributed environment, properly handling errors is extremely important because errors will happen due to the simple fact that there is a network between two systems making a call.

In systems that do not properly handle errors, one service could bring down an entire application when issues arise. We've seen many times a not-so-important service A start to return errors that are not properly handled by its clients, and thus generate a series of "cascading failures" that can potentially bring down other services or entire applications.

Timeouts

The main cause of failures in a microservices architecture will probably be timeouts, due to the network between client and server. In order to handle those types of errors, you should have timeouts—ideally with exponential back-offs—on connections and requests to all services you connect to. When services take too long to respond, a client can't possibly know if the delay is caused by expensive computation, or because the connection has failed. In distributed systems, you should always assume that a slow synchronous response is a failure; and having timeout values set very low means that your client code will not wait too long for a service response, and can handle that condition faster.

We recommend you set aggressive timeouts that will keep your systems honest. If you have synchronous endpoints that are sometimes very slow to respond, you have to make sure you fix all performance bottlenecks in those services, instead of increasing the timeout on the client. We've seen clients that have very long timeouts; anything above 1 second should be unacceptable, which means that the timeout is not protecting the client from a slow service, because it's still waiting too long for a response, and probably making the a user-facing application looks sluggish and incorrect—because of the service failure.

Circuit Breakers

A well-known pattern for handling service failures is the *circuit breaker*, also known as the *feature flag*. The circuit breaker design pattern is used to detect and isolate repeating failures, preventing system-wide failures caused by an issue with a specific endpoint/service. Circuit-breaker libraries usually allow their users to set a group of settings that characterize the circuit to be defined. Some of the properties that are usually defined in a circuit are

- **Timeout:** As discussed in the previous section

- **Retries:** The number of times a service call should be retried, in case of errors

- **Threshold:** The number of errors that will cause the circuit to open

- **Window:** The period of time to keep the circuit open before a new connection is attempted

In our sample bookstore application, we display a classic shopping cart icon in the top right of the user interface, and display the number of items currently in the cart, alongside the actual cost of the items in the cart. That interaction point is a good use case for a circuit breaker, and we have a circuit breaker in place. In that specific case, we should have a very slow timeout setting, we don't really need retries in case of failures, and we have code in place to render an error scenario that doesn't look like a failure. With the circuit breaker in place, our code properly handles failures, and it stops sending requests to the service in failure state, until it (hopefully) recovers and starts responding appropriately.

```
class BooksService
  include CircuitBreaker

  def find_book(id)
    ApiClient::Books::Book.find(id).first
  end
  circuit_method :find_book

  circuit_handler do |handler|
    handler.logger = Logger.new(STDOUT)
    handler.failure_threshold = 5
```

```
    handler.failure_timeout = 2
    handler.invocation_timeout = 10
  end
end
```

We recommend you get in the habit of always having a circuit breaker setup in place. Your application will be able to withstand failures in downstream dependencies, while at the same time, it will not overwhelm those services that are under some sort of failure scenario.

So far, we've only touched on handling the errors that happen in a downstream dependency; it's also extremely important to have some information on how to actually fix those errors. The first place anyone will look when errors start to happen is in service logs; we discuss generic logging in detail in Chapter 13, but the message to convey is that your client libraries are a great location to add logging about service calls. You should log most details your client library uses when requesting data from a service.

Ideally, you should use an error-tracking system, whether built in-house or commercial, such as Airbrake (`https://airbrake.io/`) or bugsnag (`https://bugsnag.com/`). Using such tools has some advantages:

- You can have a central location where your team can see what errors are happening throughout all your services. When a user-facing application starts to experience an increase in errors, the first challenge in a microservices environment is to find out the origin of the error; so having some visibility into error rates of all services is very useful, in stressful situations.

- You can group similar errors. Some systems can start to generate a really large number of errors; in an ideal world, someone should be notified about that one error with some sort of indication that it is happening quite often. We've been in situations where services would generate tens of thousands of error emails that ended up being a single failure, but that would cause email servers to be overwhelmed, delaying the delivery of other, potentially new errors, that could be happening.

- You can link alarming to escalation and severity policies. The main feature of an error-handling system is to notify the owning team that something is wrong. Depending on how teams are set up in your organization, the error-handling tool should notify one person, and have an escalation policy to alert other individuals if no action is taken. It's also important to be able to assign a severity to errors, so that errors with a higher impact appear quickly and are given priority over other types of errors.

Performance

Performance is a critical characteristic in a microservices architecture, and we discuss it in detail in Chapter 7. From the point of view of a client library, the message we want to convey is that the performance of a service A can differ from the perceived performance from a client that calls client A. When a client calls a service, network latency, response deserialization, circuit checks, and potentially other tasks will translate into the perceived performance of each service call.

We have the following performance-related recommendations for client libraries:

- Have metrics in place to measure service response time from a client perspective.

- Only request what you need; avoid requesting 100 attributes when all you need is 2.

- Check how much time is spent in each part of a call, as seen by the client.

Updating Client Libraries

Once your client library is used in the wild, it will start to evolve, and you should have an upgrade policy for those libraries, similar to how you support only a small number of versions of the service itself. Make sure that you have rules in place that make it easy for users of your client libraries to upgrade, and be as, up-to-date as possible most of the time.

You should follow a versioning policy for all your client libraries, to better communicate what type of changes your libraries are undergoing as you release new versions. We recommend you follow "Semantic Versioning" (http://semver.org/), as it's a well-defined policy that is both easy to follow and provides clear guidelines to how the version number should change. In Chapter 4, we talked about versioning the API endpoints in the service; we believe you should never tie the version of the service to the version of the API, as those can evolve in different ways, and having strict rules will not help you move forward quickly.

Briefly, given a version number *major.minor.patch*, increment them as follows:

- The *major* version when you make incompatible API changes

- The *minor* version when you add backward-compatible functionality

- The *patch* version when you make backward-compatible bug fixes

Also make sure you have a test suite for your client library; it should most likely be slim. You just have to make sure that you can catch obvious errors before releasing a new version of the library. We cover testing in detail in Chapter 9.

Service Discovery

One of the things you will have to add to your client libraries is a way of specifying where the service endpoint for each service is to be found. This seems like a very simple configuration parameter, and can even be defined in the client library itself, as all services should follow a naming convention based on the service name and environment in which the service is running. An example of endpoints for the books service could be the following:

- Development: books.development.bookstore.net

- Staging: books.staging.bookstore.net

- Production: books.prod.bookstore.com

Having endpoints defined in their libraries is a good practice, as it makes it easy for developers to start using the library. If you decide to distribute your service endpoints in your libraries, make sure you allow the configuration to accept an override, in case developers want or need to hit a version of the service in a nonstandard host or port.

One approach we've seen and recommend at the moment is to move the knowledge of where services are to be found to service discovery tools. We've successfully used Consul (https://www.consul.io/), which is described as a tool that "makes it simple for services to register themselves and to discover other services via a DNS or HTTP interface. Register external services such as SaaS providers as well." In our sample project, we make use of Consul, and have our client libraries ask it for service endpoints, which means that you can rely on Consul knowing the correct endpoints to connect to in each of the environments where your application runs.

```ruby
module ServiceDiscovery
  class << self

    def url_for(service_name)
      client = Consul::Client.v1.http
      service_details = client.get("/catalog/service/#{service_name}").first
      # TODO raise if there is no service data
      endpoint_parts = []
      if service_details["ServiceAddress"].empty?
        endpoint_parts << "http://localhost"
      else
        service_details["ServiceAddress"]
      end
      endpoint_parts << service_details["ServicePort"]
      URI.parse(endpoint_parts.join(":")).to_s
    end

  end
end
```

We made the complete source of the Ruby service discovery library available at https://github.com/ microservices-from-day-one/service_discovery.

Summary

This chapter focused on all aspects of consuming APIs. We defined client libraries and discussed their features and responsibilities. We talked about many concerns usually covered in client library implementations, such as...

In the next chapter will focus on what can be done to optimize the APIs on the service side. We expect to build APIs that respond quickly and efficiently, and will share some of the techniques we've seen that help you keep the promise of fast APIs.

## CHAPTER 7

Optimizing Your APIs

This chapter establishes guidelines and rules of thumb for designing and implementing APIs with a special focus on performance and maintainability. The majority of the techniques described here can be used to address and—if applied at design time—avoid performance degradation, while others can help to optimize overall service-related implementation and support costs.

Measuring Performance

The great American engineer and statistician W. Edwards Deming has been credited with the quote:

In God we trust; all others must bring data.

In our experience, this rule translates very well into the realm of optimizing service APIs. Too often have we seen engineers spending significant time fixing perceived performance issues based on mere hunches rather than concrete data, often adding significant complexity to the code without noticeable improvement.

When you are trying to improve system characteristics without introducing metrics, and methods to measure the system in terms of these metrics, you are shooting in the dark more often than not.

Finding the root cause for any long-running action often requires several iterations of defining metrics, adding probes, measuring, and finally evaluating results, drilling down further and further into the issue at hand.

Here are some typical questions that we find ourselves asking on a regular basis when researching API performance issues:

- Database related inquiries: Is the bulk of the response time spent inside the database query?

- If so, are there N+1 query issues, accessing the same database table over and over?[1]

- If the number of queries seems optimal, which particular query is run and takes the bulk of the time?

- How big is the result set of the query, and do all the returned rows need to be processed in application code?

- Can I analyze the query's EXPLAIN plan to see if table indexes are optimally used?

---

[1] Note that repeatedly running inexpensive queries can at times be justified if the equivalent SQL query involving a joining of tables turns out to be more expensive. As always, make sure you measure the impact of both options before deciding which approach to take.

© Cloves Carneiro Jr. and Tim Schmelmer 2016

C. Carneiro Jr. and T. Schmelmer, *Microservices From Day One*, DOI 10.1007/978-1-4842-1937-9_7

- Service dependency-related issues:

  - Is the bulk of the response time spent making dependent service calls, and do the downstream dependencies meet their advertised Service Level Agreements (SLAs)?[2]

  - If so, can some of the calls be backgrounded, made concurrently, or replaced by calling more efficient APIs on the dependencies?

  - Are all external calls in circuit breakers with the appropriate settings (like timeouts and maximum number of retry attempts)?

  - Is the data returned by the external dependencies optimal (that is, minimal in size and complete in content)?

- Memory allocations and CPU cycles:

  - How memory-intensive is your API endpoint, and does it spend a significant amount of time allocating, deallocating, or swapping memory to and from disk?

  - Is there resource contention with other applications or processes on a co-hosted environment?

  - How many CPU cycles are spent in each section of your code (as researched and visualized by tools like gperftools?[3]

- Business logic profiling:

  - Can you add special probes to determine how much time is spent inside the business logic of your application?

  - Are you using the most efficient libraries available to deserialize and reserialize your objects? Can some of these serialization steps be avoided altogether?

  - Do you know the algorithmic complexity[4] of your calculations? Are you using the most efficient algorithms and data structures to implement your logic?

  - Would this API be faster if it was implemented in a different programming language or toolset? (The beauty of an SOA approach is that experimentation around this question can be done in isolation and fairly cost-effectively. A prototypical implementation could be done in, for example, Ruby, and—if found too slow—switched to Go without impact if the API definitions can be kept unaffected.)

A few words of caution: while gathering performance data about your service is important, please note that often such data collecting does not come for free. Therefore, investigating the performance of your metrics-collecting tool, for example of your logging framework,[5] is always advisable in order to decide how much data should be selected. Your choice of tool to collect data about your applications should be influenced by the efficiency and performance impact it has. You might, for example, decide to rely less on

---

[2]Often, such SLAs are only loosely expressed, and—unless the service dependencies are all internal to your company—unenforceable. If you cannot coerce the team owning the dependency to meet their SLAs, then moving to alternative sources, or caching results (discussed later) might be your only options.

[3]Main gperftools repository: https://github.com/gperftools/gperftools

[4]"Analysis of algorithms," Wikipedia. https://en.wikipedia.org/wiki/Analysis_of_algorithms

[5]Sarah Ervin, "The Real Cost of Logging", 17 April 2014. https://dzone.com/articles/real-cost-logging

traditional logging frameworks, and more on UDP-based (and hence connectionless and faster, but also less reliable) data collection tools like Etsy's StatsD.[6] Another thing to consider and watch is how to effectively archive and purge all the data you have collected as part of your performance-measurement efforts. Letting log files eternally accumulate on your application servers is a sure-fire way to cause system downtime. Many log archiving and purging tools exist, which can be integrated with larger data warehouse systems, such as those based on Hadoop (`http://hadoop.apache.org/`) clusters.[7]

Chapter 13 will have more in-depth information about service application monitoring.

Service Access Pattern-Based Improvements

The very first approach we will explore among the ways to improve performance and design of a microservices architecture is to study the granularity and coherence of the system's APIs.

As laid out in greater detail in Chapter 3, sometimes service APIs are best aggregated or decomposed based on client access patterns and data joining concerns. If you find that your APIs perform sluggishly, it might be because their functionalities combine write-intensive data (like a bookstore user's reading list) with read-intensive data (like the user's profile data). Separating by such access pattern lines will enable you to introduce more tailored caching strategies, and even separate specialized storage systems with different read or write characteristics optimized for the given access pattern. Similarly, your performance analysis might show that much time is spent joining data retrieved via multiple service calls. This behavior is similar to SQL joins involving multiple tables, and aggregating such often-joined data will improve your API's performance. In this case, a new service that co-locates the joined data—whether by truly combining and replacing the original downstream services into a service that stores the data authoritatively in a new data store, or simply by caching such aggregated data based on the more granular data from the downstream services—can greatly improve API response times.

Another consideration might be to optimize the size of the service response to the need of your service's clients. In situations where a human end-user is waiting for a UI to be rendered based on data vended by your service API, it makes great sense to limit the size of the result set of an API call; the service should enable (or even better, enforce) the UI rendering application to request larger result sets in manageable, coherent chunks (also known as pages). We will focus more on this point later in this chapter.

For other client use cases, bulk APIs might actually be desirable and efficient. Consider, for example, the circumstance of a nightly, offline batch process that runs to aggregate data from several source services. In our social bookstore example, this could be the `promotions-service`. As mentioned in Chapter 3, this service runs periodically as a background process, sending out emails and push notifications promoting products to users. This service will need to operate on very large sets of users (maybe all female users, as provided by bulk data from `users-service` APIs), and it will need to mesh the user data up with bulk recommendation data from the `recommendations-service`. Making such bulk APIs sufficient and maintainable on the service side might require you to add additional pieces of infrastructure. For example, if you notice that the response times of your other client-facing APIs are affected by database connection contention with the queries executed for the bulk APIs, then you could consider adding a replicated DB read-slave[8] to service the bulk API queries. If you notice that connection requests to your web server are starting to queue up significantly because of the long-running requests to the bulk APIs, you could consider routing these requests to a dedicated pool of servers that is not part of the general web-application server pool. Try to avoid mixing long-running requests (such as for entire sections of a UI) with requests for data that can be returned much more quickly (like service requests that return within 10 milliseconds).

[6]Ian Malpass, "Measure Anything, Measure Everything", 15 February 2011. `https://codeascraft.com/2011/02/15/measure-anything-measure-everything/`

[7]Peter Dikant, "Storing log messages in Hadoop", 15 April 2010. `http://blog.mgm-tp.com/2010/04/hadoop-log-management-part2/`

[8]"Master/slave (technology)", Wikipedia, `https://en.wikipedia.org/wiki/Master/slave_(technology)`

Another fairly recent development pattern in the microservices community is to provide a very specialized façade service with APIs highly tailored for particular front-end applications. Some companies even go so far as to add one back-end API service per user experience, as Sam Newman lays out in his article on this "Backend for Frontend" (BFF) pattern.[9] Companies like REA and SoundCloud appear to have separate BFF services for their iOS app, another one for their Android app, and a third one to feed UX-specific JSON data to their desktop web application, fronting the rest of their SOA infrastructure and providing the client UIs with data in exactly the format that they need to render the desired experience.

The Blessing and the Curse of Caching

When asked to optimize the performance aspects of their web applications, for many developers the first (and often, only) tool of choice is caching.

A loose definition of this approach is to temporarily hold recently retrieved or computed information in a data store (for example, in the server's RAM, in a distributed object cache like Memcached,[10] or in a key-value store like Redis[11]) in the hope that future access to this information from that temporary data store (*cache store*, or simply *cache*) will be faster than reretrieving or recalculating it. Updating of the information held in the cache with refreshed information is usually triggered by a preconfigured timer expiring, but it can also be manually or programmatically triggered.

Caching in the API Consumer

The fastest API is call is one that isn't made in the first place. As mentioned briefly earlier, the API consumer should consider caching if it can live with information that is slightly out of date. The rest of this section will mainly focus on caching approaches in the information providing service. Please see Chapter 6 for details on how to implement techniques for client-side caching.

Caching in the API Provider

The advantages of caching seem rather obvious and convincing at first. Computing resources—client- and service-side—can be saved, and network calls can be avoided, resulting in faster information load times for the clients and more responsive websites and more enjoyable, and hence more revenue-generating,[12] end-user experiences.

As is often the case with optimization approaches, caching has its advantages but is not a silver bullet. While caching might work very well for relatively static content and for APIs where clients have a certain tolerance for stale data, it is often untenable for information that is very dynamic, very large, or where the clients have very low tolerance for data staleness. Consider the case of the inventory count of a given book in our bookstore example; this count will change very rapidly for popular books, while it might change much more slowly for others, so finding the right time-to-live for a cache for this information is very hard. Additionally, basing any sort of "sold out" decision on a cached count will be very unreliable.

Additionally, adding caching and with it additional pieces of infrastructure (like Memcached, for example) adds cost and general complexity to an application. The process of procuring, configuring, integrating, and maintaining such solutions (and the related cache writing and retrieval code) is often nontrivial.

---

[9]Sam Newman, "Pattern: Backends For Frontends", 18 November 2015; http://samnewman.io/patterns/architectural/bff/
[10]https://memcached.org/
[11]http://redis.io/
[12]Sean Work, "How Loading Time Affects Your Bottom Line", April 2011; https://blog.kissmetrics.com/loading-time/

Also, adding caching might actually turn out to be harmful to performance. It is not uncommon for engineers to discover that refreshing the information they were caching overall took less time than storing it to, and fetching it from, the cache storage they introduced. This even sometimes applies when the information authoritatively lives in a relational database that needs to be queried, especially if the cache store is distributed and hence also only reachable over a network boundary.

In such cases, the developers fell prey to the cardinal sin of "early optimization," adding complexity without reaping any benefits (or worse, actually degrading performance). Other dangers of caching are the unintended layering of several caches: services might cache information retrieved from downstream services, not knowing that the downstream service already introduces a caching layer around the very same data. As a result, the worst-case staleness of the data exposed to the clients of the first service is the accumulated time-to-live of all downstream caches.

Finally, there are often unintended interactions between the deployment of new code and the expiry of cache stores in an application. If the information stored in the cache stores has interactions with the newly deployed code, the deploying engineer will only truly be able to determine compatibility between the new code and the cached information once the cache store expiry has taken effect (which could sometimes be hours or days after deployment of the code regression).

Caching API-provided data also doesn't always have to happen inside the providing service itself or downstream from it (as seen from the client) in a key-value store or Memcached server. A caching proxy that is inserted between the client of an API and the API provider might be a useful tool, which we will explore in the next section.

Make Your Service Work Less

Retrieving information from a data store and subsequently serializing it to vend it to clients takes valuable time in your API's request/response cycle. In this section we describe two ways to reduce, or even entirely avoid, incurring this time.

Use the Standard

The HTTP standard comes with a set of built-in caching support methods, collectively known as *HTTP conditional* GET. These cache support functionalities are all implemented using a set of HTTP request and response headers.[13] We will not explain the full set of all the HTTP headers, but here are a few to be noted.

If-Modified-Since and Last-Modified

The If-Modified-Since request header and the Last-Modified response header work as a pair, as depicted in Figure 7-1.

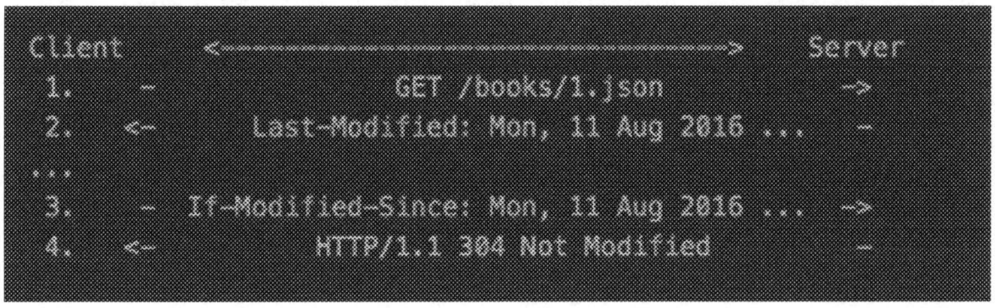

```
Client    <-------------------------------------->    Server
  1.    -                GET /books/1.json               ->
  2.   <-        Last-Modified: Mon, 11 Aug 2016 ...      -
 ...
  3.    -    If-Modified-Since: Mon, 11 Aug 2016 ...      ->
  4.   <-           HTTP/1.1 304 Not Modified              -
```

Figure 7-1. *Last-Modified and If-Modified-Since headers*

---

[13]"List of HTTP header fields", Wikipedia; http://en.wikipedia.org/wiki/List_of_HTTP_header_fields

In this example, the client (left) makes its first request for the book with ID 1 as JSON, not sending any caching-related request headers. The service responds with the serialized book data, and it includes a `Last-Modified` response header with the last modification date and time for the book resource. The client now can store that date/time, until it is time to make the next request for the same book's data. In step 3, when the client sends a request for the same book, it can add the date/time retrieved in step 2 as an `If-Modified-Since` request header. If nothing has changed since the requested modification time, then the server can return a simple `304 Not Modified` response.

Even though no direct data caching is involved for the second request/response cycle, there are several advantages to this scenario. First, the data transferred over the network is relatively small, as only headers are transferred, but no JSON data about the book.

As a corollary, the server will also not spend time serializing the book object retrieved from storage to JSON; the service will only need to calculate the modification time stamp and compare it to the time sent in the `If-Modified-Since` request header.

On the client side, efficiency is gained because the `304` status code of the response tells it that it can simply reuse the data retrieved in the previous service response's body; no renewed deserialization of JSON-encoded data into programming language objects is needed.

However, note that here, as well as with the `ETag` and `If-None-Match` headers discussed next, you will still incur the costs of making network calls and retrieving the result object from the data store.

ETag and If-None-Match

Another such pair of request and response headers is `If-None-Match` and `ETag`. Figure 7-2 illustrates a similar example scenario as in the previous section, but adapted to this header pair.

```
Client   <--------------------------------->   Server
 1.    -           GET /books/1.json              ->
 2.   <-        ETag: "3e86-410-3596fbbc"         -
...
 3.    -   If-None-Match: "3e86-410-3596fbbc"     ->
 4.   <-        HTTP/1.1 304 Not Modified         -
```

Figure 7-2. *ETag and If-None-Match headers*

In this example, the client again first makes a request without sending any related headers. The server responds with the data and a response header with a unique *Entity Tag* (also called `ETag`) for the data, calculated server-side. Any string that uniquely identifies the content of the resource will do, and many implementations simply calculate an MD5 hash[14] of the content to serve as this tag.

In step 3, when the client next requests the same book, it now adds the `ETag` it has last received (and subsequently stored) into the `If-None-Match` header of the request it sends to the service. The server again calculates the entity's unique hash and, in this case, finds that the requested entity's tag has not changed when compared to the tag sent by the client.

As a result, the service can skip the book object JSON serialization, and can simply respond with an empty-body `304 Not Modified` response. The client can now also react to this 304 response appropriately by reusing the previously retrieved book object. In short, the performance and efficiency advantages encountered in the early `If-Modified-Since` / `Last-Modified` remain the same for `ETag`.

---

[14]"MD5", Wikipedia; `https://en.wikipedia.org/wiki/MD5`

The Cache-Control Header

The HTTP Cache-Control response header can be used to help the service control all caching entities along the request/response chain to the end-clients. This includes intermediate (and potentially caching) proxies, browsers (which are built to adhere to this header), and other consuming clients (like language or platform code libraries).

We will not exhaustively explain all the cache directives that can be included (and combined) in the Cache-Control header, but here are some important ones we advise knowing and using in an SOA:

- private: Browsers and client-side caches can freely store the response marked with this directive; shared (intermediate) caches and proxies are not allowed to cache the content.

- no-cache: Sending this directive in the Cache-Control header forces all caches (intermediate *and* end-client based) to resubmit the request to origin server before releasing a cached copy; this is often useful for API endpoints that require user authentication and authorization.

- public: This directive marks responses as cacheable (as private is the default).

- max-age=[secs]: This directive indicates the maximum time in seconds the result should be cached and considered fresh, relative to the time of the request. The max-age directive is usually combined with the private or public directive.

The advantages of using cache control headers in your microservices infrastructure are manifold for performance optimization. It is an approach to caching "done right," as it lays the responsibility of cache expiry on the service, so there is a central place to expire it. It also helps to enable caching proxies (discussed shortly) to function as a transparent part of the tech infrastructure (via the public directive), thereby relieving the service itself of any additional unnecessary load. Finally, it enables clients to entirely prevent making potentially expensive network calls by letting them know how long the previously retrieved response should be used unchanged.

Framework Support for HTTP Conditional GET

As mentioned in Chapter 6, many programming languages provide client-side libraries that can process, and appropriately react to, the HTTP headers for conditional GET functionality. An example is the faraday-http-cache Ruby gem (https://github.com/plataformatec/faraday-http-cache), which works together with the lower-level HTTP communication gem faraday. Apple's iOS operation system and URL Loading System[15] come with built-in support for iOS mobile client apps that use foundation classes like NSURLConnection or NSURLCache. Similarly, the popular OkHttp library for Android (https://github.com/square/okhttp) also supports the cache control headers for storing previous results, and it reacts to ETag headers appropriately.

On the service side, there are also a large number of frameworks and libraries that support generating the necessary request headers. As an example, see Figure 7-3, which shows a Rails code snippet found in our bookstore sample application's users-service.

---

[15]Mac Developer Library, "About the URL Loading System", https://developer.apple.com/library/mac/#documentation/cocoa/conceptual/urlloadingsystem/urlloadingsystem.html

```
##
# Returns a user's data for a given user by uuid
#
# @path [GET] /users/{id}
# @response_type [User]
#
# @error_message 404 User not found
#
def show
  user = User.find(params[:id])
  if stale?(etag: user, last_modified: user.updated_at.utc)
    render json: user.to_hash
    expires_in 5.minutes, public: true
  end
rescue ActiveRecord::RecordNotFound
  render json: { error: "no user with ID #{params[:id]}"}, status: 404
end
```

Figure 7-3. *Users#show action with HTTP cache control*

This example shows the entire Ruby code necessary to implement the API to data about a given bookstore user account, based on the user's UUID. The important parts in relation to the topic of HTTP conditional GET are the stale? and expires_in helper methods that are built into the Ruby on Rails framework.

Calling the stale? method here with the :etag and the :last_modified option results in Rails calculating a hash value for the passed user object (as retrieved from the database), and a date of last modification of the user, based on the date its database row was last updated. Both of these data points are then automatically included in the API's response headers (as an ETag and a Last-Modified date, respectively). Additionally, Rails checks these two data points against the If-None-Match and If-Modified-Since headers from the incoming client request. If these request headers do not match the :etag and :last_modified options provided to the stale? helper, the user resource is considered stale, and the user JSON representation is generated by serializing the user object hash. Otherwise, the user resource is seen as fresh and the JSON will not need to be regenerated; the service API can simply reply with a bodiless 304 Not Modified response.

The expires_in helper call, which is executed only if the user resource is considered stale, sets the Cache-Control response header's max-age directive to 300 seconds (5 minutes), and indicates via the public option that intermediate proxies can cache the user resource.

The following cURL commands show this API's conditional HTTP GET behavior:

```
tim$ curl -v \
> http://localhost:5002/users/3a07468a-f97d-4242-9057-8437385efb29
*   Trying ::1...
* Connected to localhost (::1) port 5002 (#0)
> GET /users/3a07468a-f97d-4242-9057-8437385efb29 HTTP/1.1
> Host: localhost:5002
> User-Agent: curl/7.43.0
> Accept: */*
```

```
>
< HTTP/1.1 200 OK
< X-Frame-Options: SAMEORIGIN
< X-XSS-Protection: 1; mode=block
< X-Content-Type-Options: nosniff
< ETag: "616210ace8e9681c485ad8c71efcc5b2"
< Last-Modified: Sun, 28 Feb 2016 06:37:23 GMT
< Date: Mon, 04 Apr 2016 02:48:24 GMT
< Content-Type: application/json; charset=utf-8
< Cache-Control: max-age=300, public
< X-Request-Id: 028cb9d3-1965-4f5a-be28-0db8a06c3086
< X-Runtime: 0.128530
< Transfer-Encoding: chunked
<
* Connection #0 to host localhost left intact
{"user_id":"3a07468a-f97d-4242-9057-8437385efb29","name":"Tom Copeland","email":"tom@books.
com"}
tim$ curl -v \
> -H 'If-None-Match: 616210ace8e9681c485ad8c71efcc5b2' \
> http://localhost:5002/users/3a07468a-f97d-4242-9057-8437385efb29
*    Trying ::1...
* Connected to localhost (::1) port 5002 (#0)
> GET /users/3a07468a-f97d-4242-9057-8437385efb29 HTTP/1.1
> Host: localhost:5002
> User-Agent: curl/7.43.0
> Accept: */*
> If-None-Match: 616210ace8e9681c485ad8c71efcc5b2
>
< HTTP/1.1 304 Not Modified
< X-Frame-Options: SAMEORIGIN
< X-XSS-Protection: 1; mode=block
< X-Content-Type-Options: nosniff
< ETag: "616210ace8e9681c485ad8c71efcc5b2"
< Last-Modified: Sun, 28 Feb 2016 06:37:23 GMT
< Cache-Control: max-age=0, private, must-revalidate
< X-Request-Id: 1bde6ef0-dc77-4647-b7b8-0cfc1a73dde4
< X-Runtime: 0.003823
<
* Connection #0 to host localhost left intact
```

As can be seen, the first cURL request for a user (in which we send no additional headers) returns the HTTP/1.1 200 OK response with the serialized user object in the response body. But also pay attention to the relevant headers returned by the users-service:

```
< ETag: "616210ace8e9681c485ad8c71efcc5b2"
< Last-Modified: Sun, 28 Feb 2016 06:37:23 GMT
< ...
< ...
< Cache-Control: max-age=300, public
```

The Rails helper-generated ETag, Last-Modified, and Cache-Control headers are present as expected.

In the second cURL request, we include an If-None-Match request header whose value matches the previous response's ETag header value. This time, the Rails stale? helper can match the values, and the user resource is considered fresh. As a result, the service responds with a simple, empty-body HTTP/1.1 304 Not Modified, thereby saving service-side serialization and client-side deserialization of the user object.

Caching Proxies

Even if service clients do not send or honor HTTP conditional GET headers, reverse proxies added between your clients and your service will be able to do so. For its most-trafficked internal API services, LivingSocial relies heavily on Varnish (https://www.varnish-cache.org/), a reverse proxy that has excellent performance and scaling characteristics. Using Varnish, we saw some endpoints speed up by a factor of 50. It is effectively just constrained by the speed of the network. Figure 7-4 shows a diagram of inserting Varnish into the request path.

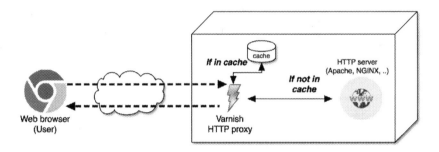

Figure 7-4. *Varnish inserted into the request/response path*

Under normal configuration settings, Varnish respects Cache-Control headers, caching content only when the service tells it to do so (via the public directive). Varnish can be configured to insert the If-Modified-Since and/or If-None-Match request headers if the service APIs' clients do not send them by themselves, thereby alleviating load on the service, but still be able to serve the content as requested to the clients.

Varnish comes with a grace mode, in which it uses objects in its cache even if their TimeToLive has expired. This means it can deliver old content while concurrently fetching the latest content from the back-end server.

Varnish is also flexible enough to function as a "hold the fort" cache: if the service fronted by Varnish is down, the proxy can return to the clients the last "good" response it received (that is, the last one carrying HTTP status code 200) from the backend service. This helps overall system uptime, as Varnish can continue to serve stale data while no healthy back-end service is available.

It can be administered to cache based on a full URI, including or excluding headers. Three tips for configuring your reverse proxy for maximum efficiency and correctness:

- Try making all query parameters sorted, so that any reverse proxy can yield a higher cache hit rate.

- Make sure all parameters that do not directly affect the API's JSON response bodies (for example, a client device platform) are sent in request headers, and instruct Varnish to ignore these headers for its cache key.

- Exclude API endpoints that require authentication and authorization from being cached in the proxy.

Size Matters

One of the most common reasons we have seen for sluggish APIs is that no consideration is given to the size of the results returned by a single call to the endpoint. Large results, or sets of results, do not scale, as they hurt performance in at least three key areas:

- **In the service:** Large amounts of memory might need to be allocated and deallocated to generate the object from which the results are generated. Once the result objects are created, time is spent serializing them into a wire format (JSON, XML, or the like).

- **In transit:** A large number of consecutive packages need to be transferred via TCP over the network. This can be especially harmful in an infrastructure with low bandwidth, low reliability, or high latency, for example when cellular networks are involved.

- **In the client:** Clients need to spend a significant amount of time waiting for the arrival of the complete data set. Even if the data connection is broken, a larger timeout needs to be set on circuit breakers to detect failure conditions correctly, so resources will be tied up for a longer time. Once the data *has* successfully been transferred to the client, significant time is spent deserializing large amounts of serialized data into objects, for which memory again needs to be allocated.

The rest of this section discusses ways to help you reduce the size of your services' API responses.

Result Representations

Not every client needs all the information the service can expose about a given resource or set of resources. Some clients might just need two or three attributes out of potentially tens, or even hundreds, of existing properties to implement their logic.

A good way to provide flexibility with regard to the amount of information returned about an API resource is to honor requests for different representations of an entity. Try to make it easy for clients to define (and iterate over) the best representation for their use case.

Consider a client calling an API in our books-service that returns information about a (set of) book(s). All the information about a book that is available to the books-service includes such properties as a full description, a synopsis, and maybe a list of all customer reviews. While it might be entirely appropriate for some clients to retrieve all of this information (maybe in order to display it to the web site user on a detail page), there are many use cases in which the vast majority of this information remains unused (for example, when there is just a small "product tile" about the book to be displayed in an up-sell scenario on another book's detail page).

Another good candidate for information that might be worth removing from a resource's representation is any detail information about secondary resources. In the previous example, it might often just suffice to include a book review "star count," review title, and the review resource ID on an API response for the book resource representation vended to the book's detail page. The full information (if needed) about a particular book review can later be requested from a reviews-service.

Implementing a given set of well-known, predefined representations is often done entirely inside the service that is the system of record for the resource to be retrieved in different representations. Taking the example of our books-service, it gets to define which properties of a book any given named representation includes; clients just request the resource by specifying the name of the representation in which they would like to receive it.

The communication of the requested format is most commonly either sent in an Accept header:

```
GET /books/841a1420-fabe-11e5-9d14-0002a5d5c51b HTTP/1.1
Accept: application/vnd.bookstore.full+json
```

Or it is sent as an additional representation query parameter, as shown here:

```
GET /books/841a1420-fabe-11e5-9d14-0002a5d5c51b?representation=full HTTP/1.1
```

The service then often stores an internal mapping between the requested representation name (here full), and a presenter class (in this case FullBookPresenter) that has the serialization logic for the resource.

The advantage of this service-side control of the properties of a representation comes to light when a presentation requires change. All updates will immediately be made available to all clients that use this representation, and the code change was done in a single place.

The flip side of the previous point is that in a purely service-controlled representation definition scheme, changes requested by (internal or external) client teams often require cross-team communication and coordination, as the service is most often owned by a different set of engineers than the client applications.

This is what the partial resources pattern discussed next is trying to address, and we prefer that pattern because it leads to better decoupling and separation of concern in a microservices architecture.

Partial Resources

In contrast to the service-controlled resource representation approach, this technique for reducing response sizes is driven by the client.

When applying the partial resources pattern, the client specifies the exact subset of resource attributes of a full set of attributes for a resource it requires as part of the request to the service.

As an example of how this can be implemented, let's consider the Google Calendar service API.[16]

To request a partial resource from most Google exposed APIs, the clients can add a fields query parameter. The value of that parameter can then be configured to specify a custom set of the fields the client wants returned.

Let's assume we have the following full representation of a book resource, requested via GET http://localhost:5000/books/582cbc4f-6e04-4d77-a129-616efe01251c:

```
{
        "book_id": "582cbc4f-6e04-4d77-a129-616efe01251c",
        "title": "The Story of Diva and Flea",
        "slug": "the-story-of-diva-and-flea",
        "description": "Diva, a small yet brave dog, and Flea, a curious streetwise cat,
        develop an unexpected friendship in this unforgettable tale of discovery.",
        "isbn": "978-1484722848",
        "price": 9.87,
        "full_price": {
                "currency": "USD",
                "value": 987,
        "exponent": 2
        },
```

---

[16]Google Calendar API documentation, "Partial response", https://developers.google.com/google-apps/calendar/performance#partial-response

```
    "weight": null,
    "height": null,
    "width": null,
    "depth": null
}
```

Requesting a partial response for the book resource that will only include the book's UUID, its title, and the ISBN number will look like this:

```
GET http://localhost:5000/books/582cbc4f-6e04-4d77-a129-616efe01251c?fields=book_
id,title,isbn
```

The resulting JSON body of the service response should then be as follows:

```
{
    "book_id": "582cbc4f-6e04-4d77-a129-616efe01251c",
    "title": "The Story of Diva and Flea",
    "isbn": "978-1484722848"
}
```

This is a very simplistic example of what is possible with Google's partial response approach. The supported syntax of the `fields` parameter to specify the elements to include in the response JSON is loosely based on XPath (`https://www.w3.org/TR/xpath/`).

This "tell, don't ask" approach to representation definition is very convenient if the clients and the service are not under the control of the same team or even company. As a disadvantage, it will be harder to deprecate or change certain fields of a given resource if there is no control over which properties are requested and exposed to client applications.

HTTP Compression

Another way of condensing the response size without removing attributes from resources is to condense the actual response.

HTTP compression[17] is the standard supported way to losslessly reduce the response body size. The two most common compression schemes are

- GZip (`http://en.wikipedia.org/wiki/Gzip`)
- Deflate (`http://en.wikipedia.org/wiki/DEFLATE`)

Compressed HTTP resources are requested by using the `Accept-Encoding` request header (for example, `Accept-Encoding: gzip, deflate`). The service will then indicate in the `Content-Encoding` response header which type of encoding (if any) has been applied to the response body (`Content-Encoding: gzip`).

Anyone should consider leveraging GZip to compress JSON Responses. Many implementations of this scheme we have seen have reached a 60–80% reduction in response payload size.

Implementations of these compression schemes are widely available in many languages and frameworks. JVM-based languages can use `java.util.zip.GZIPOutputStream`,[18] while Ruby applications can use the Rack framework middleware `Rack::Deflater`[19] for both Deflate and GZip-based compression.

---

[17]"HTTP compression", Wikipedia; `http://en.wikipedia.org/wiki/HTTP_compression`
[18]Java Platform Standard Edition 8 Documentation, "Class GZIPOutputStream." `https://docs.oracle.com/javase/8/docs/api/java/util/zip/GZIPOutputStream.html`
[19]RubyDoc, "Class: Rack::Deflater"; `http://www.rubydoc.info/github/rack/rack/master/Rack/Deflater`

A more centralized place to handle HTTP compression outside the application server is at the web server level. Examples here are mod_deflate for the Apache web server and ngx_http_gzip_module for NGINX. We recommend compressing inside the web server if only for efficiency.

Semantic Paging

Much as there are service clients that will not need all the information a service can expose about a given entity, clients will very often not need all objects in a single response of API endpoints that vend lists of resources (such as search endpoints). Requesting a chunked (often called *paged*) set of the full result list is often a good way to reduce the size of such API responses.

In this scheme, the service regulates how many entities for a given resource list can be included in the response. While the client might request the entire list of entities, the service will not allow such a potentially huge response to be returned. If the API were to return all instances of a given resource (for example, all books in the store), then it could easily overrun the memory and processing capacity of the consumer. Instead, the service returns a subset of all requested entities (a *page*), and a set of links that indicate how to request the previous and/or next page of the result set.

There are quite a few ways to implement a URI and parameter scheme, but we suggest using pagination parameters called offset and limit at a resource list's URI to enable paging. An example URL for our books-service to retrieve 25 books, starting at a book with ID 582cbc4f-6e04-4d77-a129-616efe01251c would be the following request:

```
GET http://localhost:5000/books?offset=582cbc4f-6e04-4d77-a129-616efe01251c&limit=25
```

The limit parameter is fairly self-explanatory; it simply signifies the maximum size of the page, so that in this example no more than 25 books ever get returned.

The offset parameter has semantic meaning, though. It is meant to contain the value of a sortable property of the resource (such as a UUID, ID, or the creation or update date) based on the most optimal way to access the resource's data. This semantic offset approach gives the engineer who creates the API a chance to choose an optimal way to do an offset into a result set.

Good APIs do not require the consumer to know much about the details of this semantic offset, or even an ideal page size limit value. Service APIs should lead consumers through the consecutive API invocations to help them along while returning the full result set page by page. This means leading the consumer forward and backward through the full set of results, rather than making them guess or keep track of where to go next.

In order to achieve this guidance, each API result set should include hyperlinks that provide URIs to the next and previous pages (if available). This is one of a set of principles that are collectively called Hypertext as the Engine of Application State (or HATEOAS).[20]

In a very simply implementation of a HATEOAS approach, based on the draft IETF standard for HAL (JSON Hypermedia API Language),[21] here is how an example response to the earlier request to our books-service might look:

```
GET /books?offset=582cbc4f-6e04-4d77-a129-616efe01251c&limit=25
{
    "_links": {
      "self": {
        "href": "/books?offset=582cbc4f-6e04-4d77-a129-616efe01251c&limit=25"
      },
```

---

[20]"What is HATEOAS and why is it important for my REST API?" The REST CookBook. http://restcookbook.com/Basics/hateoas/

[21]M. Kelly, "JSON Hypertext Application Language", 3 October 2013; https://tools.ietf.org/html/draft-kelly-json-hal-06

```
    "next": {
      "href": "/books?offset=e52cbf4f-6eeb-2067-b249-2345ecd02587&limit=25"
    },
    "prev": {
      "href": "/books?offset=1345bc34-4ab2-23f3-02da-235ee01234fa&limit=25"
    }
  },
  "items": [
    {
      "book_id": "582cbc4f-6e04-4d77-a129-616efe01251c",
      "title": "The Story of Diva and Flea",
      "slug": "the-story-of-diva-and-flea",
      ...
    }
    ...
  ]
}
```

In this example, the "_links" property provides links to help the API client navigate through the result set:

- "self" is the URI identifying the current result set.

- "next" is the URI for the next set of results with the same page size.

- "prev" is the URI for the previous result set with the same page size.

A Word of Caution

Front-end applications (like web applications) often need to render end-user–exposed views with paging links with data from the API result's _links section.

For example, when a web application displays a user view containing paginated lists of (for example, book) data, a next link must be embedded into the view, so that the client web app knows where to fetch the next page of API data. Developers should avoid trying to construct new URLs to the API, but rather depend on the next and previous links returned by the API.

In an attempt to prevent Denial of Service attacks to the internal backing API service, it is recommended to encrypt the pagination URIs embedded in client views, so that it will be harder for attackers to make arbitrary calls to the (internal) back-end services.

Given the example results in the previous section, a client web app might generate links in its book list view that are similar to the following Ruby On Rails/ERB template example:

```
<a href="/results?page=<%= encryptor.encrypt_and_sign("/books?offset=582cbc4f-6e04-4d77-a129-616efe01251c&limit=25") %>">Next Page</a>
```

The code in the end-user–facing web application that renders the /results view can use the value of the page parameter to fetch the next page of data from the backing books-service API, while at the same time shielding books-service from direct exposure to malicious requests.

Optimizing for Efficiency of Development and Support

When designing distributed systems you will encounter many situations in which there is no clear "silver bullet" solution to a problem. The same holds true for the trade-off between incurring development and maintenance costs by duplicating code in a client application, and increasing complexity by introducing an additional dependency in your service' clients.

In our experience, engineers in companies that are new to implementing an SOA side with the "copy and paste" (that is, code duplication) alternative as their default choice. To clarify our use of "copying and pasting," we even consider extracting common functionality into a library that is shared among client applications a duplication of code (albeit slightly better than literally copying code from one repository to another).

While there might be good reasons to take such an approach, it is often taken without much further analysis or foresight, motivated rather by a focus on the extreme short term, based on the perception that this strategy will unblock a task with the least effort.

Because it's our experience that the balance is heavily skewed in favor of code duplication in the real world, we have focused this section on listing a number of indications and scenarios where we think that a centralized implementation of a feature should be strongly considered:

- **Distributed ownership:** If not all client code is not owned and maintained by the same team, then the cost incurred in making changes (such as bug fixes or enhancements) is augmented by overhead for coordinating the owning teams, and to line up their respective timelines.

- **Risky upgrades:** Assess the risk for upgrading and deploying the client(s), and compare it to the same assessment for making a change centrally in the service. We have often found that a central change (with the same option to also revert the change centrally) appears to have less risk involved.

- **Availability of sane defaults:** One of the main risks in centralizing functionality is that a single point of failure is introduced in the dependent clients. This risk can be mitigated by building default values or functionality into the clients to fall back to in case the service API fails. Those defaults could even be delivered as part of a service access library, or a client could be programmed to store the last known good service result, and choose to fall back to it.

- **Public client apps or libraries:** If the client applications are released externally, for example, as native applications on mobile or desktop platforms, or as code libraries, you will often find yourself in a situation where you will need to support them quasi-eternally. Update cycles to such public clients are usually much longer than for internal apps. Placing functionality in a central service API to be accessed by thin client-side access code will enable quicker maintenance and extensibility.

- **Need for immediacy of change:** We have often encountered situations where there is a need for a change to take effect immediately in all clients. This point is related to the previous use case, but it's even applicable to internal clients. One example could be if an item (such as a book) is available for purchase via client applications. If such a decision was made purely client-side (for example, by calculating an inventory count based on sales numbers, or based on a cut-off date and time), then accounting for more dynamic changes in business logic would be very hard or impossible to achieve. What if you encounter all of a sudden that a book has been declared out of print by its publisher, or that your inventory is otherwise defective? If your make the clients rely on the service to answer the question of book availability, you can much more quickly adapt your business logic across all channels.

- **Experimentation:** Often you don't know ahead of time what the best (most revenue-driving, most convenient, most visually appealing, and so on) behavior to implement in your clients will be. Building several options and feature toggles into your clients and collecting data about such experiments in the service is often the best way to address this. Once you have identified a clear winner among the client-side options, you can direct the clients from the service-side experimentation logic to henceforth only use the optimal option.

- **Sorting and filtering of lists:** Imagine you initially planned to implement the book list view in your bookstore clients' search result display logic solely on sales numbers (or another criterion). But then your store strikes a deal with a publisher, who will pay you money to always make their books appear near the top of the search results. Implementing sorting on the service side enables this change to be immediate. Additionally, this helps to reduce payload sizes of results, and enables paging schemes, as the clients do not need to retrieve, and hold in memory, the entire list to sort appropriately.

- **Complex logic:** Functionalities that are nontrivial, or expensive to implement, are better maintained in a centralized place. Often clients don't all conform to the same programming language or framework, so such logic would need to be implemented, tested, and maintained in several different versions (for example, in JavaScript for single-page apps, in ObjectiveC or Swift for iOS apps, and in Java for Android). Because of the complexity, errors would be more likely, and with the larger number of implementations, they would be more expensive to fix. For memory-, CPU-, or I/O-intensive logic, this might become especially prohibitive if the client is particularly constrained (such as bandwidth- or memory-constrained mobile devices).[22]

Talk Less, Listen More

Splitting up your business domain into a large number of small, focused systems of record can potentially have a negative impact on performance: clients that need to mesh up information from different systems of record will often need to make several orchestrated requests to downstream service dependencies. If the requests are made in a traditional, synchronous matter (for example, using an ordinary RESTful scenario), then each of these requests to dependencies has the potential to fail, or to be slow and generally impede the responsiveness of the client performing the aggregation (no matter if the client itself is another service or the edge of the call chain).

An alternative to the described synchronous dependency calling approach is the "publish and subscribe" pattern. This is, in rough and general terms, an asynchronous approach that relies on clients registering with an information-providing service, and subsequently waiting for the service to notify the clients whenever the information subscribed to is updated.

While there are certainly other ways to implement this pattern, most mid- to large-scale companies introduce Enterprise Service Bus (ESB) solutions to handle reliable, monitored, and persisted message registration, marshalling, and distribution. We will not explain particular ESB solutions or patterns in detail, as that would go beyond the scope of this book. We can recommend Hohpe and Woolf's excellent book *Enterprise Integration Patterns*[23] to readers interested in further information.

---

[22]This should not be taken as an invitation to neglect resource efficiency when implementing functionality in a service! You don't want to have long-running service code make clients wait and tie up resources, which might cause client-side circuit breakers to trip, or worse make them entirely unresponsive.

[23]Gregor Hohpe, Bobby Woolf: *Enterprise Integration Patterns: Designing, Building, and Deploying Messaging Solutions*. Addison-Wesley Professional 2003.

A popular message bus that we have used successfully for more than a year at LivingSocial is Apache Kafka (`https://kafka.apache.org/`). Originally developed at LinkedIn, Kafka is a distributed publish-and-subscribe messaging system with a special design focus on scalability, performance, and message persistence. In Kafka, the basic point of interaction is a *topic*, which can be thought of as a log where messages are constantly stored in an append-only fashion. *Messages* written to a topic can be identified by their positive integer offset, which indicates a message's location in the storing topic. A topic has a (configurable) rolling window for retaining messages that defaults to seven days. *Producers* generate messages to be published to a topic, while *consumers* read and consume messages from a topic. Every consumer registers itself as part of a *consumer group*, which tracks up to which offset messages have been processed. Consumer groups also ensure that messages are only processed once and round-robin-distributed among multiple consumer processes in the consumer group. To guarantee strong durability and fault-tolerance, Kafka *brokers* are distributed among several servers in a cluster, and they replicate topic messages among each other. Kafka's design allows for guaranteeing that messages are reliably delivered to consumers in the order they were consumed, albeit in very rare cases more than once. While we will not further explain the concepts behind Kafka; this Apache project comes with an extensive amount of excellent documentation.

In LivingSocial's case, the engineering best practice is to design a system-of-record service such that it publishes messages about any change event to entity-type–specific topic. This enables current and future client applications that need information about the published entities to consume some or all of the information in these change events.

As a result, when synchronous requests are received by these upstream client applications, they are no longer required to make secondary synchronous requests to the system of record to check for information about entities for which a change event topic exists; they can instead subscribe to the entity's topic(s) and asynchronously retrieve, store, and finally use the information broadcast therein.

▓ **Note**   For the scenario just described, it is not advisable for client applications to simply store full copies of all entities owned by downstream services that they depend on, as that would effectively recreate the system of record's entire data store in each and every client. The goal for the dependent client should instead be to pick out only the limited amount of information about downstream entities that is needed for the aggregating client to perform its own purpose.

A LivingSocial-internal example for such an approach is `catalog-service`, which was first mentioned in Chapter 3 to illustrate the "aggregation to aid system performance" application-partitioning pattern. The service vends data about all disparate types of products in a uniform and searchable manner. In order to do so, it consumes Kafka topic streams published by the various systems of record for each of the product types, plus additional Kafka topics about data regarding product classifications, and so on. The topic consumers for `catalog-service` live in an entirely separate demon process than the service's APIs that provide the catalog information to `catalog-service`'s clients. The topic consumers consume, aggregate, and store the topic information into the `catalog-service` database, while the API process uses read-only access to query the database; no secondary service requests are needed when clients call the `catalog-service` APIs.

Finding a message-based approach in our fictitious bookstore example laid out in Chapter 3 is similarly easy. The `bestsellers-service`, `purchase-service`, and `refund-service` can communicate in an entirely decoupled manner. When a purchase is made, a record with the number of copies for each book sold is created in `purchase-service`, which then turns around and creates a message on a purchase-creation related topic, and the message includes the IDs and sales count for each sold book. Similarly, creation of a `refund-service`-owned refund record will trigger the publication of a message to a refund-creation topic, and this message also includes information about the number of copies for books that are returned and refunded. The aggregating `bestsellers-service` consumes both the purchase-creation and the refund-creation topics, and it keeps a count for copies sold and refunded for each of the books listed in these messages, in order to calculate the data it proffers to its own clients (that is, lists of books in various categories, ordered by net sales). No synchronous requests to either the `purchase-service` or the `refund-service` need to be made as part of the request cycle to any `bestsellers-service` API, as the information to calculate the bestseller lists has been precollected via asynchronous topic consumption and stored locally in the bestseller database.

One of the changes that reliance on a messaging system like Kafka brings along is that your data will only be eventually consistent across all your services that consume the update messages. One such example could be that a user updated her credit card data as part of the purchase flow, but the user's account detail page still needs some time to catch up on consuming the data change, and hence is still showing the previous details.

If this behavior seems unacceptable, then a synchronous call to the true data source needs to be made, or workarounds need to be implemented; for example, a secondary (AJAX) request could be made after the account details page is initially rendered, or WebSockets could be used to update the credit card information element upon receipt of the Kafka update message.

Summary

In this chapter you learned about ways to reduce our APIs' consumption of resources (both computer and human). We first discussed the importance of measuring performance before trying to improve it. We suggested some aspects to measure: database queries, service dependencies, memory and CPU consumption, as well as logic probes.

We next discussed analyzing how service APIs are accessed by their clients and then optimized accordingly for maximum client performance. Making sure that the information vended is grouped based on the underlying entity's write. Similarly it was explained that data that is often joined together should best live inside a single service, so that cross-service joins can be avoided. Adding separate bulk APIs for the retrieval of very large data sets and using very focused BFF façade services were also explained and proposed as effective improvements.

The advantages and the potential pitfalls of for caching information in the API-providing service were noted, before schemes to employ the benefits of HTTP conditional `GET` and its `ETag`, `If-Modified-Since`, and Cache-Control headers (including service-side implementation approaches in Ruby on Rails) were discussed. The related option of inserting a caching proxy between the client and the service was also laid out, listing Varnish as a viable option for this.

Next we showed the importance of controlling the size of API responses, along with several ways to do that, including specialized representations, vending resources partially, HTTP compression and semantic paging as ways to help issue responses of optimal size.

We then addressed the inefficiencies involved in developing and maintaining duplicated code in the clients, and gave a list of eight indicators to consider, each of which might justify centralizing functionality inside a service if these benefits outweigh the cost of introducing an additional service dependency.

Finally, we explained ESBs in general, providing specific detail by using Apache Kafka. We described a real-world use case of employing a message-based approach to improve API performance by obviating the need for secondary service calls. We also described how Kafka could be of use to vending bestseller lists in our bookstore example.

In the following chapter we will look at a number of ways to handle the nontrivial task of managing the development environment in microservices architectures more efficiently, thereby making it less cumbersome and hence more productive to implement.

## PART III

Development and Deployment

CHAPTER 8

Development Environment and Workflow

Software engineering in a microservices environment requires a specific mindset, as well as tools to make development and deployment simple. Any friction caused by a high number of deployment units will put a damper on overall productivity.

In this chapter we will explain the advantages of a list of measures any organization should take to make developing in a microservices environment enjoyable and efficient.

The Premise

Your company has decided to wholeheartedly embrace microservices. Given the size and complexity of your business application, and the requirement to be quick and nimble, you have to implement a design with a large number of RESTful services, front-end applications, and backing data stores. Even for smaller applications, having 25–30 individual deployment units is more usual than not; LivingSocial's production environment is made up of hundreds of interconnected deployment units.

You are a software developer who is tasked with making changes to one of the customer-facing web applications, which also requires enhancements in one of the company's service APIs that provide all the data to the web-applications to be rendered to the end user. Both the web application and the service you need to extend have additional, direct and indirect, service and data store dependencies.

How do you set up your development environment to make sure you are correctly implementing the feature you are tasked to develop?

How do you run your test suite?

How do you pass this feature on to your QA team, and how do they go about testing your changes for regressions and new features?

Any engineering organization should strive to answer these and other important questions in order to adopt microservices successfully. The following list of attributes of the development environment they should aspire to implement stems from our experience in the matter.

The Development Environment Wish List

The following 12 subsections list circumstances and properties of the software development process that should be present in companies that want to be successful in operating in a microservices environment.

© Cloves Carneiro Jr. and Tim Schmelmer 2016
C. Carneiro Jr. and T. Schmelmer, *Microservices From Day One*, DOI 10.1007/978-1-4842-1937-9_8

Ease of Development Tool Setup

To increase productivity from day one, organizations should avoid requiring their engineers to perform time-consuming and tedious busy work, simply to get their development machine ready. The set of tools needed to be productive as a software engineer in your organization should be easily and quickly installed, and preconfigured, on every new developer's machine.

Note that these setup steps should be convenient and useful, but they should not be entirely opaque to the developer. Instructions on what is installed and how to customize it should be available to someone joining your team on day one.

Ease of Application Setup

Additionally, any of the many code repositories for the services or other applications that make up your microservices architecture should provide an easy and preferably uniform way to install (and uninstall) its own specific requirements to develop in, run, and test the application locally on the engineer's computer.

This way, your engineers aren't bogged down in trying to understand how any given application they need to change is set up on their development machine.

Automation of Application Tests

Automated test suites exercising as many as possible of the five microservice testing layers laid out in the next chapter should exist, and instructions (preferably uniform across projects of the same framework) or—even better—commonly adopted conventions for how to run them need to be included.

This decreases the risk of introducing regressions in the service behavior, and it also gently nudges developers in the direction of adding test coverage for new functionality by making this step easy. While we focus in much greater detail on the advantages of microservices testing in the next chapter, the main take-away is that automated test suites reduce the chance for costly bugs to make it into the production environment.

Availability of Sample Data

When running any application during local development, sample data to exercise both "happy paths" and exceptional behavior should be available for manual testing. Additionally, it needs to be easy for a developer to extend the sample data sets with new data that exercises the logic that was altered or extended by the code changes under development.

The arguments for this point are similar to those for test automation (that is, reducing the likelihood of defects), plus the added efficiency during the actual feature development, when developers tend to explore their code changes by manually exercising new and existing code paths.

Up-to-Date Dependencies

It is burdensome to all your developers when they have the responsibility of keeping up to date all the service dependencies for the application(s) in which they develop. First, keeping other applications' code and data fresh is a—sometimes rapidly—moving target when there are multiple engineering teams developing in parallel. Second, updating all the applications on the developers' computers is potentially time-consuming and distracts the engineer from the coding task at hand.

Addressing the freshness of application dependencies adds to your developers' velocity, while at the same time helping with the accuracy and reliability of the test scenarios you exercise during development.

Fast Developer Machines

A related point is that a microservices company should aim to avoid obliging developers to run dependent services (let alone the entire SOA system) on their development machine. This will invariably waste resources on the developers' machines, thereby slowing down their computers and by that token the entire software development process.

Note that using resources more efficiently on a developer's workstation does not mean we are advocating making developers use outdated or subpar computing hardware. Quite to the contrary: the cost difference between providing a developer with a slow versus a fast laptop computer is usually not more than $1,000, which averages over a year of work at around $4 per working day. That is a very modest expense, with great return on investment considering the ensuing gain in developer happiness, efficiency, and productivity.

Concurrency of Development

Successful software development organizations want to foster developer collaboration. While some of this can be done via pair programming on the same task in a single service's code base (side-by-side in the same physical location, or remotely using tools like Screenhero[1]), developers should also be able to collaborate while working in tandem on code bases for separate services.

Collaborative Development

Revisiting the premise in the opening section, two or more developers can team up, so that one of them makes changes in the front-end web application while the other developer simultaneously extends the backing service's API to provide the web app with the functionality. Both developers should immediately be able to see changes and receive feedback via their respective development branches of the web app and the service communicating.

This increases productivity for the developers involved, as they will not need to spend time on elaborate code branch synchronization procedures to experience the results of each other's most recent work.

Privacy of Development

Developers of software that lives at the edges of your company's microservices architecture (that is, engineers coding native applications on mobile devices and desktop computers, or web-applications serving HTML and JavaScript to consumer browsers) should be able to test their software without releasing any changes to publicly exposed resources. This means that they should be able to run all their edge systems on local development devices. Additionally, they also need to be able to test their software against unreleased code branches of services they depend upon.

That way, they will not be obliged to sit idle while waiting for code of service dependencies to be released to production before they can develop features in their own applications. Also, they will be able to provide feedback to the service-providing APIs prior to their public launch, thereby helping to prevent launching (and having to maintain and support) service endpoints that need to be revised soon after launch—it is often very hard, or even impossible, to recall or change APIs once publicly released.

---

[1]A collaboration tool that enables remote pair programming. https://screenhero.com/

Immediacy of Change Feedback

Once a service-side change or extension has been implemented by a developer, it should get exposure to, and exercise from, all the potential client applications. This should best happen in as many real-world usage scenarios as possible. This service-side change should be visible as immediately after completion as possible, and it should even be visible during the ongoing development and QA cycles of the dependent client applications, and definitely before the changed code is released to a production environment.

This approach helps finding any breakages or adverse effects of the changed code as early as possible, and it can be seen as an extension of (and sometimes as a replacement for) component-level testing.[2]

Ease of Service Generation

When generating new applications in your microservices environment, developers should not be left guessing about which libraries to use, or what design guidelines, coding style, test tools, and documentation approach to follow.

The advantages of such out-of-the-box consistency among the services in an organization are manifold. For one, developers save time when setting up new services includes sane defaults. Also, support and maintenance costs are decreased when only a smaller set of library, storage engine, and similar dependencies need to be supported. Additionally, it helps synergy and reduces risk for a company if developers can more easily switch between code bases to which they contribute. Making sure that there is a level of uniformity and familiarity among the applications reduces the switching overhead for developers and hence reduces cost.

Accessibility of Documentation

Being able to learn about a service's purpose and capabilities is crucial in an environment where potentially hundreds of such microservices and surrounding applications might exist. Developers (and computers) should be able to discover services they need, learn about their APIs and specifications, as well as explore the services' functionalities prior to using them in any code of their own.

This goal aids in reducing duplication of effort, as chances of reimplementing a functionality that an existing service already provides decrease when a developer can easily find out about what is already there. Additionally, being able to explore, and therefore ultimately better understand, service dependencies that your code will need to rely on helps to produce quality code with less time spent on fixing bugs that are due to incorrect assumptions.

Making the Wishes Come True

Now that we have clarified the software development conditions that need to exist in an organization that wants to successfully adopt microservices, let's look at some processes and tools that can help in implementing these conditions.

Automating Developer Machine Set-Up

In order to make setting up the development tools for any developer easier, a very effective measure is to generate, and keep up to date, scripts to set up development machines. These automated scripts should include the main tools that are common across your engineering organization (such as version and source control tools, programming languages, IDEs or text editors, and communication tools like instant messaging clients or Slack).

---

[2]See Chapter 9 for an explanation of component tests.

There are a large number of configuration management software systems (commercial as well as OSS) that can help in automatically setting up, and keeping up to date, all the computers in your organization. Explaining the differences between all the available solutions is a rather fast-moving target and certainly outside the scope of this book. At the time of writing, some of the most popular open-source systems are Ansible, Puppet, CFEngine, and Chef, all of which support Unix-like and Microsoft Windows platforms. Wikipedia has a very thoroughly researched article[3] that compares the various OSS solutions and their feature sets.

The LivingSocial engineering team has automation in place which can install and configure software on the developers' company-provided Apple MacBook Pro laptops. This script will take a computer from a freshly installed OSX image to having the development environment needed to be productive at the company set up on the laptop in less than an hour.

The project is called sudo-make-me-a-laptop, and it consists of a set of scripts that automatically install `git`, the Java SDK, `rbenv`, `homebrew`, `gcc`, `kafka`, `emacs`, `nginx`, `mysql`, Memcached and Redis, as well as some essential internal services.

The set of scripts in use at LivingSocial is based on Pivotal Labs' Pivotal Sprout toolset,[4] and it uses Soloist (`https://github.com/mkocher/soloist`) and Librarian-Chef (`https://github.com/applicationsonline/librarian-chef`) to run a subset of the recipes in Pivotal Sprout's *cookbooks,* which is the name for a group of scripts used by Chef (`https://github.com/chef/chef`). A more detailed discussion of the background of the Pivotal Sprout project can be found in a presentation by Pivotal Labs' Brian Cunnie and Abhi Hiremagalur, hosted at `http://sprout-talk.cfapps.io/`.

Automated Application Set-Up

Similar to providing scripts that install and update the basic tools that any developer needs to contribute on a daily basis, the specific project code under development should also be installed in an automated fashion.

The responsibility for encoding the specialized knowledge about set-up, build, execution and testing steps should lie with the team that owns the specific service or application under development.

Consistently Named Scripts

An approach to automating application set-up that we have seen work well is to include shell scripts that programmatically set up the specific application and all its required parts as part of the application's source code repository. This approach should best be paired with organization-wide conventions defining where to find the scripts. For example, there could be a convention to have a `bin` directory as part of all code repositories, which should include two scripts: `install.sh` to check for, and potentially set up, all dependencies required for an application to run on a developer's computer, plus an `uninstall.sh` script to remove all components set up by the install script.

Regardless of having a convention about set-up and tear-down scripts, your team should adopt a convention about shipping each code repository with a file that contains human-readable instructions for setting any given application up for development purposes. Our team adopted a common template for a Readme file included in all GitHub repositories, and this template includes a section entitled "Setting Up Your Environment." That section defaults to simply listing that a developer should run the well-known scripts (for example, `bin/install.sh` mentioned earlier), but it should include exact descriptions for any additional steps that cannot be automated (for example, if certain permissions need to be granted via an approval process that involves human intervention).

[3]See "Comparison of open-source configuration management software," Wikipedia: `https://en.wikipedia.org/wiki/Comparison_of_open-source_configuration_management_software`
[4]See `https://github.com/pivotal-sprout` for an overview of Pivotal Sprout tools and recipes.

Docker and Docker Compose

There are many ways to implement the actual dependency declarations and installation automation process. We have seen configuration management tools like Chef, mentioned in the previous section on developer machine set-up, being also used for describing and setting up dependencies of individual code repositories.

At LivingSocial, the engineering team is in the process of employing container technology via the use of the Docker tool chain (https://www.docker.com). The Docker open-source project aims to automate installation and deployment of applications inside *LXC* containers.[5] It provides a layer of abstraction and automation on top of LXC containers, and it allows multiple applications to run independently within a single Linux host.

In order to run Docker on our development Apple computers, we are also using Docker Machine (https://docs.docker.com/machine/), which enables us to install and run Docker on a Mac.

We also use the Docker Compose tool (https://docs.docker.com/compose/) to define, combine, and run multiple Docker containers to run the dependencies of our application under development.

Note that for now, we are installing Docker Machine and Docker Compose in a separate step for newer service projects. As these tools become more widely used, they should be moved into the general developer machine set-up scripts.

As an example, let's walk through the set-up in one of the services we use in our day jobs.

The service allows for fast geolocation-based searching of offer data, based on data aggregated from the systems of record for the products on offer. We chose to implement it as a light wrapper service that fronts an instance of Elasticsearch, or ES (https://www.elastic.co/products/elasticsearch). The service populates its ES instance with offer data retrieved by subscribing to Kafka topics about product data updates.

The Docker Compose configuration file used to declare ES and Kafka as dependencies is shown in Listing 8-1.

Listing 8-1. docker-compose.yml file for the search service

```
version: '2'
services:
  messaging:
    image: "spotify/kafka"
    ports:
      - "9092:9092"
      - "2181:2181"
    environment:
      - "ADVERTISED_PORT=9092"
    env_file:
      - ./config/docker/kafka.env

  es:
    image: "elasticsearch"
    ports:
      - "9200:9200"
      - "9300:9300"
    volumes:
      - /mnt/sda1/var/elasticsearch/data:/usr/share/elasticsearch/data
```

---

[5]Linux containers, a way to virtualize multiple, isolated Linux systems on top of a single Linux host machine. See https://en.wikipedia.org/wiki/LXC

After declaring the docker-compose file format version, the services section in the file lists the search service's dependencies that will be run as Docker containers. In this case, those prerequisite applications are labeled messaging for Kafka messaging and es for the Elasticsearch. Both container images for ES and Kafka will be retrieved from the official Docker Hub container repository (https://docs.docker.com/docker-hub/).

The ports section defines that host ports for zookeeper and brokers (for Kafka), as well as for the native transport and RESTful API of ES are forwarded from the host machine to the containers' equivalent ports.

The environment and env_file sections help you declare Unix shell environment variables, which are resolved to their values on the machine on which Docker Compose is running.

Finally, the volumes section allows for mounting paths or named volumes from the container into the host's filesystem, so they can be accessed on the host.

Docker Compose defined containers are then installed (on first use) and launched based via the docker-compose up command, which is based on the docker-compose.yml listed earlier. Listing 8-2 shows bin/start_docker.sh, a short bash script that makes Docker use the default machine, adds the Kafka host into the container's environment variable, and finally starts all the containers via docker-compose up.

Listing 8-2. bin/start_docker.sh script to start the docker containers

```
#!/usr/bin/env bash

eval $(docker-machine env default)
mkdir -p config/docker
echo "ADVERTISED_HOST=`docker-machine ip default`" > config/docker/kafka.env
docker-compose up $1
```

Using Consistent Start-Up Scripts

Another convention adopted at LivingSocial engineering to make running applications on developer machines homogenous is to use the Foreman Ruby gem (https://github.com/ddollar/foreman).

Foreman helps with defining a set of processes simultaneously. The list of processes to run by Foreman is managed via a file called a *Procfile*. Its aim is to allow you to run your application directly by executing a single command, like so:

```
foreman start
```

The nice thing about this abstract approach is that one can easily combine Foreman and Docker containers. See Listing 8-3 for an example.

Listing 8-3. Procfile for the search service, executing bin/start_docker.sh

```
docker: bin/start_docker.sh
service: bundle exec rails s -p3052
```

The Procfile has entries for two processes to start. The service entry starts our Rails-based search service mentioned earlier, while the docker entry starts the Docker Compose script.

Making Testing Efficient with Common Tools

Much as it does with setting up the prerequisites of an application for development efforts, the responsibility of making testing as easy and efficient as possible lies with the development team owning the service.

Consistent Process and Documentation

A first step for this could be to make sure there is uniformity in running an applications test suite. A well-structured template for a Readme file for all your code repositories featuring a "Running the Tests" section will go a long way. In addition to tips about how to trigger a run of the automated test suite, such a section can (and should) include detailed instructions for how to run any additional smoke tests that— for whatever reason—cannot be, or simply are not, automated. Our team implemented a similar approach by including a checklist of manual verification steps to perform as part of a change request. The checklist, in the form of a to-do list, is included in the GitHub pull request template[6] for our repositories.

Such a Readme-based documentation template can supplement, but will never fully replace, the approach of using a script with a well-known name and location in the code repository as the agreed-upon convention to run all tests.

LivingSocial engineering therefore is in the process of introducing a shell script—uniformly named `run_tests.sh`, and located in any project's `bin/` directory—that every developer (and ancillary automated tool) can expect to exist in a repository.

Anointing a Test Framework

Another great way for an engineering organization to help make the testing process more efficient is to settle on a very small set of test frameworks, ideally one test framework per language in use. This reduces the cognitive load for every developer new to a project.

As an example, all of LivingSocial's Clojure developers use Stuart Sierra's `clojure.test` test framework for unit tests (`https://clojure.github.io/clojure/clojure.test-api.html`). This was not just a subconscious choice or coincidence. The decision to use this framework was deliberate and preceded by thorough discussions and comparisons with other frameworks (like Brian Marick's Midje, `https://github.com/marick/Midje`). On the other hand, for Ruby applications in the same engineering organization, such a discussion had not happened for a long time, leading to a very wide range of different testing frameworks in the wild. This has been recognized as a deficiency and a cause for much loss of efficiency, which is why new Ruby applications have recently been unified to adopt the RSpec, Cucumber, and Capybara frameworks.[7]

If an organization sees a reason to replace one recommended test framework with a different one, then we recommend slowly updating any existing test suites using the deprecated frameworks in an "as you go" manner. In our experience, justifying the (often large) effort to switch all old-style tests to the new framework in a single project is very hard. A more practical approach would be to write all additional tests using the new framework, while only moving the existing test case to the new framework whenever it, or a small set of tests that include the given test case, needs modifying.

Implementing Test Code Guidelines

But just picking a (set of) supported framework(s) does not entirely suffice to help reduce maintenance effort and to flatten the learning curve for test-related code. Widely published style guides should exist not just for coding, but also for tests. Software consultancy Thoughtbot (`https://thoughtbot.com`) has published a succinct yet effective style guide for their developers to follow when writing tests using RSpec and Cucumber. Figure 8-1 shows the succinct but effective guide at the time of writing.[8]

---

[6]For a description of how to set up Pull Request templates in your repository, see `https://help.github.com/articles/creating-a-pull-request-template-for-your-repository/`.

[7]See `http://rspec.info/`, `https://cucumber.io`, and `http://jnicklas.github.io/capybara/`; more details on how to use these frameworks will be presented in Chapter 9.

[8]See `https://github.com/thoughtbot/guides/tree/master/style/testing` for the full test style guide at Thoughtbot.

▦ README.md

Testing

- Avoid the `private` keyword in specs.
- Avoid checking boolean equality directly. Instead, write predicate methods and use appropriate matchers. Example.
- Prefer `eq` to `==` in RSpec.
- Separate setup, exercise, verification, and teardown phases with newlines.
- Use RSpec's `expect` syntax.
- Use RSpec's `allow` syntax for method stubs.
- Use `not_to` instead of `to_not` in RSpec expectations.
- Prefer the `have_css` matcher to the `have_selector` matcher in Capybara assertions.

⌥Acceptance Tests

Sample

- Avoid scenario titles that add no information, such as "successfully."
- Avoid scenario titles that repeat the feature title.
- Place helper methods for feature specs directly in a top-level `Features` module.
- Use Capybara's `feature/scenario` DSL.
- Use names like `ROLE_ACTION_spec.rb`, such as `user_changes_password_spec.rb`, for feature spec file names.
- Use only one `feature` block per feature spec file.
- Use scenario titles that describe the success and failure paths.
- Use spec/features directory to store feature specs.
- Use spec/support/features for support code related to feature specs.

Factories

- Order `factories.rb` contents: sequences, traits, factory definitions.
- Order factory attributes: implicit attributes, explicit attributes, child factory definitions. Each section's attributes are alphabetical.
- Order factory definitions alphabetically by factory name.
- Use one factories.rb file per project.

Unit Tests

Sample

- Don't prefix `it` block descriptions with `should`. Use imperative mood instead.
- Use `subject` blocks to define objects for use in one-line specs. Example.
- Put one-liner specs at the beginning of the outer `describe` blocks.
- Use `.method` to describe class methods and `#method` to describe instance methods.
- Use `context` to describe testing preconditions.
- Use `describe '#method_name'` to group tests by method-under-test
- Use a single, top-level `describe ClassName` block.
- Order validation, association, and method tests in the same order that they appear in the class.

Figure 8-1. *Test-related section of Thoughtbot's coding style guide*

Introducing Concurrency of Test Runs and Development

Another valuable tool to support developer efficiency during the development and test phase is Guard (`https://github.com/guard/guard`). While Guard is a generalized automation tool that triggers customizable actions whenever observed files or directories are modified, it becomes particularly useful when integrated with the development and test cycle.

Many Guard plugins for test frameworks exist,[9] and we use guard-rspec (`https://github.com/guard/guard-rspec`) to support automatically running tests on Ruby-based projects. The guard-rspec gem allows you to specify rules that determine the correct subset of all tests to run, based on which file containing business logic changed.

Guard can be configured based on a file called a Guardfile, in which you can specify files and directories to watch, and which action to take based on changes to the watched entities. Actions and watch definitions can be expressed in a DSL. Listing 8-4 shows an excerpt from a sample Guardfile from guard-rspec's documentation,[10] which is focused on auto-executing the RSpec specs for a prototypical Ruby on Rails application.

Listing 8-4. Guardfile for a typical Rails application

```
guard :rspec, cmd: 'bundle exec rspec' do
  watch('spec/spec_helper.rb')                          { "spec" }
  watch('config/routes.rb')                             { "spec/routing" }
  watch('app/controllers/application_controller.rb')  { "spec/controllers" }
  watch(%r{^spec/.+_spec\.rb$})
  watch(%r{^app/(.+)\.rb$})                             { |m| "spec/#{m[1]}_spec.rb" }
  watch(%r{^app/(.*)(\.erb|\.haml|\.slim)$})            { |m| "spec/#{m[1]}#{m[2]}_spec.rb" }
  watch(%r{^lib/(.+)\.rb$})                             { |m| "spec/lib/#{m[1]}_spec.rb" }
  watch(%r{^app/controllers/(.+)_(controller)\.rb$})  { |m| ["spec/routing/#{m[1]}_routing_
spec.rb", "spec/#{m[2]}s/#{m[1]}_#{m[2]}_spec.rb", "spec/acceptance/#{m[1]}_spec.rb"] }
end
```

The guard command block specifies that RSpec should be run (via cmd: 'bundle exec rspec'). The watch statements define directories or filenames (directly, or via regular expression matching), and the blocks following the watch expressions list all the test files for which to re-execute the specified cmd if a particular watched (set of) file(s) has changed.

Using Guard or other automated test execution frameworks, like Autotest (`https://github.com/seattlerb/zentest`), provides developers immediate feedback about the effect of their changes in a potentially unfamiliar code base. Forgetting to run, or deliberately choosing not to run, the application's test suite at the end of the contribution cycle will no longer be an option. And because test runs are incremental and only focused on the files currently under change, the cost and impact on productivity of running tests is drastically reduced.

Integrating Static Analysis Tools into the Test Process

The introduction of static analysis tools can also help with teaching (and enforcing) coding guidelines and testing etiquette. The Code Climate platform (`https://codeclimate.com/`) is a commercial tool that runs a configurable set of analysis steps on every code commit, and then generates reports on adherence to coding standards, code complexity, code duplication, or percentage of test coverage. Figure 8-2 shows the summary page of a LivingSocial-internal service repository monitored by an on-premise installed version of Code Climate.

---

[9]For a full list of plugins, see `https://github.com/guard/guard/wiki/Guard-Plugins`
[10]See the *"Typical Rails app"* section at `https://github.com/guard/guard-rspec#typical-rails-app`

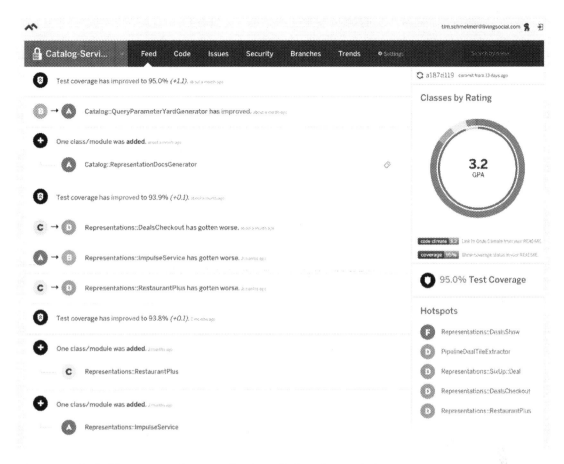

Figure 8-2. *Code Climate report for an application called catalog-service*

A simpler and, for commercial use,[11] less costly approach to encouraging attention to test coverage in the Ruby environment is SimpleCov (`https://github.com/colszowka/simplecov`), a code coverage analysis tool that makes use of Ruby's built-in coverage-tracking mechanism to collect data about code coverage. SimpleCov lets the developer easily process, format, and display the code coverage data collection results in just a few lines of Ruby code.

In order to guide developers into adhering to safety and maintainability standards for a given code base, the development team should explore whether a service's test suite can be made to fail whenever code coverage falls below an acceptable threshold value. When using the RSpec test framework and SimpleCov in the Ruby world, you can configure RSpec to fail the run if SimpleCov reports a decline in coverage percentage.

A Spec helper file that implements this for whenever coverage falls below 85% is shown in Listing 8-5.

---

[11]Code Climate analysis can be added for free to any open-source project.

Listing 8-5. spec/spec_helper.rb that fails test suite runs below 85% coverage

```
require "simplecov"

SimpleCov.start

RSpec.configure do |config|
  config.after(:suite) do
    simplecov = RSpec.describe('Test coverage')
    example = simplecov.example('must exceed 85 percent'){
      expect( SimpleCov.result.covered_percent ).to be > 85
    }
    simplecov.run

    if example.execution_result.status != :passed
      RSpec.configuration.reporter.example_failed(example)
    end
  end
end
```

Continuous Integration to Improve Code Reviews

If you want to use a less forceful approach than failing the entire test suite, but still want to keep track of declining code coverage numbers, you can instead (or additionally) try and integrate coverage checks into your Continuous Integration (CI) build system.

When using the Jenkins project's CI system (`https://jenkins.io/`), it can easily be extended with plugins to set up a workflow that processes SimpleCov-generated code coverage data. The DocLinks plugin (`https://wiki.jenkins-ci.org/display/JENKINS/DocLinks+plugin`) can be used to display formatted coverage reports, as shown in Figure 8-3.

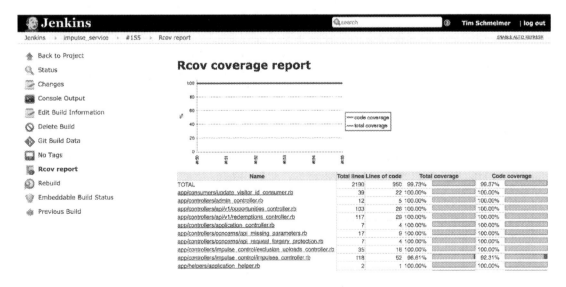

Figure 8-3. *Jenkins shows SimpleCov reports via the DocLinks plugin.*

The RubyMetrics plugin (`https://wiki.jenkins-ci.org/display/JENKINS/RubyMetrics+plugin`) for Jenkins can be configured to adapt the CI build symbol and status based on the SimpleCov coverage percentage (see Figure 8-4).

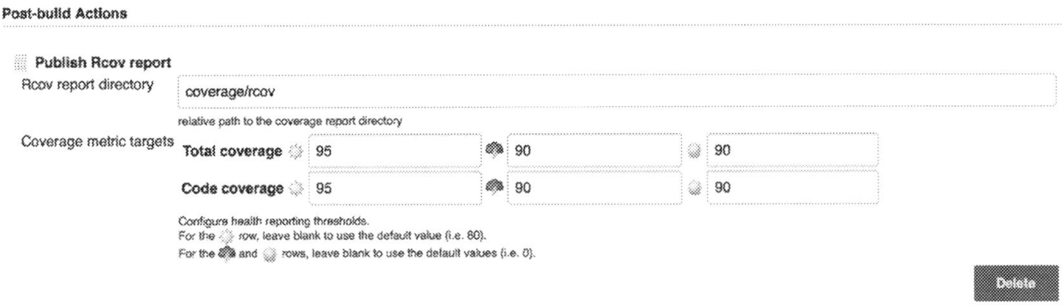

***Figure 8-4.** Jenkins RubyMetrics plugin configuration for build health assessment*

Configuring your RSpec test suite is easy, and Listing 8-6 shows how it is done. It presents a Spec helper file that implements this for whenever coverage falls below 85%.

Listing 8-6. spec/spec_helper.rb that generates reports processable by the DocLinks and RubyMetrics plugins

```
require "simplecov"
require "simplecov-rcov"

SimpleCov.formatters = [
  SimpleCov::Formatter::RcovFormatter,
  SimpleCov::Formatter::HTMLFormatter
]

SimpleCov.start
```

Another great use case for Jenkins that makes testing newly developed code more efficient is to integrate it directly with the code version control system. Many engineering organizations set up Jenkins to detect new branches or pull requests for a given GitHub repository, and they execute the test suite automatically. This helps the development team owning the service to review any change requests within a shorter feedback loop.

Shipping Sample Data with the Code

During the development cycle, engineers usually do not want to rely only on test-driven development (TDD) and automated tests to implement their features. A seasoned developer will also try to start the service they are altering locally, to see the changes made in effect immediately, and as perceived by clients. This also helps in efforts to use exploratory testing[12] to verify new features or other code behavior changes.

---

[12]See the next chapter for further notes on exploratory testing.

Two Types of Data Sources

Let us first define the two main categories of data sources for which we will need to provide sample data when making changes to a service: a *data store* in which the service application keeps the data it owns itself, as well as another *service application* that provides data to the service under development.

The rest of this section will be structured around several different ways that we have seen successful microservices applications set up such development-time sample data, starting with sample data for entities owned by the service itself, and then addressing sample data and logic provided by a service dependency.

Providing Samples for Data Owned

Here are some ways in which samples of service-owned data can be procured for local development.

Seeding Scripts

Probably the most common set-up to run a service application in which you have made changes and now want to explore locally on your development machine is to also run the application's data store on the development machine.

In this situation, running automated scripts to populate—or reset and clear out—the service-owned data store is often a viable option to provide sample data.

We do not recommend any particular automated approach to performing such seeding tasks, as many development frameworks allow for easy implementation of adding data to a store. As always, we recommend using a standardized approach across your organization applications to foster familiarity by consistency.

In Ruby on Rails, for example, developers often use the rake tool to run this automation. For example, the built-in rake db:seed reads and executes the Ruby code contained in the db/seeds.rb file in a Ruby on Rails project.

Another, very similar, option is to populate the development instance of your service with the data sets that are used for your automated unit tests. In Rails, this data often lives in so-called fixture files, and Rails provides you with the db:fixtures:load rake task to use these fixtures and move them into the development environment.

Production Snapshots

Another approach we have seen used in cases that require more exhaustive, or more authentic and "production-like," data is to work on snapshots of the production data store.

One way to implement this scenario is to take periodic snapshots of the data store in the production environment (for example, dumping the tables of a SQL database to a file).

These data dumps are then stored (and optionally compressed) on an internal file server to which all developers have access. To use the dumps locally, the service code base could again run automated bootstrapping scripts to download, decompress, and then install the dumps into the locally running data store.

▓ **Note** If you take this approach, make sure to scrub the production data of any sensitive information, such as personally identifiable information about your customers, passwords, financial information, and the like. You should anonymize, randomize, remove, or otherwise obfuscate sensitive data.

Connecting to a Shared Data Store

Some microservices companies follow a pattern in which they provide a sandbox environment where all the services are instantiated and running, outside and in addition to their production environment.

While we will explain more about the advantages of such a set-up later in this chapter, it is relevant to the sample data discussion as well, as it allows the service-owned data to live outside the developer's machine. Instead, the service instance under local development will in this scenario be configured to connect to the data store(s) that serve(s) the instance(s) of the same service in the sandbox environment.

This way, not every developer is obligated to install and update the sample data on their local machine, as the sample data can be centralized in the sandbox data stores.

A downside to this approach is certainly that it will be impractical to use for development of changes in the service that require a breaking change to the schema of the sandbox data store, as that would effectively incapacitate the sandbox instances of that same service. Also, it needs to be clear that the mutable state of the shared data store that is in use in the sandbox environment can change at any time in unpredictable ways. For example, purchases made or users created in a sandbox for our bookstore example cannot easily be coordinated across developers concurrently using the sandbox.

Providing Samples for Downstream Services

Next we will show to address dependencies on sample information for services upon which the application under development depends.

Providing Client-Side Samples

When a service has other services as downstream dependencies, then usually these service dependencies run remotely and outside of the dependent service's process boundaries and are accessed over a network boundary.

However, the development scenario discussed here removes cross-process boundary invocations and instead replaces them with in-memory calls. As a consequence, this means that all code that is reaching out to other services in a production scenario needs to be intercepted and rejiggered to respond with sample data that is generated inside the service process that is under test.

One option to implement this would be to first record live sample communications between the service under test and all its dependencies in production, and then change the service's development configuration to replay the recorded conversations appropriately when the service under development is run locally.

Even though there are options available in almost all programming languages and frameworks to address this record-and-replay approach, it is cumbersome to set up and expensive to maintain for any environment with more than a handful of service dependencies. See the next chapter's section "Out-Of-Process Component Tests" for more examples of such frameworks.

A slightly lower-effort (because more centralized) way of generating all service responses client-side is to have the teams that maintain downstream services ship libraries that can simulate sample data and behavior of their service. This technique is explained at length in the "Pluggable Back-Ends" section of the next chapter. While the focus in that chapter is on using this feature in an automated test suite, it can certainly and easily be adapted to be used in a general development environment.

The least costly manner in which to stub service dependencies in-process is to auto-generate the client-side, in-process service stubs. This can be done either by promoting stubs generated by contract-testing frameworks[13] to be used in the development stage with the service responses or by auto-generating a pluggable back-end library for each service based on the service's API specifications document. Support for the latter approach is unfortunately very service-framework specific and not a widely available option.

---

[13]Chapter 9 offers insights into frameworks for this purpose, such as `pacto`, in the sections on contract testing.

Mocking Services with Data

A twist on the just-described approach of providing mock data for a service dependency is not to alter the service under development to use in-process/in-memory doubles for their service dependencies. Instead, you provide mocks for the downstream services run remotely and out-of-process, just as the actual downstream dependencies do in a production environment.

The level of automation involved in generating these service doubles is again the deciding factor in assessing the technique's usefulness at scale. As a rule of thumb, if your organization employs more than a handful of interdependent services, hand-coding mocks for each one of them is going to be a productivity killer.

Thankfully, most service definition frameworks come with options to generate such mock services in an automated way, based on a computer-readable document that describes the APIs. The next chapter describes some of these tools in the "Contract Testing" section. Other (commercial and free) frameworks exist, such as RepreZen (`http://reprezen.com/swagger-tools`) and vREST (`https://vrest.io/`) for the Swagger tool chain.

Connecting to a Shared Environment

As mentioned in the section "Connecting to a Shared Data Store," many organizations using microservices run an additional shared sandbox environment for all their services.

This approach can be used to provide desired realistic sample data without having to run the downstream services locally. The service under test will be configured to rely on the sandbox instances of its dependencies. This service configuration can of course take place outside the service under development itself; for example, in a DNS, or a Consul (`https://www.consul.io/`) install, which resolves the locations of the dependencies.

In this scenario it is most advisable to have an organization-wide development policy in place which states that outages in the sandbox environment should be treated with an urgency that is only trumped by tackling issues currently surfaced in the production environment. If your organization cannot adequately implement such fast-response support for the shared environment, developers will be left only with the option of resorting to running service dependencies locally on their workstations. This has the disadvantages mentioned earlier, like slowing down the developers' machines, and the use of potentially out-of-date dependency code, but it is still better than having no end-to-end testing facilities prior to promoting code to production.

Maintaining a Development Sandbox

As alluded to in two of the previous sections, a key approach for making development in a microservices environment more effective and fun is to provide a shared sandbox environment.

This can be seen as a switched, self-contained network fabric whose topology is such that only the participating service nodes interconnect. In this scenario, the fabric of services is solely meant to enable an improved software development and testing process, in order to shorten release cycles while at the same time decreasing defects shipped to production.

Figure 8-5 shows a set-up of three separate network fabrics (sandbox, staging, and production) into which the entire microservices application is deployed.

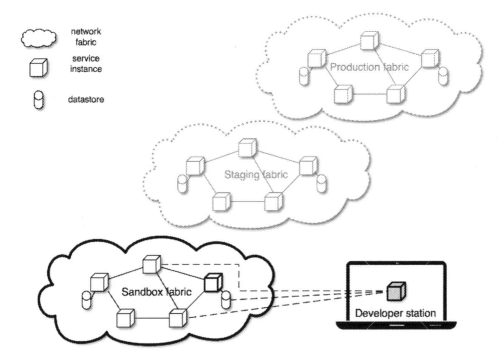

Figure 8-5. *Interconnected services in the sandbox fabric*

Software developers who need to make changes to a service will alter and run just the particular service under change on their developer workstation. If the service in which they develop, and which they hence need to run on their workstation, depends on other services or data stores, then the locally running service instance will be configured to use the service and data store dependencies deployed to the sandbox environment.

Integrating a sandbox environment into the development process can address many items on our developer wish list. Let's look at each of these items in a little more detail.

▓ **Note**   The use of a dedicated sandbox environment is our own recommendation based on our years of experience in developing in microservices architectures, but the approach introduced here is by no means uncontested. As our former colleague Evan Phoenix, CEO of VEKTRA Innovation (http://vektra.com/), poignantly describes in a post on his personal blog:[14]

The industry needs a common set of practices for how to develop microservices.

[…]

Microservice development is still in its infancy. Teams are slowly figuring out solutions to their specific problems and largely hacking something together.

---

[14]Evan Phoenix, "Microservice Development - Who Runs What Where", April 17, 2016. http://phx.io/posts/ microservice-dev/

Providing Up-to-Date Dependencies

In a scenario where developers can rely on the development sandbox to run all services and systems that the code base they are currently altering is running, they are relieved of many cumbersome and time-consuming chores.

They will no longer need to make sure they have the latest version of their service's dependencies running locally on their own workstation. They simply have to make sure that their local setup is communicating with the service and data dependencies in the sandbox fabric.

Note that this has an impact on the discipline of your development process. The responsibility for keeping each of the microservices in the organization fresh in the sandbox resides with the teams that own them. This means that there needs to be internal monitoring and support dedicated to making sure that the systems in the sandbox are running during business hours.

As an example, Amazon's development organization ensured this by making sure that owner teams of sandbox services were easily identifiable, and it was acceptable to page the owning team's engineer on-call when outages were perceived.

Saving Resources on Developer Workstations

The point of reducing load and resource consumption on the developer workstations is to increase developer velocity by not wasting their time waiting for unresponsive applications.

Running the majority of the systems and services making up your microservices architecture on dedicated computing resources definitely helps to offload developer stations: no memory, CPU processing power, or disk space needs to be dedicated to install and run the service dependencies locally.

Fostering Concurrent and Collaborative Development

In our many years of experience we have learned that there is no better way to increase the productivity of your development team than to encourage forming close-knit working relationships. Creating an environment in which solving problems and developing features is fun, and which leverages the combined skills of everyone on the team, is key to the successful growth of your engineering organization. Software development organizations are most successful where collaboration is engrained in the culture. A development sandbox helps greatly with these efforts.

Imagine a situation in which a new feature is to be added to our sample bookstore application, to enable customers to save favorite searches, and to be notified by a tool of their choice (for example, via email, mobile push notifications, or pop-up messages on the site). This feature requires changes in various pages in the bookstore front-end, the mobile applications, and a fair number of back-end services (new functionalities to associate users and searches, to periodically re-execute the searches offline, to notify the users of new results, and so on.).

Typically, these changes are most efficiently performed when expert developers focus on the various parts: front-end specialists take care of the HTML, JavaScript, and CSS changes in the desktop and mobile web applications, iOS and Android developers change the native apps, and back-end developers from each of the teams that own the backing services are adding or changing service APIs.

In this very common situation, having an environment where developers from all these teams can collaborate by pushing their latest code branches to the application instances running in the sandbox fabric has a number of advantages. For one, the velocity of development is increased by having subject matter experts focus on making the changes concurrently. Additionally, communication and collaboration between the participating developers is encouraged very early on in the feature development cycle, so that less time is wasted on hunting down missed or unclear requirements, or potential bugs.

▓ **Note** In situations where only a few applications need changing to implement a feature, we have seen organizations encourage collaborating developers to use a *single* workstation to develop the changes in all affected systems. In this scenario, the participating engineers would all be given access to a shared workstation, which they would use to make the changes to the two or three services involved. They would then run these development branches of these services simultaneously on the workstation, and connect them with each other, while still utilizing the sandbox environment for all other dependencies. If the resources needed to change and run the applications under development locally do not noticeably slow down the workstation, then this route can cut down feature development time even further, as it obviates the need for deployment of the development branches to the sandbox instances.

Shortening the Feedback Loop for Changes

Another advantage of using a sandbox environment stems from the fact that all developers will use the services deployed there. It means that all engineers will exercise the services deployed there day in and day out, as the code running on their own developer workstations depends on the proper functioning of the services in the sandbox.

This simple fact greatly increases the chances of finding bugs and regressions very early on, even during the development cycle of a new feature and before any other quality assurance measures. Additionally, for companies whose release process includes quality assurance on an end-to-end basis, the QA team can use the sandbox environment to perform such application-wide testing well ahead of releasing any code changes out into a production environment.

One caveat of using the sandbox for true QA purposes is that it would be advisable to enforce a brief code-freeze during QA times for the sandbox, so that verification results are not invalidated by any mid-test changes.

In order to prevent these inaccuracies and the potential slow-down to ongoing development efforts, many companies introduce an additional network fabric, often referred to as "staging" (see Figure 8-5 earlier). This is an interstitial environment between sandbox and production, which is mostly prepopulated with production-like data sets, so that end-to-end QA efforts can happen in a setting that very closely mirrors actual production scenarios.

Using a Rewriting Proxy for Edge Device Development

As mentioned in the wish list section under "Privacy of Development," it is important that applications installed on edge devices (like iOS, Android, or other native OS applications) can be tested against service-side changes *prior* to releasing these changes to a production environment. This not only aids in security and stability concerns, it also benefits development velocity, as developers will not need to wait for changes to be deployed all the way through the stages out into a development fabric before they can be tested with the native applications.

The best way that we have seen this situation addressed is via the use of a proxy service. In this approach, the developer would perform the following steps:

1. Install a proxy server in the same network fabric where the service instances under change are running (usually either on the local developer workstation or inside the company's VPN in the sandbox fabric).

2. Change the network settings on the edge devices (for example, iPhones or Android tablets) participating in the development to direct all traffic via the previously set up proxy server.

3. Configure the proxy server with a rewriting rule, so that requests from the edge devices to the production domain of your application are being rerouted to the internal (workstation- or sandbox-hosted) instances of your services.

4. Make sure the edge device is able to join (for example, via Wi-Fi) the network in which the proxy server is exposed, so that subsequently all requests from the device can be routed via the proxy to the respective services under development.

While there are many proxy services available that will allow these features to be implemented, we have found CharlesProxy (`https://www.charlesproxy.com/`) to be very feature-rich, yet easy to use, and available for all major desktop operating systems (Mac OSX, Windows, and Linux).

Figure 8-6 shows the CharlesProxy rewrite settings page, configured such that any device sending requests for resources in the `books.com` domain would instead be serviced by the equivalent hosts in the `int.books.dev` domain (which you can configure to be the domain for your workstation or sandbox fabric, for example).

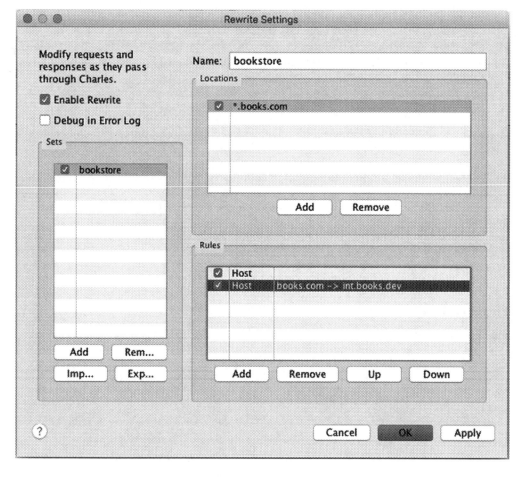

Figure 8-6. *Example host rewriting settings in CharlesProxy for our fictitious bookstore*

Codifying Internal Standards via Generation Tools

Any development organization should make sure to take the guesswork out of setting up new services and applications. Doing so will aid in three areas:

- Development speed

- Efficiency in application support and maintenance

- Fostering standards and familiarity across applications and frameworks within the development team

Our advice is to develop scripts and tools that can automatically generate service repositories or internal libraries. The code for the service applications so generated should be prepopulated with the approved libraries, configuration files, and preferably even skeleton code and test examples. A newly generated library could simply add certain artifacts (like a change log or Readme file) in consistent places in the directory tree as defined by the organization's conventions, thereby getting the developers started down the right path.

Examples for such generation tools can be found in many companies that have successfully adopted microservices. Amazon is running an internal web application which sports a web wizard that walks developers through all the steps to generate a service stub conforming to their internal Coral service framework. Developers can choose from options like the programming language to use, and the internal organization and code repositories in which to create the artifacts.

LivingSocial is streamlining the application generation process through a set of templates-based Ruby scripts. The tool is called `ls-forge` and is very easy to invoke from the command line:

```
$ ls-forge rails create ./path/to/new_service
```

This command starts an interactive shell-based questionnaire to generate a new Rails API based service. During its course, it asks the user about choices regarding the use of test framework options, selection of approved data store options, the use of crontasks, caching back-ends (like Memcached) and the need for messaging (for example, by including Kafka support), and so on. The generated applications include standard gems (both internal and external) and code stubs that are preconfigured to support test frameworks, circuit breakers, documentation tools, and monitoring and alarming.

The generated code often does nothing more than expose a "Hello World!" API functionality. Still, the trivial example code can be used to showcase an acceptable coding style and other API design guidelines, thereby setting the tone and "soft-enforcing" consistency and best practices. In LivingSocial's case, for example, one feature of the generated application is that APIs are documented via Swagger specifications, and a Swagger UI explorer can be launched locally.

The main point for such tools is to help consistency between applications, so that developers do not have to overcome a high barrier when switching between them during development.

Making Documentation Search-Efficient

With the adoption of a large number of fine-grained service applications also comes the need to make it easy to discover documentation about things like service specifications, characteristics, mission, ownership and development roadmap. Aiding both humans and computers in discovering service attributes can have a great effect on maintainability, stability of your infrastructure, and time-of-production for your business-critical features.

In our time working with microservices we have not seen many universally accepted solutions to this challenge. The only common thread we have been able to determine is that most organizations discover the need to address inconsistencies or lack of documentation rather late in their service adoption process.

It is fairly easy to start small, though. Amazon, for example, started out with the introduction of nodes describing each service on their company-internal Wiki installation. LivingSocial has adopted Atlassian's Confluence (`https://www.atlassian.com/software/confluence`) as a company-wide documentation tool, and teams have generated page templates to use for each service they own. These templates include information on team contact details, additional documentation, URL for an API explorer web tool, configured alarms, monitoring dashboard links, production console access, standard operating procedure in case of outages, as well as operational support and SLA agreements.

A really useful addition to service documentation is a web UI that lets you easily explore the APIs exposed by a service. One such example is to describe your APIs using Swagger and then publish the documentation using the Swagger UI explorer.[15] To aid documentation and specification even further, it helps to introduce conventions defining where API specifications and the explorer are hosted. As an example, all services using the Swagger toolchain host their API specifications at the `/swagger/api` path, with the service explorer accessible at `/swagger/docs`. Additionally, the services' API specifications are pushed to another centralized service, which both other services and humans can use to retrieve a full list of all available services.

This last approach last can be seen as the beginning of implementing a true service registry that can help in programmatically discovering available services and their capabilities. We will not go into detail about private service discovery tools such as Weaveworks Weave (`https://www.weave.works/product/`), AWS Route 53 (`https://aws.amazon.com/route53/`), or HashiCorp's Consul (`https://www.consul.io/`).[16] Nevertheless, such tools play an important role in helping effectively manage both development and production environments, and they become essential when running medium to large-scale microservices architectures.

Summary

Any organization that wants to be successful in adopting microservices needs to make sure that a list of processes and tools are in place for engineers to be set up to support the business goals effectively and efficiently.

The first part of this chapter explains the most essential 12 properties of a successful microservices development environment, detailing the rationale behind each of the items on the list.

In the second part, we describe practices and tools to address each point on the first part's wish list. Each of the recommendations we make is backed up by our practical experience with those tools gathered over the course of our careers.

Now that we have explained general development concerns, the next chapter will focus on what is involved in testing microservices applications to verify them in an exhaustive fashion, and what to look out for in particular.

---

[15]For more details on the Swagger UI, see the *"The Swagger User Interface"* section in Chapter 5.
[16]See Chapters 6 and 9 for more information on the Consul tool.

CHAPTER 9

Testing with Services

Automated testing is crucial in any software development project. Manually testing a system built from microservices is tedious and error-prone. In some cases, it is well-nigh impossible to test all the possible failure modes by simply exercising the application through exploratory tests executed by human QA personnel. Automating these tests will save hours of time, and it will prevent those bugs that could cost your business millions in profits.

Testing becomes even more important in a microservices architecture where the components of the system are highly distributed across network boundaries.

This chapter first discusses the five system layers at which testing can and should be done:

- Unit testing

- Integration testing

- Contract testing

- Component testing

- End-to-end testing

Next, we will show approaches to testing a single microservice component in isolation from other, external microservices with which it interacts. The pros and cons of each approach are discussed, and example code to illustrate implementing them is explained.

We then move on to showing how tests can support services in guaranteeing that they meet their published API contract. The goal is to shield the service clients from unexpected breakages caused by service-side changes.

Last but not least, we demonstrate how system-level, end-to-end tests can be specified, in order to exercise the functionalities that make up an application that is composed of multiple interacting microservices.

Layers of Microservice Testing

As discussed in Chapter 1, microservice architectures enforce clearer, more pronounced internal boundaries between the components of an entire system than monolithic applications typically do.

This can be used to the advantage of testing strategies applied to microservices; more options for places and methods to test are available. Because the entirety of the application is composed of services with clear boundaries, it becomes much more evident which layers can be tested in isolation. This section describes each of the conceptual layers at which tests can be introduced.

The Five Layers of Testing

An application designed in a microservices architectural style can be viewed at several levels of granularity. Starting from the outside in, end users will interact with the system as a whole. At the next level down, the system internals can be viewed as a series of communications between each of the underlying services. Finally, the services themselves can be described as the code modules that make up each of the services. Testing strategies should aim to cover all these levels or layers, as well as interlayer communication.

■ **Note**   We use the terms *layer* and *level* interchangeably when referring to a set of tests that exercise the same layer of the microservices application, and hence conceptually belong together.

The diagram in Figure 9-1 was inspired by one that Toby Clemson of ThoughtWorks used in a presentation on microservices testing,[1] published on Martin Fowler's blog. It illustrates five layers of tests, and where they are applied in a system designed with microservices.

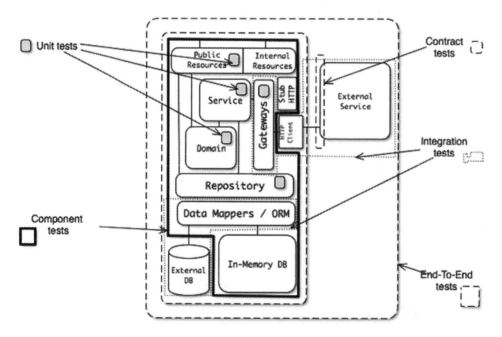

***Figure 9-1.** Diagram of the five layers of testing applied to microservices*

Unit Testing

As the lowest level of testing, unit tests exercise the smallest piece of testable software in the application to determine whether it behaves as expected. The emphasis here is on trying to identify the truly smallest independent piece of logic to be tested.

---

[1]Tobias Clemson, "Testing Strategies in a Microservice Architecture," November 18, 2014. http://martinfowler.com/articles/microservice-testing/#conclusion-summary

An example in the realm of our bookstore could be the functionality of displaying the user's name correctly. The underlying logic specifies that the first choice is to display a name the user has entered via the bookstore app itself, with a fall-back to a name as vended by a third party (like Facebook), and finally a name deduced from the user's email address data. The various conditions and fall-back scenarios should be exercised via unit testing.

When you find yourself struggling to implement unit tests for a code module, such difficulties often indicate that the design of the module needs improvement: the cause could be that logic needs to be broken down even further, and that responsibilities allotted to the module need to be further separated.

Even at this very low level of testing, the code under test often relies on collaborating with other modules. When running unit tests, the tester has two options for setting up such interactions with these collaborators: either the unit under test is exercised in isolation from all its dependencies, or it is not (meaning that collaboration with external units continues to happen). In his book *Working Effectively With Unit Tests* (Leanpub 2014), Jay Fields calls these two options for approaching unit testing *sociable* (where collaborators stay involved), and *solitary* (where dependencies are not exercised).

Both solitary and sociable testing are important when verifying microservices architectures. A good example of where sociable tests are usually preferred is the domain logic of a service, as these tests usually involve observing changes in state of the unit under test. It is an approach that can best be described as black-box testing that examines the unit under test while interacting with its external interface, and having all collaborating external modules present in their true form adds much to the level of confidence such tests provide.

On the other hand, when testing "plumbing" code (like gateway code to other services or data stores) or "orchestration" logic (which simply coordinates the message flow with other modules), solitary tests are most often used; the respective external services, data stores, or coordinated modules are replaced by test doubles to facilitate faster, and potentially more reliably repeatable, tests. A word of caution on the solitary testing approach, though: it makes it all too easy to neglect testing mocked responses from dependencies that simulate *failure conditions or exceptions*. Don't fall prey to the *fallacies of distributed computing*!

Integration Testing

Compared to unit tests, integration tests are more coarsely grained: their purpose is to verify that each module of a service correctly interacts with its collaborators. They are meant to detect any defects in how modules should communicate with each other, so that a new feature, or a code change, can be safely deployed to production.

To achieve that end, they exercise communication paths through the service in order to find incorrect assumptions each module might have about how to interact with its communication partners. Also, make sure not to test just for the "happy paths" of successful communication, but also cover basic failure and exception scenarios of the integration module—an advisable approach, which is not just limited to the realm of integration testing, but which should be heeded for testing at all levels.

When testing integration with components that are external services, you should prepopulate external components with an agreed-upon fixed set of representative data that is guaranteed to be available. This aids repeatability of your tests in an automated integration test suite.

Testing a service's persistence layer at an integration level should include tests that confirm that the schema assumed by the code matches the one actually available in the data store. As is often overlooked, timeouts and network failures can happen for data stores, as well, since they usually exist across network boundaries. Therefore, the service's ability to fail gracefully under such conditions also needs to be verified.

An integration test scenario for our bookstore example would be to exercise the communication between the cart-service and the books-service, where the cart-service's code base would include verifications that it can successfully retrieve and process product data (such as pricing information) provided by books-service. Additionally, the integration tests should assert that the cart-service can still continue to function— albeit most likely in a limited fashion—in case of a books-service outage.

While integration tests should generally *not* rely on involving test doubles, it can sometimes be difficult to trigger exception behaviors, like timeouts or slow responses, in an external service. This is especially true if the external service is not under the control of the team that is writing the integration tests. In such cases, stubbing failures in predetermined ways can be helpful.

Note also that integration tests can start failing not only when the integration module itself regresses, but *also* if the external component that is being integrated with suddenly becomes unavailable, or breaks its contract. Therefore, our advice is to write a few truly sociable integration tests, but to focus more attention on unit tests, plus contract tests (which are discussed next) on either side of the integration boundary.

Contract Testing

When implementing and maintaining a service, it is essential that the service's exposed APIs (collectively also known as the *service contract*) meet the requirements and expectations of all its consumers. A service contract consists of expectations of input and output data structures, side effects, and nonfunctional points like performance and concurrency characteristics.[2] If the microservice is subject to change over time, it is important that the contracts of each of the service consumers continue to be satisfied. Contract testing is meant to verify that a service boundary behaves as advertised.

As contract tests are aimed at the boundary of a service and its consumers, they are usually bifurcated into two parts. The maintainers of each consuming client application write tests suites that verify only those aspects of the producing service that are in use by the client. On the other hand, the maintainers of the service itself run contract tests to determine the impact of their changes on their consumers; these service-side tests are ideally just the bundle of all its consumers' contract test suites. If breaking changes in the service's APIs are to be made, running all the consumers' contract tests will tell the service maintaining team which of its clients would be broken. Then, either all broken clients need to be convinced to move to the new API in lock-step, or versioning of the API is needed, which leaves existing client-exposed API versions untouched.

The nature of contract test suites also makes them valuable when a new service is being defined. Service consumers can help to drive the design of the service's API by building contract tests ahead of time, so that the consumer's requirements can be taken into account in the earliest stages. This pattern of service development is usually called *consumer-driven contracts*.[3]

There are some test tools available for various technology stacks, which are aimed at supporting contract testing (for example, Pacto, Pact, and Janus[4]). Later in this chapter, we will show examples of such tests.

Component Testing

At this level of testing in a system that is composed of a set of microservices, the unit under test is one of the services in its entirety. Component tests provide a controlled testing environment for the service, aiming to trigger any applicable error cases in a repeatable manner.

The scope for these tests is intentionally limited to the single service as a component of the whole system. This means that a service is set up to be isolated from any other external components, which are usually replaced with test doubles, usually injected via special start-up configuration of the service under test.

As a consequence, this level of testing cannot make sure that the microservices all work together as a whole to satisfy business requirements; more coarse-grained, end-to-end testing (discussed below) will be necessary for such comprehensive purposes.

---

[2]Testing nonfunctional requirements will not be shown in this book. Such specifications are most likely the hardest to verify, and short of a full load-testing environment probably impossible to assert.

[3]Ian Robinson, "Consumer-Driven Contracts: A Service Evolution Pattern," June 12, 2006. http://martinfowler.com/articles/consumerDrivenContracts.html

[4]Pacto, https://github.com/thoughtworks/pacto; Pact, https://github.com/realestate-com-au/pact; Janus, https://github.com/gga/janus

One advantage of component-level tests compared to end-to-end tests is that they provide more accurate test feedback about the service itself; the service's APIs are directly driven through tests from the perspective of a consumer, as opposed to indirectly via the execution of a higher-level interaction of an end-user with the entire system. Component tests also usually run faster than tests that are aimed at the entire system.

When implementing component tests, there are principally two options where the tests will be executed: in-process, or out-of-process. The next two sections will discuss these options in more detail.

In-Process Component Tests

In-process tests for a service component execute in the same CPU process as the service code under test. Test doubles for outside resources (like external services the component depends upon) live inside the service at the time of executing in-process component tests. Data stores that the service might use for persistence are held in-memory, so that access to them does not cross network or process boundaries.

To achieve in-process testability, tests often communicate with the microservice through a special internal interface that allows requests to be dispatched, and responses to be retrieved, without making actual (HTTP) network calls to the service-under-test's API. This way, in-process component tests can get as close as possible to the (out-of-process) alternative of executing real HTTP requests against the service, without incurring the additional overhead of true network interactions.

As an advantage of this approach, in-process component tests do not touch the network, and thus execute much faster and are generally less complex.

Other external services upon which the component under test depends are usually replaced with in-process test doubles. These doubles serve canned responses that cover not just regular service responses, but also failure codes and other communication edge cases.

Using an in-memory database, like H2 DB, or an in-process implementation of Cassandra or ElasticSearch, improves test performance compared to accessing external DBs, as network calls are unnecessary. The argument for using such in-memory replacements is that any persistence-layer integration tests will provide sufficient coverage for communication with the actual data store in use by the component.

A disadvantage is that the microservice being tested has to be altered for testing purposes to be started in a "test" mode, which differs from its usual production mode. Dependency injection frameworks can help with setting services up for tests, but the fact remains that the service is not configured exactly as it would be in a production scenario.

Out-Of-Process Component Tests

Out-of-process tests treat the service component as a black box and verify it via tests that execute in a different process and exercise the service over the network, using its publicly exposed APIs.

Test doubles for external service dependencies are still in use, but they live outside the service. They execute in their own process, and they are reached only across a network.

Similarly, data stores used in these out-of-process component tests are real data stores. They provide the service under test with sample data.

Out-of-process testing allows more layers and integration points to be exercised than is possible with the in-process variant; all interactions make use of real network calls, and the deployment unit can remain unchanged. If the microservice under test has complex integration, persistence, or startup logic, then this approach is the only way to test it at a component level.

Tests in this category verify that the microservices have the correct network configuration and are capable of handling true network requests. The modules that communicate with other service resources, as well as the persistence-access modules, are tested in full integration with external dependencies, which live in separate processes.

External service dependencies can be stubbed in various ways: the tester can either build a set of actual stub services that expose the same contract or have them dynamically generated. Tools like Moco[5] or Mountebank[6] can help with this task. To make the data returned by such mock services more realistic, it can again be either manually crafted or prerecorded from interactions with the real service (using tools like VCR[7]).

The trade-off to be aware of when choosing this approach is that the complexity of isolating the microservice under test from its dependencies is pushed into the test harness. The harness will be responsible for starting and stopping external stubs, coordination of network ports, and other configuration options. Also, using external stub services and actual out-of-process data stores will most likely result in slower tests than in-process approaches can achieve, because of the additional network communications.

We will show practical examples of setting up component-level tests for a bookstore-related service later in this chapter.

End-To-End Testing

End-to-end tests aim to exercise the entire application in order to verify that it meets all external requirements and that all goals are met.

Compared to previously discussed component tests, they are concerned not just with a single microservice, but with the entire set of communicating services and technology components making up the system. This is why they are sometimes also referred to as *full-stack tests*.

They exercise as much of the fully deployed system as possible, manipulating it through public interfaces, such as GUIs and service APIs. This level of testing allows microservice architectures to evolve over time, as they assert that the system remains intact during large-scale architectural refactorings. When actions like splitting, combining, or decommissioning some of the services that make up the entire system becomes necessary or desirable, they serve as a means of verifying that no regressions are caused to the overall application functionalities and expectations.

One complication often encountered in end-to-end testing is how to address potential dependencies of the application under test on truly external services, provided by third parties. Similar complications arise if the dependencies are simply flaky or unreliable.

In such systems it may not be possible to write end-to-end tests that are repeatable and side effect free; tests can start to fail for reasons outside of the testing team's control. Under these circumstances it can be beneficial to sacrifice a certain level of confidence in the true end-to-end nature of the tests by introducing stubs or other test doubles for the external services. What is lost in complete fidelity is gained in greater stability in the test suite.

For systems that require direct user manipulation via a GUI, tools such as Selenium WebDriver[8] can help to drive the GUI to trigger particular use cases within the system. For headless systems without a GUI, end-to-end tests usually directly manipulate the microservices through their public APIs (for example, via HTTP client libraries, or even just direct cURL command-line tool calls).

As a general rule, end-to-end test suites carry higher costs than lower-level testing efforts. Given their asynchronous nature, their long run times (as they execute entire application-level usage scenarios), and the fact that there are typically many moving parts involved, each of which can be broken, they are more laborious to implement, and larger efforts are necessary to maintain them.

To address this problem, it can be prudent to set a fixed limit on the total runtime budgeted for end-to-end test suites. This introduces a forcing function to purge particularly long-running tests once the budget is exceeded.

---

[5]https://github.com/dreamhead/moco
[6]https://github.com/bbyars/mountebank
[7]https://github.com/vcr/vcr
[8]http://docs.seleniumhq.org/projects/webdriver/

To determine which tests to keep, it can help to design the test scenarios around the various user roles, and to formulate stories how these users interact with the system. Another approach would be to order the tests by financial importance. For example, a test that exercises interactions with an external payments gateway might take a quarter of your time budgeted for end-to-end testing, but it is verifying a functionality considered business-critical; it is still considered a worthwhile assertion.

This helps to focus on the parts of the application that provide the highest value. Coverage for the lesser concerns can be addressed by lower-level types of testing.

In order to make it easier to have the engineering and business organizations of your company collaborate on defining user stories, many practitioners use domain-specific languages (DSLs) to implement their test cases. The intent is to make the verification steps human-readable while maintaining the properties of keeping them machine-executable. Popular tools to support test DSLs include Cucumber[9] and Gauge.[10] We will show examples of end-to-end tests written in Cucumber later in this chapter.

Another problem to specifically address in end-to-end tests is setting up the entire system with test data that makes these tests reliably repeatable.

The most efficient way to handle this is to apply the same DevOps techniques that one should generally apply to deploying microservices architectures to setting up test beds, as well. Much reliability is gained if pristine test environments are spun up as part of the test initialization process. These environments should already be populated with known test data (provided via DB imports or by populating the services involved via the APIs they expose).

Because of the effort involved in getting end-to-end testing right, there are many teams that simply skip this extra layer of testing. They would rather rely on more stringent production environment monitoring and alarming, paired with a handful of manually executed, exploratory smoke tests once changes have been deployed.

You can find an example scenario for end-to-end testing in our bookstore application later on in this chapter.

The Test Pyramid

We are adopting Mike Cohn's metaphor of a test pyramid[11] to express the notion that the number of tests written at each testing level should decrease the more coarsely grained the view of the unit under test becomes.

The diagram in Figure 9-2 shows Toby Clemson's depiction[12] of the relative number of tests in the various testing layers just described.

---

[9]https://cucumber.io/
[10]http://getgauge.io/
[11]http://martinfowler.com/bliki/TestPyramid.html
[12]Tobias Clemson, "Testing Strategies in a Microservice Architecture," November 18, 2014. http://martinfowler.com/articles/microservice-testing/#conclusion-test-pyramid

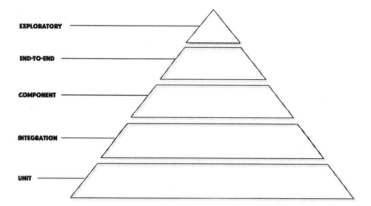

Figure 9-2. *The testing pyramid shows the relative number of tests in each layer*

At the very top we find a layer we haven't specifically talked about yet: exploratory tests are executed manually by human testers, and they interact with the application directly through a user interface. These tests can help to educate the testers' efforts of writing and improving automated tests. They can also be used as a sanity-checking tool to make sure a recently released change has in fact taken effect.

As we move down the pyramid, the scope of each of the tests executed decreases, while the number of tests in a given layer becomes larger compared to the layers above.

The metaphor of a pyramid expresses the general advice about where to spend time and effort for writing tests. If the advice is taken, it is easier to arrive at a test suite that minimizes maintenance costs and total runtime while at the same time maximizing utility.

Testing Examples

Now that you've seen the various layers at which microservices can be tested, the following sections will show examples for approaches to some of the less obvious and commonplace levels of testing. Most of these examples are based on actual test suites we have encountered in our work experience.

In-Process Stubs for Component and Unit Testing

As described in the sidebar, although stubbing external dependencies has its disadvantages, it helps with increasing the speed and isolation of test suites. In order to take advantage of these pros, we have spent some time trying to address the cons.

WHAT IS STUBBING?

For the remainder of this section, we will be using the terms *stub* and *stubbing* generically for any case where you replace a production object for testing purposes. This aligns mostly with Gerard Meszaros' general term *test double*,[13] disregarding the more nuanced differences between the various types of doubles.[14]

---

[13]http://xunitpatterns.com/Test Double.html
[14]For a more nuanced distinction between types of doubles, see Fowler's "Marks Aren't Stubs" article, January 2, 2007. http://martinfowler.com/articles/mocksArentStubs.html

Concretely, this means that the application under test uses test doubles for every call to an external web services made in the exercised code. This way, no service calls ever leave the process in which the component under test is running. Results of the service calls are predefined, or "faked," so that the rest of the code under test can be exercised based on these assumptions.

There are a large number of such test double frameworks out there. Just in the Ruby ecosystem, projects like Mocha or RSpec Mocks[15] can help to prevent service calls by stubbing out methods of the service clients' access objects. Other gems (such as Webmock[16] and FakeWeb[17]) tie in at the HTTP request level, letting you define mock responses for all requests to predefined URL patterns.

The main advantage of using stubs when testing applications with external dependencies is speed. Calling external dependencies can really slow down a test suite. If no time has to be spent in your tests for making expensive network calls, then you will be much more productive. Another advantage is that you can truly test your component in isolation, and dependencies do not need to be available during test runs. Additionally, your component's test runs will be resilient to changes in the dependent services' data.

Traditional stubbing does come with disadvantages, though. For one, testing never happens on a true "integration" level, as the request round-trip between the application under test and the service will never happen.

Another danger is the potential for the dependent APIs to change. If you rely solely on testing the interactions with test doubles, your tests will still pass, even if the API contract or behavior on the service side changes, and you run the risk of not detecting issues that will show up only when deployed to the production environment.

Finally, setting up stubs often introduces distracting boilerplate code into your tests simply to bootstrap your test scenarios.

The direction we took was to build test doubles right into the service's client library, and to evolve and maintain them in lock-step with the changes in the service APIs. Here are some key points of the stubbing approach taken. We will summarize with an explanation of the main benefits of this approach.

Pluggable Back-Ends

When building a client library (or in our case, a Ruby gem), we provide a way to configure (at least) two back-end alternatives: one that makes actual HTTP calls to the respective service in order to assemble the library's response objects; and a second "fake" back-end, which never makes actual network calls to retrieve response objects, but instead chooses them from a pool of well-known response objects.

First, Listing 9-1 shows the common "abstract class" that defines the interface for both the real and the mock back-end.

---

[15]https://github.com/rspec/rspec-mocks
[16]https://github.com/bblimke/webmock
[17]https://github.com/chrisk/fakeweb

Listing 9-1. Abstract backend class

```
module BookStore
  module Books::Backends

    class BackendUnimplementedMethodError < StandardError; end

    # This class defines the API that backend implementations need to follow
    class Backend

      def self.find(id)
        raise BackendUnimplementedMethodError.new
      end

      def self.find_by_slug(slug)
        raise BackendUnimplementedMethodError.new
      end

      def self.get_all
        raise BackendUnimplementedMethodError.new
      end


      ...
    end
  end
end
```

Next, Listing 9-2 shows the actual back-end that connects to the service in question. It implements the methods defined in BookStore::Books::Backends::BooksService.

Listing 9-2. Class for implementing communication with the book-service

```
module BookStore
  module Books::Backends

    class BooksService < Backend

      def self.api
        @api ||= Faraday.new(url: ServiceDiscovery.url_for(:books), ...)
      end

      def self.find(uuid)
        raise BookStore::Books::BookNotFoundError unless
            BookStore::Books::ArgumentChecker.valid_uuid?(uuid)
        response = api.get(URI.escape("/books/#{uuid}"))
        raise BookStore::Books::BookNotFoundError unless
            response.status == 200

        response_to_book_container(parsed_response(response.body))
      end
```

```ruby
    def self.find_by_slug(slug)
      raise BookStore::Books::BookNotFoundError unless
          BookStore::Books::ArgumentChecker.valid_slug?(slug)
      response = api.get(URI.escape("/books/slug/#{slug}"))
      raise BookStore::Books::BookNotFoundError unless
          response.status == 200

      response_to_book_container(parsed_response(response.body))
    end

    def self.get_all
      response = api.get("/books/")
      raise BookStore::Books::BookNotFoundError unless
          response.status == 200

      parsed_response(response.body).map do |book|
        response_to_book_container(book)
      end
    end
    ...
  end
end
```

Listing 9-3 shows the implementation of the stubbed back-end that serves canned responses to all gem clients.

Listing 9-3. Implementation of a back-end stub

```ruby
module BookStore
  module Books::Backends

    class Stub < Backend

      def self.find(uuid)
        raise BookStore::Books::BookNotFoundError unless
            BookStore::Books::ArgumentChecker.valid_uuid?(uuid)
        book = @books.detect {|book| book.uuid == uuid}
        raise BookStore::Books::BookNotFoundError if book.nil?

        book.backend_data
      end

      def self.find_by_slug(slug)
        raise BookStore::Books::BookNotFoundError unless
            BookStore::Books::ArgumentChecker.valid_slug?(slug)
        book = @books.detect {|book| book.slug == slug}
        raise BookStore::Books::BookNotFoundError if book.nil?

        book.backend_data
      end
```

```
      def self.get_all
        @books.map(&:backend_data)
      end
      ...
      def self.reset_all_data
        @books = BookStore::Books::TestStubs.all_books
        ...
      end
    end
end
```

Finally, the main accessor class of our gem allows for setting a back-end, and then delegates all API calls it exposes to the currently set back-end, as shown in Listing 9-4.

Listing 9-4. The gem's main access class

```
module BookStore
  module Books

    ...
    class << self
      attr_writer :backend

      def backend
        @backend ||= BookStore::Books::Backends::BooksService
      end

      def stubbed_mode!
        @backend = BookStore::Books::Backends::Stub
        @backend.reset_all_data
      end

      def get(uuid)
        BookStore::Books::Book.new(backend.find(uuid))
      end

      def get_all
        backend.get_all.map do |book|
          BookStore::Books::Book.new(book.id, :backend_data => book)
        end
      end

      def get_by_slug(slug)
        books_service_response = backend.find_by_slug(slug)
        BookStore::Books::Book.new(books_service_response.uuid,
                               :backend_data => books_service_response)
      end
      ...
    end
  end
end
```

Realistic Canned Responses

The well-known response objects served by the stubbed back-end expose the same API as the objects returned from actual network service calls (in fact, they are instances of the same model classes), and they come preloaded inside the stubbed back-end's registry of responses. Listing 9-5 shows an extract from the code that demonstrates how the test stub objects are exposed.

Listing 9-5. Class to provide book test stubs

```
module BookStore
  module Books
    class TestStubs

      def self.diva_and_flea
        Book.new('f81d4fae-7dec-11d0-a765-00a0c91e6bf6',
                 backend_data: BookStore::Books::BookContainer.new(
                                 'f81d4fae-7dec-11d0-a765-00a0c91e6bf6',
                                 'The Story of Diva and Flea',
                                 'the-story-of-diva-and-flea', ...))
      end

      def self.winnie_the_pooh
        Book.new('481dfebc-7fa5-22c0-a765-01b0c83e5ce4',
                 backend_data: BookStore::Books::BookContainer.new(
                                 '481dfebc-7fa5-22c0-a765-01b0c83e5ce4',
                                 'Winnie-the-Pooh',
                                 'winnie-the-pooh', ...))
      end
      ...
      def self.custom_book(attributes={})
        book = diva_and_flea.backend_data
        attributes.each_pair {|k,v| book.send "#{k}=", v}
        Book.new(book.uuid, backend_data: book)
      end

      def self.all_books
        [ diva_and_flea, winnie_the_pooh, ...]
      end
      ...
    end
  end
end
```

Running Tests in Stubbed Mode

Introducing the test approach just described into our service access library has some immediate advantages when setting up and customizing test scenarios.

Ease of Test Set-Up

As part of their test suite set-up, applications under test place the service client library into stubbed mode, thereby configuring it to serve responses entirely out of the stubbed back-end's registry of preloaded response objects. As can be seen from the preceding code samples, all that these applications need to do is place the line shown in Listing 9-6 into code that is executed as part of their test harness set-up.

Listing 9-6. Code to make sure the tests are using stubs

```
# Applications under test just place this inside a test_helper.rb, or the like
BookStore::Books.stubbed_mode!
```

▓ **Note**   When the client application is running in a production environment, the production-specific setup will of course need to configure the client library to use the actual HTTP service-based back-end instead (which is the default for our client gem anyway).

Customizing the Stubs

To serve the needs of special-case, nonstandard situations, the client library allows for creating additional stub objects, and for adding them to or removing them from the mock back-end's business object registry. While the idea here is similar to stubbing response objects corresponding to given request patterns at the transfer protocol layer (as is implemented by some HTTP client libraries, such as the Typhoeus concept of a direct stubbing mechanism[18]), it differs in that we leverage test doubles at a higher (application logic) level, where the test double behavior is defined in terms of model objects that expose exactly the same interface and behavior as the client gem's result objects as they are generated in a production environment.

Listing 9-7 shows a code example of how our client gem can be convinced to customize the test mocks stored in the mock back-end.

Listing 9-7. Customizing which stubs are used in the tests

```
# turn on stubbed_mode
BookStore::Books.stubbed_mode!
# add a couple of books to the stubbed mode's backend data
my_test_books = [
  BookStore::Books::TestStubs.custom_book(
    uuid: '6291ba52-7e45-1423-b764-01b0c83e5ce4',
    title: 'Peter Pan',
    slug: 'peter-pan'),
  BookStore::Books::TestStubs.custom_book(
    uuid: '62bae4a6-54a6-162d-a654-7281fb3a6ce7',
    title: 'Pete The Cat',
    slug: 'pete-the-cat')]

BookStore::Books.backend.add_books(*my_test_books)

# ...
```

---

[18]See the "Direct Stubbing" section of the Typhoeus gem's Readme, https://github.com/typhoeus/typhoeus#direct-stubbing

```
# Remove some of the objects added above from the stub backend's data
BookStore::Books.backend.remove_book(*my_test_books)

# ...

# Reset the backend data to the 'well-known' set of books
BookStore::Books.backend.reset_all_data
```

Why use Pluggable Back-Ends?

The approach to include several service back-ends and realistic test responses we've described allows the mock objects to evolve in lock-step with the client library version. This will increase the client application's confidence that it is testing against the same API as the actual objects returned by the latest service API version.

Additionally, none of the usual cumbersome and boilerplate code to create and register stub objects for the various tests needs to be written; the stubbed back-end comes preconfigured with a variety of standard responses, which the application code under test will simply use without any additional configuration.

Out-Of-Process Component Testing

The sample code that accompanies this book comes with a project called api-testing. In this project, we are testing the books-service in a black-box manner. This means that the test suite executes in a separate process than the books-service itself, and it verifies its proper functioning via calls to the service's externally exposed API.

As described in Chapter 6, we are using a tool called consul.io (https://www.consul.io/) for independently configuring and discovering the services that make up our entire application in each of our system stages.

Setting Up the Environment

Prior to starting up our component test suite, we need to announce to our local consul.io discovery service that we have a (Rust) service called books running logically at port 5000:

```
echo '{"service": {"name": "books", "tags": ["rust"], "port": 5000}}' | sudo tee /etc/
consul.d/books.json
```

Next, we start our Consul service:

```
consul agent -dev -config-dir=/etc/consul.d
```

This command reads all the services configured from the data files in the Consul configuration directory, and also launches a web UI to administer the consul.io service (see Figure 9-3).

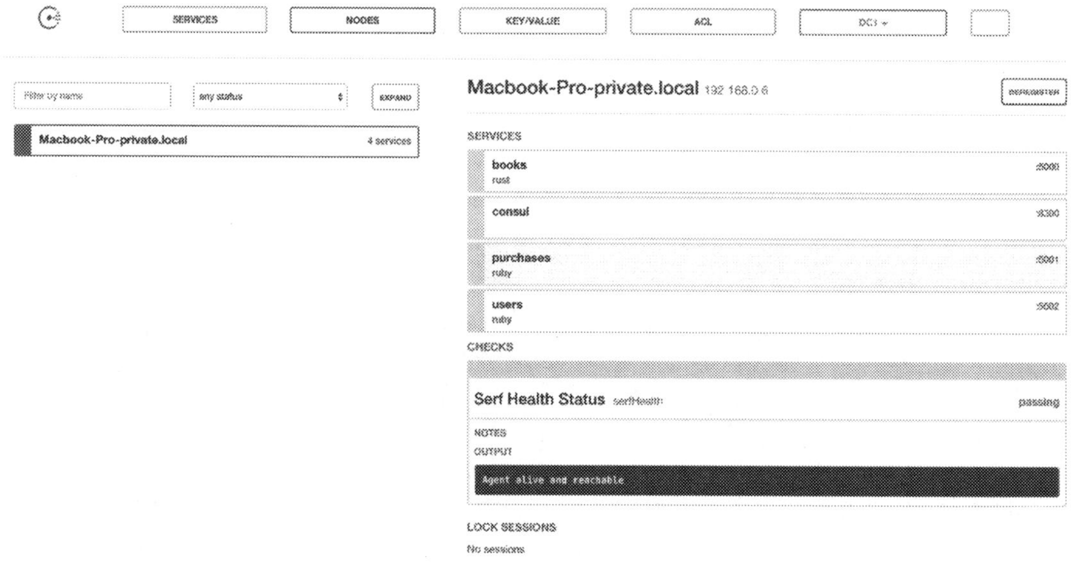

Figure 9-3. *Adminstration Web UI for consul.io*

Later on, in the test suite, we will show code that simply looks up the currently running books-service instance by contacting and searching the local consul.io registry.

Next is starting the actual books-service. This service (implemented in the Rust[19] programming language) will be configured at startup to use a test database, which is destroyed at the end of running the full suite. To that end, we will set an environment variable for the database URL, which will be honored by the service code when setting up the DB connection:

```
DATABASE_URL="postgres://tim@localhost/books_componenttests" cargo run
```

Let us emphasize this again: the test DB is a real data store, running outside the books-service process. It has, however, been preconfigured to include sample data for the component test runs.

Writing Your Test Cases

While there are a very large number of testing frameworks for implementing component-level tests, we have decided to demonstrate this level of testing using Cucumber.

Cucumber includes a DSL called Gherkin[20] for formulating test cases that mostly read like "plain English" (or any of over 60 other languages). The self-described (and might we add, rather lofty) goal Cucumber is trying to achieve is that it "merges specification and test documentation into one cohesive whole." By writing system requirements in "executable specifications," this tool aims to make collaboration between people who define the business goals and people in engineering positions easier.

Cucumber tests revolve around *features*, written down in the Gherkin language, and stored in .feature files in your test project. Features are there to describe software capabilities and requirements at a high level; they are simply a grouping of related scenarios.

---

[19]https://www.rust-lang.org/
[20]https://cucumber.io/docs/reference

You define a feature in Gherkin by starting a line with the `Feature:` keyword, followed by a name and an optional description.

A scenario is a "concrete example that illustrates a business rule." Its Gherkin keyword is `Scenario:` and just like a feature, it can have a name and further descriptive text. After that, a scenario consists of a list of steps, which first describe the outset of the test (starting with a `Given` keyword), then an event or set of events to occur (via the `When` keyword), and finally the expected result of the event under the described circumstances (in a `Then` clause). several `Given`, `When`, or `Then` steps can be logically combined via the `And` and `But` keywords.

Step definitions can take arguments, which come in handy when your step definitions don't easily fit into a single line. One particularly handy way of defining step arguments is as a Gherkin *data table*. The contents of such tables can easily be accessed as key-value-pairs in the code behind the step definitions.

Let's look at a very simple example scenario from our `books-service` component test suite:

```
Feature: books endpoints
As an API user
I want to call CRUD endpoints to manipulate books

Scenario: POST to add a new book
  Given I send a POST request to "/books" in "books-service"
    | title        | price | price | isbn       | brand | description   |
    | Pete the Cat |   500 | 650   | 0062303880 | HP    | New York Times ...|
  Then the response status should be "201"
```

This first feature describes the simple *Create-Read-Update-Delete* (CRUD) endpoints for the books resource in our service.

Our scenario describes adding a new book to the service, which can be done via an HTTP POST method call as listed in the `Given` clause. The data table passed to the `Given` step describes the parameters to send, plus example values for each of the fields. The outcome described and tested for in the `Then` step is that the service's HTTP response should carry a 201 status, indicating that a new book resource was created.

While Gherkin parsers exist in many programming languages, we chose Ruby to implement the steps, as shown in Listing 9-8.

Listing 9-8. Step definitions for the POST scenario

```ruby
# in `http_steps.rb`
  ## Uses service as parameter
  Given(/^I send a POST request to "([^"]*)" in "([^"]*)"$/) do |api_path, service, table|
    url = File.join(ServiceDiscovery.url_for(service.to_sym), api_path)
    @response = Faraday.post(url, table.hashes.first)
  end

  # in `json_steps.rb`
  Then(/^the response status should be "([^"]*)"$/) do |code|
    assert_equal code.to_i, @response.status
  end
```

The most important line to discuss here is the following:

```ruby
url = File.join(ServiceDiscovery.url_for(service.to_sym), "/books")
```

As mentioned earlier, we are using a service discovery tool to configure our microservices environment. This code looks up the books-service service in the service registry before making test calls to it. This approach enables us to execute these steps unchanged against a version of our services where external dependencies are replaced for test purposes (like connecting to test database content), or against the actual unaltered production service, simply by changing the service registry's entry for the books-service.

To conclude this out-of-process component tests section, we are showing our test suite's console output, as produced by the Ruby cucumber test runner tool, in Listing 9-9.

Listing 9-9. Shell output of running the Gerkhin tests

```
api-testing tim$ bundle exec cucumber
  Feature: books endpoints
    As an API user
    I want to call CRUD endpoints to manipulate books

    Scenario: POST to add a new book                         # features/books.feature:5
      Given I send a POST request to "/books" in "books" # features/step_definitions/http_
      steps.rb:2
title                      | price | full_price | isbn       | brand        | description|
| Pete the Cat: Scuba-Cat | 500   | 650        | 0062303880 | HarperCollins | New York Times
bestselling author and artist James Dean brings Pete the Cat's world to life under the sea
in this new I Can Read book. |
      Then the response status should be "201"               # features/step_definitions/json_
      steps.rb:1

    Scenario: POST to add a new book without required attributes # features/books.feature:11
      Given I send a POST request to "/books" in "books"          # features/step_
      definitions/http_steps.rb:2
        | price | full_price | isbn       | brand        | description
|
        | 500   | 650        | 0062303880 | HarperCollins | New York Times bestselling
        author and artist James Dean brings Pete the Cat's world to life under the sea in
        this new I Can Read book. |
      Then the response status should be "422"                   # features/step_
      definitions/json_steps.rb:1
      And the JSON response should be:                           # features/step_
      definitions/json_steps.rb:15
        """
        {
          "missing": "title"
        }
        """

    Scenario: GET book details by slug for a book                # features/books.
    feature:23
      Given I create a dummy book                                # features/step_
      definitions/setup_steps.rb:1
      And I send a GET request to "/books/slug/:book_slug" in "books" # features/step_
      definitions/http_steps.rb:8
      Then the response status should be "200"                   # features/step_
      definitions/json_steps.rb:1
```

```
    Scenario: GET book details by slug for an invalid book            # features/
books.feature:28
        Given I send a GET request to "/books/slug/not-a-real-book" in "books" # features/
step_definitions/http_steps.rb:8
        Then the response status should be "404"                      # features/
step_definitions/json_steps.rb:1

    Scenario: GET book details by book id for a valid book     # features/books.feature:32
        Given I create a dummy book                           # features/step_definitions/
setup_steps.rb:1
        And I send a GET request to "/books/:book_id" in "books" # features/step_definitions/
http_steps.rb:8
        Then the response status should be "200"              # features/step_definitions/
json_steps.rb:1

    Scenario: GET book details by book id for an invalid book
# features/books.feature:37
        Given I send a GET request to "/books/d3f764a5-2f09-457e-8a94-0128cd46ad3e" in "books"
# features/step_definitions/http_steps.rb:8
        Then the response status should be "404"
# features/step_definitions/json_steps.rb:1

    Scenario: POST to add a new category                      # features/books.feature:41
        Given I send a POST request to "/categories" in "books" # features/step_definitions/
http_steps.rb:2
          | name        | description        |
          | Tech Books  | Books for techies  |
        Then the response status should be "201"                  # features/step_definitions/
json_steps.rb:1

    Scenario: GET list of categories                          # features/books.feature:47
        Given I create a dummy category                       # features/step_definitions/
setup_steps.rb:17
        And I send a GET request to "/categories" in "books"  # features/step_definitions/
http_steps.rb:8
        Then the response status should be "200"              # features/step_definitions/
json_steps.rb:1
        And the response should be valid JSON                 # features/step_definitions/
json_steps.rb:20

  8 scenarios (8 passed)
  21 steps (21 passed)
  0m0.139s
```

Examples of End-to-End Tests

Much as for component tests, as shown in the previous section, Cucumber can also be very useful in end-to-end testing of an application, especially when combined with two other projects: Capybara (`http://jnicklas.github.io/capybara/`) and Selenium 2.0 (`http://www.seleniumhq.org/projects/webdriver/`).

Capybara is another domain-specific language that aims to help in testing web applications. The DSL is aimed at simulating how a user would interact with the web application via a web browser. In order to connect to the various browsers installed on the computer executing the end-to-end test suite, it can be configured to make use of the Selenium project, which exposes an API abstraction layer and drivers to connect to the most common browsers, like Google Chrome, Firefox, Apple Safari, and even mobile browsers for Android, or headless browsers that don't require a GUI.

When loaded into the same Ruby project, the Cucumber and Capybara DSLs complement each other quite naturally to create a very powerful toolchain for acceptance testing.

The sample bookstore project accompanying this book also comes with a very rudimentary Cucumber-plus-Capybara test suite.

Let's look at the showcase.feature file that describes the very basic use case of navigating to the bookstore homepage, and then locating and following a link to the detail page of a book. On the detail page, we make sure we see the correct ISBN number for the book listed, and we can find a link to add the book to the user's shopping cart:

```
Feature: Browse books in the store

Scenario: Navigate to a book detail page
 Given I am on the Bookstore homepage
 When I click on the "/products/the-story-of-diva-and-flea" link
 Then I should see the text "ISBN : 978-1484722848"
 And I should find the "ADD TO CART" link
```

Next, Listing 9-10 shows the Cucumber step definitions that make the feature description text executable.

Listing 9-10. Step definitions for the end-to-end tests

```
Given(/^I am on the Bookstore homepage$/) do
    url = File.join(ServiceDiscovery.url_for(:bookstore), "/")
    visit url
end

When(/^I click on the "(.*?)" link$/) do |link_path|
    find(:xpath, "//a[@href='#{link_path}']").click
end

Then(/^I should see the text "(.*?)"$/) do |expected_text|
    assert page.has_content?(expected_text)
end

And(/^I should find the "(.*?)" link$/) do |link_text|
    assert page.find_link(link_text)
end
```

The Given step navigates to the bookstore's homepage using the Capybara visit command. This command instructs the underlying Selenium webdriver to connect to a browser (by default, Firefox) installed on the test machine, and then navigate to the URL given as an argument.

As you can see, we again use our service discovery tool's application registry to look up the URL for the bookstore web site. This helps in being able to run the acceptance test suite against several different instances of the whole system without needing to change any code in the test suite.

Next, the When step uses the Capybara find command to execute an XPath query on the HTML DOM rendered by the browser for the homepage. In this particular case, we verify that a link (or anchor, expressed by the HTML <a> tag) with an href property matching the path quoted in the step's input can be located and clicked.

Once we get to the book's detail page, the Then step verifies that the book's correct ISBN number text is displayed. This is done by using Capybara's page object and executing the has_content? method with the step's input.

Once we verify that this text can be found, the final And step makes sure the page shows a link with the text *ADD TO CART*, which is proof enough for our purpose of verifying that the book can be added to the shopping cart.

Contract Testing Examples

The following examples are taken from our work experience at LivingSocial's engineering organization. As mentioned in Chapter 4, we use swagger_yard as a tool to generate API specifications in the Swagger interface definition language (which is conforms to the JSON Schema specifications).

Based on those tools, LivingSocial also built a Ruby gem called ls-api_validation. This tool works on top of the json-schema[21] gem, which helps with validating JSON objects against a JSON Schema definition.

The use cases of ls-api_validation are mainly the following:

- **Validation of API requests:** The gem can be configured to validate the request parameters and interrupt the service's request cycle and return an error response if the request validation fails (by default via indicating an Unprocessable_Entity[22] to the clients).

- **Validation of API responses:** Responses can be sampled and validated (at a configurable percentage of traffic). If response validation fails, log entries are created that explain which properties of the JSON schema API definition are violated.

- **Contract test support:** The validations of API request parameters and service responses conforming to the published API contract can be integrated into a service's test suite.

It is the last use case that we are going to demonstrate in this section. But let's first take a look at some swagger_yard API endpoint and response data type definitions. Here is a snippet of defining documentation that describes an endpoint that allows for searching for offers in a "geo box," specified by a set of latitude and longitude coordinates:

```
# @path [GET] /api/v0/search/geo
#
# @summary Returns geo search results
# @parameter city_id(required) [integer] User's current city ID
# @parameter vertical [enum<local,shop,escapes,all>] Vertical filter for ...
# @parameter top_left_latitude(required) [double] Top edge of geo box
# @parameter top_left_longitude(required) [double] Left edge of geo box
# @parameter bottom_right_latitude(required) [double] Bottom edge of geo box
# @parameter bottom_right_longitude(required) [double] Right edge of geo box
# @parameter expandable [boolean] Optional allow geo box to expand to find ...
# @parameter query     [string] Optional query text
```

---

[21]https://github.com/ruby-json-schema/json-schema
[22]http://www.restpatterns.org/HTTP_Status_Codes/422_-_Unprocessable_Entity

```
# @parameter category [string] Optional category name
# @parameter page      [integer] Optional page number
# @parameter per_page [integer] Optional results per page
#
# @response_type [GeoCollection]
#
# @error_message 422  Unprocessable, if city service reports a city not ...
# @error_message 503  Unavailable, if city service or inventory service ...
```

As can be seen from these specifications, the API endpoint will return data of the type GeoCollection. That data type (also referred to as an *API model*) is defined next:

```
#
# @model GeoCollection
#
# @property page(required)              [integer] Current page
# @property per_page(required)          [integer] Count of entries per page
# @property total_entries(required)     [integer] Count of entries in collection
# @property total_pages(required)       [integer] Total count of pages
# @property collection(required)        [array<OfferTile>] Collection items
# @property top_left_latitude(required) [double] Top edge of geo box
# @property top_left_longitude(required) [double] Left edge of geo box
# @property bottom_right_latitude(required) [double] Bottom edge of geo box
# @property bottom_right_longitude(required) [double] Right edge of geo box
```

As you can see, the specification describes the return type in a reasonably complete manner. While we leave out further details about the exact definition of an OfferTile, note that all attributes of this API model are required, and their data types are also defined (as integer values, double-precision decimal values, and an array of OfferTile JSON objects).

Listing 9-11 shows how we use ls-api_validation in our test suite to verify the API's contract.

Listing 9-11. Contract tests evaluation schemas and error responses

```ruby
require 'test_helper'

class VO::SearchControllerTest < ActionController::TestCase
  include LS::ApiValidation::TestHelpers::Minitest
  #...
  context "GET geo" do
    should "fail request validation for missing geo-box definitions" do
      get :geo, city_id: 1
      assert_response :unprocessable_entity
    end

    should "successfully search offers in geo box" do
      VCR.use_cassette('search_geo_city_1') do
        get :geo, city_id: 1,
            top_left_latitude:     34.28181943724182,
            top_left_longitude:    -116.533715291111,
            bottom_right_latitude: 33.03275371591785,
            bottom_right_longitude: -115.5809313949477,
```

```
      expandable: false,
      category: ""
    assert_response :success
    assert_passes_schema_validation request, response.body
  end
 end
end
#...
end
```

This test code shows an example of validating the API's contract both regarding the incoming parameters and the data that is returned.

When the API is called without the required `top_left_latitude`, `top_left_longitude`, `bottom_right_latitude`, and `bottom_right_longitude` parameters, the validation code intercepts the request cycle and returns an HTTP response with status code 422 (expressed as `:unprocessable_entity` in the Rails framework).

The second test case first ensures that the test request is successfully executed, by confirming the response status to be of HTTP status code 200, or—as Rails allows you to refer to it—`:success`. Note that we are using VCR in this example to increase test speed and reliability by isolating the contract test from direct access to a downstream external service that the service under test depends on.

The more interesting verification is the `assert_passes_schema_validation`. This method is provided by the `LS::ApiValidation::TestHelpers::Minitest` Ruby mixin, and it is passed the request object and the JSON response body generated by the service's API code. The `ls-api_validation` test helper code now uses information from the request to locate the Swagger JSON API definitions associated with the requested API endpoint (as defined earlier in this chapter). It then takes the JSON response body and simply runs JSON Schema validation code to ensure that the response JSON conforms to the JSON Schema that defines the response type published as part of the API contract; in this case, it compares the response JSON with the definition of the `GeoCollection` model defined above.

Just to illustrate the usefulness of this approach, here is some sample output generated by validation failures. In this case the latitudes and longitude data returned by the API no longer is encoded as a JSON number, but as a JSON string instead:

```
The property '#/top_left_latitude' of type String did not match the following type: number
in schema 1191bb4f-6d99-5a3c-8aa8-d4c0cee3908f
The property '#/top_left_longitude' of type String did not match the following type: number
in schema 1191bb4f-6d99-5a3c-8aa8-d4c0cee3908f
The property '#/bottom_right_latitude' of type String did not match the following type:
number in schema 1191bb4f-6d99-5a3c-8aa8-d4c0cee3908f
The property '#/bottom_right_longitude' of type String did not match the following type:
number in schema 1191bb4f-6d99-5a3c-8aa8-d4c0cee3908f
```

These failure examples are taken from an actual regression that happened in a service we worked on. We had changed the Ruby gem that is used to generate JSON responses, mostly to take advantage of the new library's performance improvements for JSON serialization. Running our contract test suite found this change in the default behavior of JSON serialization for Ruby decimal number objects, and we were able to prevent contract breakages before launching the change.

While the LivingSocial engineering department often releases internal tools as open source software, the `ls-api_validation` gem has not been released publicly at the time of writing. However, there are quite a number of other open source contract testing tools, such as `pacto` from ThoughtWorks, as well as Realestate.com.au's similarly named `pact` tool.

Both of these tools provide additional functionalities to define the client applications' expectations regarding the API-providing service in the clients' test suite, and record those expectations to a file (a *pact*). These pact files are then used in the service's test suite as input to the contract test suite. This enables the API provider to verify that the clients that provided such pacts will not suffer from service-side changes.

Summary

This chapter first introduced you to the five layers of testing a microservices architecture:

- Unit testing
- Integration testing
- Contract testing
- Component testing
- End-to-end testing

After discussing how to best apply them in your projects, we showed an implementation of using pluggable back-ends in service client libraries to aid in making test code less verbose and more realistic when using dependency mocking.

We then focused on examples for out-of-process component testing, using tools like Gherkin, Cucumber, and Capybara, and we illustrated how these domain-specific languages could be combined to specify end-to-end features of our sample bookstore application.

We concluded Chapter 9 by showing real-word examples of contract testing and how it is used, and how it helped us find regressions prior to launching changes to our production environment.

The next chapter will address deployment-related aspects of introducing a microservices architecture into your business.

CHAPTER 10

■ ■ ■

Deploying and Running Microservices

Being able to deploy a new service easily should be a goal of any company that embraces microservices. While there is much more risk involved in each deployment of a monolithic application, the processes involved with getting it deployed are much simpler than deploying small, but highly connected and interdependent services. In this chapter we will show that not only should new services be built, deployed, and configured in an automated and repeatable way, but that they need to be staged prior to releasing, in support of the overall stability and availability of your business during development efforts.

In this chapter, we focus on the aspects of building and deploying microservices in a continuous, automated, and repeatable way.

We will also discuss how to utilize preproduction rollout strategies to make sure you can release changes to production with confidence, so that running microservices has a positive impact on the overall availability of your production application.

Finally, we will explain how to design and utilize an infrastructure that is based on multiple stages and can support the benefits introduced by adopting microservices.

Automation Is Key

Before we go into any detail about deployment and operational aspects of microservices later in this chapter, let us emphasize something we have learned from our experience.

Any organization that is serious about entering into employing microservices needs to fully embrace DevOps practices. Without a culture of automation, the productivity of your engineering department is bound to suffer enormously. While your organization might have gotten away with manually executing tests, builds, releases, and monitoring for a single deployment unit, such processes will be ground to a halt by the effort involved in repetitively executing these very automatable tasks for tens—or potentially hundreds—of microservices, each of which should be its own deployment unit.

In a successful microservices environment, developers build and run their software. Because their time is very valuable, everything—from provisioning computing resources to building, testing, and deploying artifacts, to monitoring and generating alarming for live services—needs to be self-service and scripted. When dealing with microservices architectures, it is absolutely unacceptable if provisioning and launching a new service takes any longer than an hour.

Before our mutual employer LivingSocial started adopting services, it started out with one of the largest and most high-traffic monolithic Ruby on Rails applications in existence, serving tens of millions of visitors. When the decision was made to break up the application into smaller parts, one of the main cost factors involved was that provisioning production resources to run a service would sometimes take weeks. Build and deployment tools were not unified or automated, and general service configuration and monitoring approaches were very manual.

C. Carneiro Jr. and T. Schmelmer, *Microservices From Day One*, DOI 10.1007/978-1-4842-1937-9_10

As a result, during that time quite a few less-than-optimal architectural decisions were made, misplacing functionality into existing applications, simply because that was more expedient and less cumbersome than placing them into a new service with a more focused set of responsibilities.

Focusing on introducing end-to-end automation, from committing to a code repository all the way to launching the changes in the production application, helped LivingSocial's engineering department address the bulk of these issues. Today, software development at LivingSocial is very agile and productive, even when the ratio of services per developer is roughly 2 to 1.

Therefore, it is essential that an organization evaluate the available automation tools (some of which we have mentioned earlier in the book, and to which we will return later in this chapter) and find the ones that are best suited for their engineers, in order to address the added complexity introduced by having many, many deployment units.

Continuously Integrating Microservices

One indispensable measure for automating the software development environment for microservice development is to employ *Continuous Integration (CI)*.

A Brief History

CI started out as a practice first proposed by Grady Booch in his 1990 book on object-oriented design.[1] Back in those days, most software projects would be based on a process where all feature work—done by several different developers—was never integrated into a common code base until the very end of a given development cycle. This "big-bang integration" often led to a problem referred to as "integration hell," where a significant amount of time was spent on resolving merge conflicts of largely diverging developer branches before any clean build could happen.

When the Extreme Programming movement adopted CI as one of its core practices, it greatly increased the frequency with which such integration of developer branches into a code mainline would need to happen: in their view, integration (as well as testing of the integrated code base) would need to happen several times a day. In today's increased use of agile software development with ever-shorter development and release cycles, the focus has shifted from the branch integration component toward continuously running test suites and building deployment artifacts.

The first automation support came around in 2001. With the open source CruiseControl (`http://cruisecontrol.sourceforge.net/`), ThoughtWorks developed the very first CI server for code integration, artifact building, and subsequent testing.

The Advantages of Using CI Tools

Today, there are a large number of tools available. Popular examples are Jenkins (`https://jenkins.io/`), Travis CI (`https://travis-ci.org`), Go from ThoughtWorks (`https://www.go.cd/`), and JetBrain's TeamCity (`https://www.jetbrains.com/teamcity/`).

While these tools may vary in their detailed feature lists, the principle types of tasks they fulfill are all very similar. They all do the following:

- Monitor a set of code repository for changes.

- Check out the changed code from the repository.

- Build artifacts.

---

[1]Booch, Grady, *Object Oriented Design with Applications*, Benjamin Cummings 1990.

- Verify that the code in the change set passes the automated test.

- Store the result of the CI run (often of the build artifact) in a uniquely identifiable way for later deployment.

Note that, in our experience, employing continuous integration is worth the investment only if your engineering team buys into the culture that goes along with it.

This means that it needs to be engrained in the software development process that automated tests are added for every change. Additionally, changes should be committed to the repository in the smallest possible, testable chunks, in order to avoid the inefficiencies of the *big-bang integration* approach mentioned earlier. Finally, alerting needs to happen whenever the CI system reports problems or failures, and fixing such issues needs to be addressed by your team as their highest priority.

If you can implement these conditions in your organization, then the use of CI systems can contribute some very valuable benefits to your development process:

- **Shortened feedback loop:** Automatic, change-based execution of builds and tests will surface any bugs or other code quality issues[2] early on in the development cycle. Research has confirmed that the cost of fixing a bug is higher the later it is discovered in the development process, so this can definitely be a big financial incentive to adopt CI.

- **Traceability:** CI tools can help to maintain an audit trail for code that is deployed to your production environment. Storing an identifier for the exact version of the code repository deployed (such as a Git commit SHA-1 identifier), a protocol of the verifications performed, a link to the previous and/or next build artifacts, and so on, will help operational aspects (for example, rollbacks to a known good state) and debugging efforts.

Using CI for Microservices

A finer point about continuous integration and its relationship to microservices architectures is that you should set up your CI systems to deal with each of the microservices on an individual basis.

Many of the advantages of using microservices are rooted in the fact that they enable adopters to make decisions on a very fine-grained level. In line with this thinking we recommend having no less than one code repository per service. Such a setup will make things like switching programming language, optimizing around caching and data store technologies, grasping the purpose of the repository, and transferring ownership a lot easier than if several discrete services are rolled into the same code revisioning unit.

As a corollary, having one microservice per code repository also simplifies setting up dedicated and independent CI builds.

The advantages of configuring your CI to work on each microservice separately are clear. First, CI build times are reduced so that the development feedback loop is tighter and overall productivity is improved. In environments with potentially hundreds of services, where the choice is made to run all of them in a single CI instance, it is possible that full CI runs can take a few hours, even if there is just a one-line change to a single microservice. Instead, setting up a discrete CI cycle for each microservice in this scenario means that the same one-line code change only triggers tasks that can finish in less than a minute.

Second, smaller build artifacts are produced as the outcome of a CI run. This in turn will lead to smaller packages to deploy to smaller deployment units per service.

We will return to the arguments about trying to build and promote the smallest possible deployment unit after explaining the rationale and benefits of continuous delivery.

---

[2]Chapter 8 showed examples of using Jenkins CI for running code coverage and other static analysis tools.

Continuous Code Delivery

The concept of *continuous delivery* (CD) takes the concepts behind continuous integration and applies them to the entire software release cycle. It is a practice in which the engineering team has visibility into, and automated tool integration for, every step a software deliverable takes, from code check-in all the way through to releasing the software into production.

How Do You Know You Are Doing CD?

In an article on his website,[3] Martin Fowler describes four criteria that ThoughtWorks developed to verify that continuous delivery is being practiced in an organization:

- The software artifact is deployable throughout its lifecycle.

- The owning team makes keeping the software in a deployable state a priority over feature work.

- Whenever the software is changed, feedback regarding the production-readiness of software is automated, fast, and accessible to anyone.

- Any software artifact that has been verified to be working can be released to any stage (development, staging, production, and so on) with the push of a button.

Fowler summarizes these points saying that the litmus test is

... that a business sponsor could request that the current development version of the software can be deployed into production at a moment's notice—and nobody would bat an eyelid, let alone panic.

Breaking the Release Process into Stages

Full and thorough verification can take a very long time. Before releasing code into production, it usually doesn't suffice to create code artifacts and then run automated unit and integration tests—all of which are relatively fast steps.

In many cases, you will usually want to deploy the code into a test-bed environment (for example, a staging fabric, as described in Chapter 8), in order to perform more coarse-grained (automated) end-to-end tests, or even have QA professionals expose the build artifacts to (manual) exploratory testing. This could also be a good strategy for verifying that nonfunctional requirementsof your services, like performance, are still met.

Implementing these practices requires that you build a deployment pipeline.[4] In such an approach, you split up the entirety of your release process into stages. To achieve fast feedback and best time efficiency, it makes sense to place fast stages (like unit testing) at the beginning of your pipeline, while more time-consuming steps (like manual acceptance testing) are pushed into later stages.

Figure 10-1 shows an example of how a deployment pipeline could be structured.

---

[3]Fowler, Martin "ContinuousDelivery," May 30 2013; http://martinfowler.com/bliki/ContinuousDelivery.html
[4]Fowler, Martin "DeploymentPipeline," May 30 2013; http://martinfowler.com/bliki/DeploymentPipeline.html

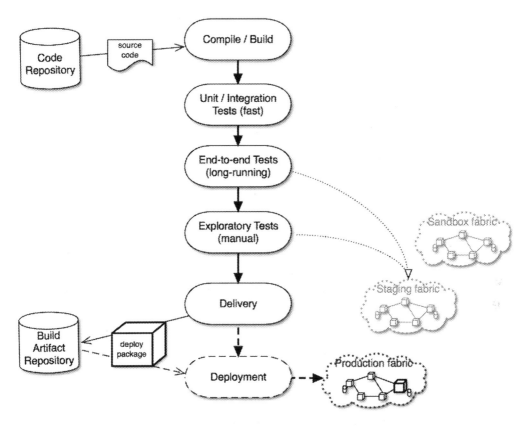

Figure 10-1. *Continuous Delivery pipeline with optional deployment step*

In this pipeline, committing code to the mainline branch of a given repository automatically kicks off the build step. If it succeeds, then the unit and integration test suites for the service are executed.

Next, the code under test is installed in a staging environment, where automated end-to-end tests are run before humans manually explore the application. Note that it is best if testers record which tests were performed alongside a particular pipeline run, so that tests can be repeatable and blind spots can be addressed.

Human sign-off on the exploratory phase triggers building an artifact that can be deployed to the production fabric, and it is checked into a repository. The deployable artifact can be an executable, an image of a virtual machine, or an application container, all based on your company's choice of production infrastructure. More on these choices can be found later in this chapter.

In some cases, the continuous delivery pipeline ends in an automated step to deploy the latest successfully delivered build artifact to the production fabric, effectively resulting in a continuous release cycle.

If any steps fail, the pipeline will stop and report failure to the engineering team that owns the code to be delivered via this pipeline, and fixing the failure needs to be that team's very first priority.

PROS AND CONS OF CONTINUOUS DEPLOYMENT

In a blog post[5] on the site for their excellent book *Continuous Delivery*,[6] Jez Humble and David Farley point out the differences between continuous delivery and continuous deployment, and which one to employ given the circumstances:

Continuous deployment is the practice of releasing every good build to users—a more accurate name might have been "continuous release."

...

While continuous deployment implies continuous delivery the converse is not true. Continuous delivery is about putting the release schedule in the hands of the business, not in the hands of IT.

...

In the world of COTS, there are good marketing and support reasons why you'd not want to have more than a few "released" versions of your software in play at any given time (although you could still do regular "developer" or "early access" builds as Eclipse and the Omni Group do). There are probably other good reasons too—the important point is that they must be business reasons.

In short, if you have constraints related to how many times your business can release software, then employ continuous delivery only. Otherwise, tweak your delivery pipeline to automatically release your builds as a final step.

If your company decides to implement continuous releasing of software, then make sure that the period of time from code commit to release to production is predictable and on the order of minutes. This way, the developer committing the change can plan to be around to verify and potentially fix the change in production.

CD and Microservices

The concepts and practices behind continuous delivery most certainly predate microservices architectures, but they become all the more essential when dealing with potentially hundreds of unique deployment units.

But how do we map microservices applications to deployment pipelines? Should there be one single master pipeline that is responsible for monitoring, building, testing, and delivering all services? If not, of how many deployment units should the results of any given delivery pipeline be comprised?

In our experience, the biggest advantages are reaped if there is a separate pipeline per service. Only by dedicating pipelines to services will we be able to make sure that each of the services that make up the full application can be released (and potentially recalled) individually, and without negatively impacting the rest of the system.

Tool Support for Continuous Delivery

When investing in starting a culture of CD, you can start fairly small and simple. For example, if you are already practicing continuous integration in your organization, you can often leverage the same toolset to trigger and monitor additional dependent steps that are gated by success of previous stages.

---

[5]Jez Humble, "Continuous Delivery vs Continuous Deployment," August 13 2010. http://continuousdelivery. com/2010/08/continuous-delivery-vs-continuous-deployment/
[6]Jez Humble, David Farley, *Continuous Delivery: Reliable Software Releases through Build, Test, and Deployment Automation*, Addison-Wesley Professional 2010

As an example, LivingSocial engineering started its own continuous delivery journey by repurposing Jenkins CI to kick off downstream deployment jobs automatically if the build-and-test CI job succeeded. Figure 10-2 shows the example of a Jenkins project configuration that triggers builds on two other downstream Jenkins project.

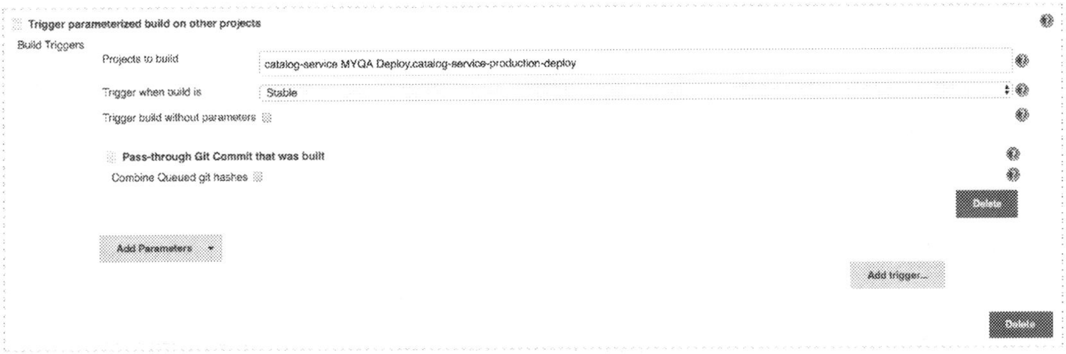

Figure 10-2. Jenkins CI project configuration that triggers dependent deployments

The projects triggered sequentially shown here are a deployment to the staging fabric (internally called *MYQA*) and a subsequent production deployment. Triggering the dependent deployment projects after the CI build hinges on the build status; only if the latest code in the mainline branch could be built and tested successfully, and is hence considered "stable," will the deployments be started.

Note that LivingSocial also developed a uniform set of tools (on top of the Capistrano deployment tool), command-line scripts collectively called `ls-deploy`, which can be used to automatically kick off deployments across all projects that can be deployed to all network fabrics. The universal usage of this tool, and the simplifications it provides, are more indications that a DevOps culture is essential to launch and support microservices architectures efficiently.

Today there are quite a few other tools available that specifically focus on supporting continuous delivery.

Amazon.com made its internal build pipeline tool available for commercial use as the generally available AWS CodePipeline (`https://aws.amazon.com/codepipeline/`). CodePipeline is a highly configurable and programmable tool that can be used independently of any of the other AWS service offerings, and it integrates with source repository, CI, and deployment solutions like GitHub or Jenkins. AWS CodePipeline workflows consist of sequential, interdependent stages that can communicate via input and output artifacts. Each stage is made up of actions that can be run in parallel or sequentially. CodePipeline provides an API that can mark single actions as success or failure, which serves as an excellent way to integrate custom actions into the flow of the delivery pipeline. CodeDeploy actions can even be directly implemented as serverless AWS Lambda functions (`https://aws.amazon.com/lambda/`), which can also directly report back results to influence the course of the pipeline.

Figure 10-3 shows the graphical UI for creating and editing CodePipeline flows, in this case a very simple test pipeline set up for an experimental service at LivingSocial.

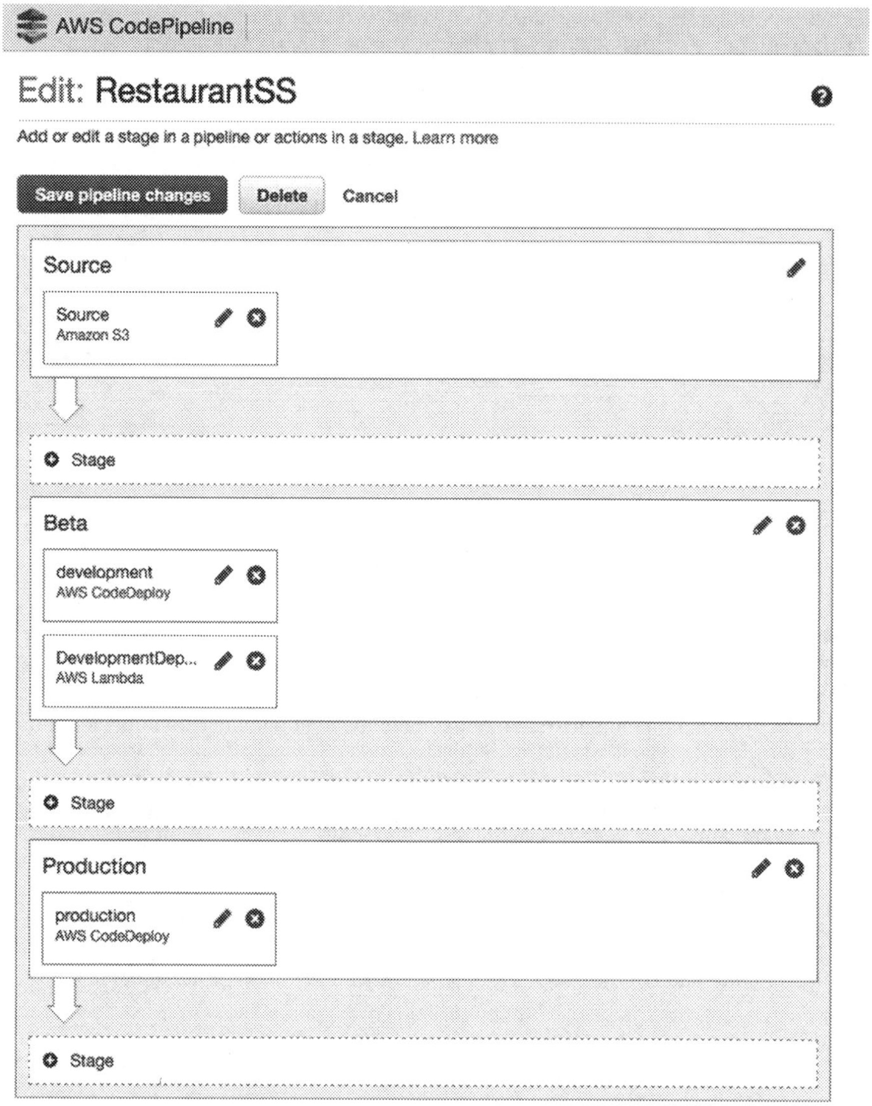

Figure 10-3. Example of a very simple delivery pipeline in AWS CodePipeline

Another relatively new arrival, but already a very promising looking CD tool, is Netflix Spinnaker (http://www.spinnaker.io/). Spinnaker is an open source project that not only allows you to build delivery pipelines, but also aims to introduce a layer of abstraction on top of the infrastructure used to run service software. It aims to support building, testing, and deploying code not only to all three major public cloud platforms (Amazon AWS, Microsoft Azure, and Google's Compute Engine), but also to private cloud installations by supporting a plugin approach for cloud back-ends. Pivotal Cloud Foundry private cloud support is already implemented in this fashion. Figure 10-4 shows the UI to set up Spinnaker pipelines.[7]

---

[7]"Global Continuous Delivery with Spinnaker," posted by Andy Glover, November 16, 2015; http://techblog.netflix.com/2015/11/global-continuous-delivery-with.html

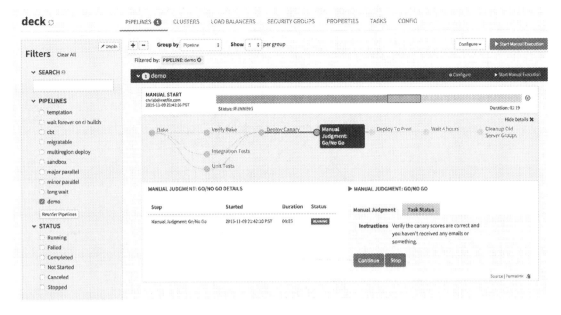

Figure 10-4. *A Spinnaker pipeline, as shown on the Netflix techblog*

Maturing Code Preproduction

In an application that is made up of many smaller interdependent service components, it is essential to increase confidence in any code changes in an integration environment.

There is only so much that testing any service can tell you when you test it in isolation, and it is unrealistic to assume that stubs or mocks for service dependencies are complete with respect to functional, as well as nonfunctional, edge cases.

The closer the integration environment is to simulating production-like conditions, the more reliable and hence valuable the feedback received from prerelease testing becomes.

The rest of this section describes our experience with the best ways to address these concerns.

Staging as a Preproduction Environment

While discussing a suitable development process for a microservices-based application in Chapter 8, we recommended maintaining several network fabrics in which to install instances of all services that make up the application.

While the discussions in Chapter 8 focused on the need for a development sandbox environment, this section will consider the use of a staging fabric. Figure 10-5 describes the scenario we recommend implementing.

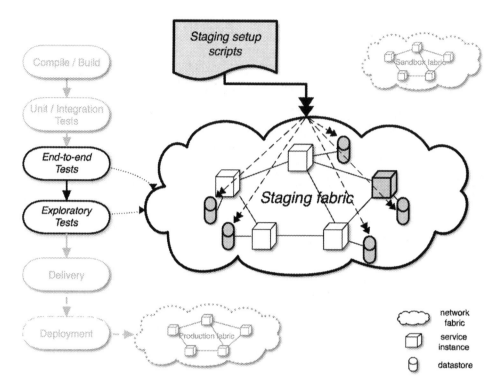

Figure 10-5. *Use of a staging fabric for preproduction testing*

Once the delivery pipeline has built all the artifacts for a given service, and all tests that can be performed in isolation have passed, it is time to deploy the service into a staging environment.

We will explore the options and our recommendations for generating an entire network fabric later in this chapter. For now it is just important to emphasize that the staging setup should aim to mirror the actual production infrastructure *as closely as possible.*

At the very minimum, this means that all interdependent microservices (other than the one that is part of the current change set under test) are deployed and running in the staging environment using exactly the same code versions that are live in production.

On top of that, you should strive to make sure that the rest of the infrastructure can mirror the production setup. Operating systems, databases, proxies, and the like should all run in the same versions as in production. The routing layer configuration (routing tables, ports, use of SSL) and hardware resources (number of CPUs, physical or virtual machines, disk space, and so on) should match what is used to run your actual business.

We realize that significant costs can be involved in provisioning additional computing resources to fully simulate the production environment; additional hardware and software licenses need to be requisitioned, set up, and so on. It may well be that the costs outweigh the benefits.

The point is that we strongly advise going through such cost-benefit analysis. Any decision to skip setting up a realistic staging environment should be preceded by a detailed risk analysis, in which cost factors are attached to each risk. For example, how likely is it that a different version of the operating systems in production will cause a 30-minute outage, and how much revenue and/or customer trust would you lose?

Once the staging environment is provisioned with the appropriate build artifacts, it needs to be brought into a state that has all the appropriate data needed for preproduction testing. This can be best achieved by maintaining set of automated staging setup scripts.

The purpose of these scripts is to automatically bring the staging fabric into known good states, so that automated and manual tests can be performed in a repeatable manner.

Tool Support for Staging Environments

Setting up a staging environment that has the same properties as your production environment follows the same rules as all infrastructure-related tasks in a microservices architecture: if you do not want to overwhelm your engineering department with busy work, then it needs to be automated with a set of tools.

The tools of choice to implement the infrastructure-as-code include Chef, Vagrant, Ansible, and Puppet. All of these tools can be used both for managing and provisioning your infrastructure and configuration based on version-controlled configuration files, rather than manually configuring hardware via interactive configuration tools.

They all can be used irrespective of your company's choice to run the physical data centers with bare-metals servers or to use a public cloud, and regardless of the choice to utilize virtual machines or application containers or not.

PaaS provider Heroku comes with very good documentation showing how to set up a staging environment,[8] and we know from personal experience that using Heroku's cloud platform for staging purposes is very easy and convenient.

Another toolset we have successfully used to set up staging fabrics is Amazon's Web Services platform, and we are very impressed with the power of the tool chain surrounding infrastructure automation. AWS provides a dedicated set of services called *AWS CloudFormation* for storing infrastructure definitions, and to automatically generate environments based on these definitions. Another very useful tool that works together with CloudFormation is the community-supported *CloudFormer*,[9] which can be used to create a CloudFormation-compatible infrastructure definition template for your staging environment from already-deployed production AWS resources.

Another very promising tool for infrastructure automation is Otto by HashiCorp (`https://www.ottoproject.io/`). We mention it here even though it is in a very early stage of development, because it promises to greatly simplify the development-to-staging-to-production fabric transitions. While it unfortunately does not yet handle any fabrics other than development on the local workstation and a production deployment, support for more stages is on the project's roadmap.[10]

As far as the staging setup scripts are concerned, their aim is to make sure that the data stores for each of the services are primed with a set of sample data that enables the end-to-end and exploratory tests to execute both normal and exceptional paths.

Such scripts are usually very business-logic specific, and are by that token often very close to the particular technology in use. As an example, when SQL-based databases are used to store service state, they often include raw SQL statements stored in seed files, which are imported into the databases for each of the services involved at staging set-up time.

Some companies, including LivingSocial, also provide access to production database dumps (which are scrubbed of sensitive information), which such set-up scripts can use to prepopulate the services' database. While exact repeatability of test situations is lost (because of the dynamic nature of production data), the advantage gained here is that the set-up will more closely match the real-world conditions in which your application needs to function.

---

[8]Heroku Dev Center documentation, "Managing Multiple Environments for an App"; `https://devcenter.heroku.com/articles/multiple-environments`

[9]AWS Developer Tools: CloudFormer template creation tool; `http://aws.amazon.com/developertools/6460180344805680`

[10]See the related discussion on the project's GitHub issue number 161; `https://github.com/hashicorp/otto/issues/161`

Safer Releases

As mentioned in the previous section, setting up a one-to-one production-equivalent staging fabric is sometimes not a cost-effective option for every business.

Also, while setting up a production-like, preproduction environment is definitely very valuable for detecting issues when integrating a microservices-based application end-to-end, it is certainly no 100% guarantee that the same will be true when exposed to production conditions.

Therefore, it is a good strategy to try to make the process of releasing code changes to production—as well as potentially rolling back defective changes—as safe as possible. The following two release strategies are aimed at supporting the *resilience and recovery* tenet you'll see in the section discussing the seven deployment tenets later in this chapter.

Using microservices, and having properly separated the services into small self-contained units, helps the roll-out of code changes incrementally to each single service without blocking other changes to other ones. This is another advantage compared to maintaining a monolithic application, where all changes have to stack up sequentially.

Blue-Green Deployment

Like so many software architectural patterns, *blue-green deployment* existed for many years as a practice before being named, and it is not entirely certain who first named the technique. In his 2010 article on the subject, Martin Fowler credits Dan North and Jez Humble with coining the term.[11]

In its essence, blue-green deployment is a technique that allows for fast cut-over of production traffic to a new code version, but only after a series of smoke tests have been successfully executed.

This is done by delivering the new code to the production environments (labelled *green*), to be installed on the service host alongside the service code version currently exposed to live production traffic (which is called *blue* code).[12]

As part of the blue-to-green switch, a set of automated smoke tests are then performed on the green code. Once the green code is confirmed to be working as expected, the service host's configuration is changed to direct all incoming requests to the green code.

Blue code now becomes unused, but still installed on the host. This sets you up for rapid rollback in case any problems are detected shortly after the switch-over, so you can easily and quickly switch back to the blue environment.

Figure 10-6 illustrates the process of blue-green deployment.

---

[11]Martin Fowler, "BlueGreenDeployment," 1 March 2010; `http://martinfowler.com/bliki/BlueGreenDeployment.html`

[12]Some implementations of blue-green deployments choose to instead install the green code on an entirely separate set of service hosts, and then change over production traffic by changing load-balancer or DNS configuration. The principles of this technique still apply unchanged, though.

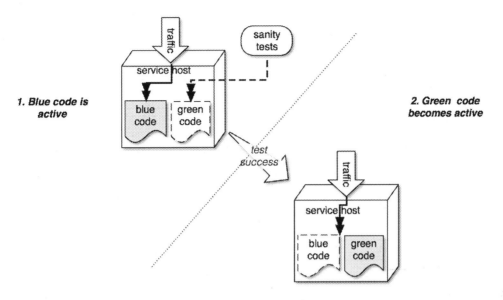

Figure 10-6. *Blue and green code are installed side-by-side, and switched upon release*

Canary in the Coal Mine

Another approach for making the release process safer and less impactful that is often used in microservices architectures is referred to as *canary release.*

Canary releasing—sometimes also referred to as *shadow deployment* or *incremental rollout*—reduces the risk of releasing new versions of software to production by means of a gradual roll out.

The diagram in Figure 10-7 describes the technique.

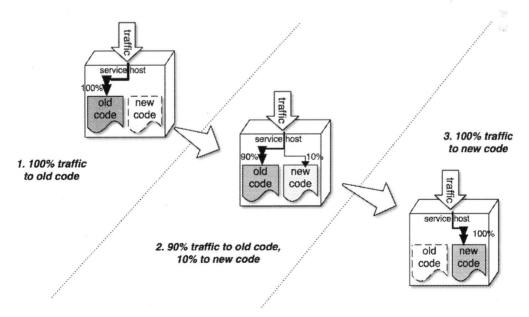

Figure 10-7. *Canary releasing in three stages of traffic to the new version*

The following steps are usually taken during incremental deployments:

- The new code is deployed alongside the code that is currently used by 100% of the production traffic (step 1 in Figure 10-7).

- Next, only a small percentage (such as 10%) of service clients is exposed to the new code version (step 2 in Figure 10-7).

- Once released to 10% of traffic, the engineering team will closely identify and monitor the performance of the change (based, for example, on feature functionality, response times, or service and client-side failure rates).

- When enough confidence is gained that the new version is functioning as desired, more traffic is diverted from the existing production code version and sent toward the new code. Monitoring continues to ensure that the new service version is behaving as designed.

- Finally, once enough traffic increase iterations have been performed satisfactorily, 100% of client traffic is directed to the new code version, and it becomes available to everybody (step 3 in Figure 10-7).

Canary releasing is very closely related to blue-green deployment in that both versions are deployed to the production service hosts simultaneously.

The main difference is that both versions coexist in production for a much longer time, as the switch-over from old to new code versions happens in stages (as opposed to the "all or nothing" traffic routing approach employed in the blue-green deployment strategy).

In a variation of the canary release process, some engineering organizations divert traffic to new code versions based on criteria other than by percentage or request. One example that we have seen practiced is to identify traffic generated by employee users, and then cherry-pick new or changed functionality only to such internal clients. Exposing new code to such a controlled user group first often also helps with monitoring changes in client-side experience.

Another twist sometimes applied to this phased rollout is to simply copy a portion of production traffic and feed it into the new service code version. You can then watch the new version handle the requests without exposing the results to the clients, which will continue to be serviced by service instances running the old production version. While the advantage here lies in additional safety (as initially no clients will receive results generated by the new code), the trade-off is that results are often less meaningful because the impact of the new service code is not verified end-to-end.

Note that neither canary releases nor blue-green deployments by themselves address the problem of mutating shared resources, such as potentially breaking migrations for database tables that might be used by both the old and the new versions of the code. These problems need to be mitigated by other means; for example, via additive-only tables and duplicated data for the new code.

Assigning Resources to Microservices

We have tried to demonstrate throughout this book that having a large number of self-contained, small services to make up your application has many upsides.

In this section, we first recap the gains achieved by adopting microservices. Next we walk through each of the current technology options for assigning the services to computing resources, and we compare how each one of them supports the microservices architecture advantages previously identified.

Tenets for Microservice Deployments

Let's start out by detailing some of the main principles that microservices architectures bring to the business when it comes to deployment and operational aspects:

- **You build it, you run it:** Development teams gain autonomy of the entire lifecycle and operational aspects of the software they produce. Developers are empowered to make their own technology choices, as they also are involved in monitoring and maintaining the infrastructure and computing resources on which their software runs.

- **Continuously and independently deliverable:** Code bases for services can be kept small and self-contained. As a result, code artifacts can be built, delivered, and deployed in isolation. Changes in one microservice can trigger a delivery pipeline that is independent from the pipelines associated with other deployment units.

- **Locality of technology choice:** As the only way to access microservices' capabilities is via well-defined APIs, the technology choices and all dependent resources (like operating systems, data stores, library dependencies, and so on) are local to any given microservice. Therefore, they can be changed or updated fairly inexpensively and without the risk of impacting other parts of the overall application.

- **Locality of configuration:** Each service has its own set of configuration properties that can be tweaked. This also means that their runtime properties can be independently optimized. Also, when specific security constraints apply to their mission (such as PII or PCI requirements), they can be secured without affecting any interdependencies with other deployment units.

- **Individual scaling:** When functionalities need to be scaled out, microservices provide the business with very fine-grained options and hence greater flexibility. Some microservices might profit most from being horizontally scaled, while others should best be scaled vertically. When horizontal scaling is best, the additional resources (such as additional hosts) can be added more cost-effectively, as the additional computing power can be added to smaller parts of the application. Partitioning services based on their expected load is also easier. Your team might own a telemetry service that needs to handle 100,000 requests per minute with very small payloads, while it also owns an internal reporting application with only 10 requests per minute, which trigger longer running data queries. These services will have very different scaling concerns, which means they should live in separate microservices, so that their constraints can be addressed with independent deployment units.

- **Self-contained codebases:** Microservices have separated and focused concerns, which make understanding, changing, and verifying their code safer and faster. Code changes can be kept more local and have less potential to affect other parts of your application. Test suites can be focused on a smaller set of scenarios and can hence have very small execution times.

- **Resilience and recovery:** Building your application based on services involves more individual service processes. While this means that the chance that any *one* process can fail increases, this risk is mitigated by the fact that the impact caused by a single process failing is much smaller. Also, the culture of employing circuit breakers and sane fallback values into clients to address dependency outages will become much more engrained in a successful development team. Mean time to recovery is usually also shorter than in a monolithic application, as independent deployment units make the cause of regressions more easily identifiable, and rolling back and launching smaller build artifacts is faster.

We will examine various strategies for assigning computing resources to microservices in the remainder of this section, paying special attention to how each of these strategies can help implement the advantages just described.

Options for Running Microservices

Ever since the invention of computers, much time and effort has been spent in the IT industry make the use of physical computing resources more and more efficient.

One of the main advances in achieving that has been the development of virtualization, which is mainly aimed at increasing efficiency of a physical server by partitioning it into smaller and smaller units, each of which roughly has the look-and-feel of being an independent host in itself.

This section will look at each of the major levels of virtualization currently in use. For each level it will explain the pros and cons of installing a single microservice versus multiple microservices in a given virtualization unit for that level, considering whether the microservices tenets discussed above can be maintained.

Running on Dedicated Hardware

The largest possible level of virtualization granularity is to not virtualize at all; all services can run directly on physical machines.

The diagram in Figure 10-8 shows the options.

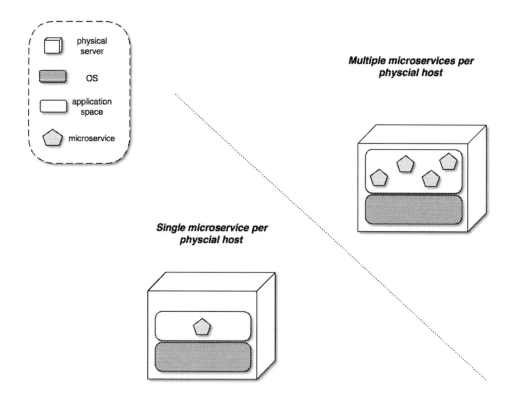

Figure 10-8. *Deploying a single microservice vs. multiple microservices directly on the physical server*

Let's first look at the scenario where each microservice would run on a dedicated physical server. We know of no microservices architectures in the wild that really even seriously considered running such a setup. Dedicating a server to each of the often hundreds of microservices in a production environment *and* duplicating such a configuration in a staging fabric, and potentially even a development sandbox, would be simply prohibitively expensive for most businesses.

Even if money was not an issue given the *"you build it, you run it"* principle, the development teams would need to provision a physical server each time they decided to start a new service project or needed to scale out the number of service instances. Lead times to procure new hardware for such situations would be too long for any team to avoid idling and would thereby decrease velocity. In most businesses, the development teams' autonomy would also vanish, as other departments are usually involved in granting provisioning requests.

A slightly more reasonable choice is to host more than one service instance on any given physical server. In this case, *"you build it, you run it"* is still affected, as monitoring and support would be complicated by the fact that resource contention (for CPU, memory, connections, storage, and so on) would need to be tracked down and addressed across *multiple* services. In our experience at LivingSocial we have run into quite a few situations where long-running, resource-intensive tasks for one service caused degradation in another service that was installed on the same physical box, and tracking these issues down takes time-intensive investigations using multiple tools.

Running more than one service on the same physical machine can also adversely affect the *"locality of technology choice"* tenet. What do you do if more two services installed on the same, nonvirtualized machine have conflicting requirements for dependencies like libraries or even operating systems or OS versions?

Team autonomy and the *"locality of configuration"* benefits are also hard to maintain if services from more than one team are deployed to the same physical host. If two services are competing for the same resources, then it will be very hard to configure the partitioning of these resources optimally, and arbitration in such situations will then have to fall to a third team that will be tasked with general infrastructure maintenance.

What if there are special requirements about the sensitivity of data held and vended by one service that is installed alongside services that do not need to follow the same stringency? Another case in point is that the desired *"locality of configuration"* will be hard to implement with co-hosted services.

Resource contention is also the reason why *"individual scaling"* would become more complicated to implement. How do you best identify the physical servers on which to install additional resources (such as another service instance, or more memory or disk space)?

Likewise, *"resilience and recovery"* will be negatively impacted if the failure or resource inefficiencies (like memory leaks or CPU stalling) of one service can negatively impact the entire server environment, and therefore the rest of the services installed and running on the server.

Running Services in an Enterprise Application Server (EAS)

The next small step toward using the physical servers more resource-efficiently is the use of an EAS technology, like Java Enterprise Edition (JEE)-compatible server products, or Microsoft Internet Information Server (IIS) for .NET technologies.

The advantage of this virtualization is that an EAS usually gives you nice features like unified service monitoring and alarming, hot service restarts, and clustering. Also, if you run several services that run on top of the Java Virtual Machine (JVM) or the .NET Common Language Runtime (CLR), they help with better use of host resources by requiring only one instance of the respective platform's runtime, which all the service code artifacts (like JEE .WAR files) share.

Employing an EAS solution where a single service is installed in each EAS incarnation is even less advantageous than running each microservice on a dedicated physical machine. Such an approach would share all the disadvantages of dedicating a server to each service, plus it would incur the costs for the overhead required to run the EAS itself.

Figure 10-9 therefore depicts running more than one service inside an EAS.

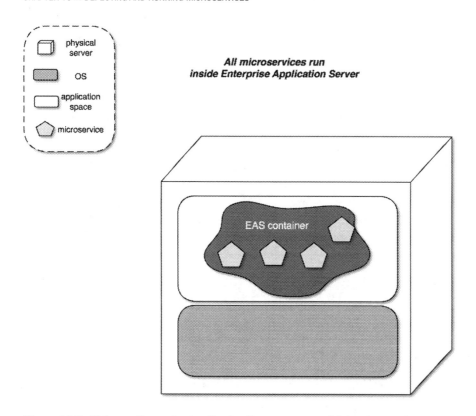

Figure 10-9. *Using an Enterprise Application Server to run multiple microservices*

Even when you choose to install multiple services inside the same EAS container, the drawbacks are nearly the same as with running the services directly on the service boxes. While the various EAS suppliers advertise benefits that address some of the monitoring and support concerns,[13] this approach introduces new impediments to the *"locality of technology choice"* tenet: when choosing an EAS, you lock yourself into a particular technology stack for your service implementations, as well (for example, services can be JVM or .NET-based only). Also, while JEE servers usually come with easy ways to redeploy just a single service's code artifact into the EAS container, this is not a given for all EASes per se, so it is well worth your time to research whether your application server allows for this. If not, the *"continuously and independently deliverable"* benefit will no longer be true.

Using VMs

In this approach to using computing resources more efficiently, additional software called a *hypervisor* is installed in the physical server—either in the server's firmware, or on top of an operating system—to enable virtualization. The hypervisor then allows you to divide the underlying single server machine into a number of separate hosts called *virtual machines* (VMs).

---

[13]Anyone who has attempted to analyze the behavior of Java threads for applications that share the same JVM process can attest that improvements to monitoring are certainly not perceived by every developer.

Each VM for all intents and purposes looks and feels very much like a separate, physical server: it runs its own operating system (including its kernel, should it have one) and application process independent from the other VMs installed on top of the hypervisor. They are also separated from any potentially underlying host operating system.

The hypervisor takes on all VM management tasks, from assigning the physical resources of the host machine to the VMs, to controlling and even potentially resizing the VMs. To perform these tasks, the hypervisor itself uses resources on the host machine, though, and the more VMs need managing, the more of the physical server's resources it will needs. This places a natural upper bound on the number of VMs that can be efficiently run on any given server.

Figure 10-10 shows how VMs relate to the physical host machine and the services running inside them.

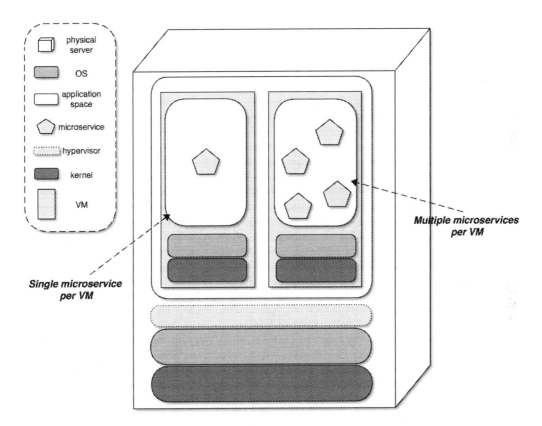

Figure 10-10. *VMs can be configured to run a single or multiple microservices on top of a hypervisor*

As was an option with physical servers directly, and also with employing EAS containers, you can choose to run more than one microservice inside any and all virtual machines controlled by the hypervisor. The problem with that choice is that you will still negatively impact all the tenets mentioned earlier when discussing the disadvantages of running more than one service per hosting unit.

On the other hand, the use of virtual machines is a great step toward avoiding the downsides involved with having to acquire and provision a new physical host for each time you decide to add services. While there is, as mentioned, an upper bound on how many VMs can be managed on a single server, you can get to the state where you host each service independently on a dedicated VM much more cost-effectively.

One particular advantage over running directly on a physical machine is good support for the *"continuously and independently deliverable"* and *"individual scaling"* tenets. This is mainly based on the fact that VM images can be automatically built for each service to be deployed in isolation, as part of the service's delivery pipeline. This will also enable automatic scaling mechanisms, as you can start to monitor service loads and respond in a scripted way by deploying a new VM for just the small set of services that experience a higher load.

Note that these advantages cannot be realized when you decide to deploy multiple services into the same VM, as you would be obligated to bundle a set of service to always be co-hosted, and thereby sacrificing their independent deliverability and individual scalability.

There are a large number of choices for software (called "type-2") and hardware ("type-1") virtualization. AWS EC2 deployable *Amazon Machine Images* (AMIs), VMWare's *VMWare Player*, Redhat's *KVM,* and Oracle's *VirtualBox* are all choices where the hypervisor runs on top of the host OS. Type-1 virtualization options include the Open Source *Xen* project, VMWare's *VMWare ESXi*solution, and Microsoft's *Hyper-V.*

Using LXC with Docker

Virtualizing at the machine level is not the only option available in order to get more isolated hosting units out of your physical hardware.

As briefly mentioned in Chapter 8, *Linux Containers* (LXC) can be used to virtualize multiple isolated Linux systems on top of a single Linux host machine.

One of the notable differences between LXCs and VMs is that only one Linux kernel is in use across all virtualization units. VMs host the entire stack of OS, kernel, and applications, while LXCs contain only the higher OS layers and applications. Reusing the same kernel allows LXCs to run without the need for hypervisor software, which VMs need to be managed and to partition host resources; physical resources for LXCs are managed by a single kernel.

As a result of these differences, LXCs are much speedier to bring into an up-and-running state than VMs, and their smaller footprint also means that a typical host can run a lot more LXCs than VMs before responsiveness is seriously impacted. This means that it will be much more cost-effective to run all your microservices in a separate LXC than it is to run them in separate VMs.

Out of the box, creating, setting up, and installing apps inside LXCs is rather cumbersome. Here is where Docker or proprietary solutions like Heroku's container management come in.

We introduced Docker in Chapter 8 when we showed how to use interdependent containers for building a development sandbox. Docker's main mission is to simplify container management and networking setup. It uses a text file called a *Dockerfile* to describe and install the applications in each container. Docker also comes with the concept of a shared repository for containers (called a *Docker registry*), so that you can reuse containers that have been contributed by others. Such a reusable container can either come from a public Docker registry like `https://hub.docker.com/`, or they can be provisioned from a private Docker registry, which you can install for your company-specific applications.

CONTAINERS ON HEROKU'S PLATFORM

The company Heroku offers a set of higher-level services often referred to as *Platform as a Service* (PaaS). It implements automated provisioning, deployment, monitoring, scaling, and high availability on top of AWS EC2 instances.

Heroku offers service-level options, mostly tiered by the amount of resources they dedicate to a hosting unit (called *dyno* in Heroku's terminology). The largest dynos are called *performance* and *performance-m,* and they are hosted on a dedicated large EC2 instance.

All other dyno types run in a multitenancy environment; that is, they run as single process inside an application virtual machine.

According to Heroku's own documentation, a dyno is a "lightweight Linux container that runs a single user-specified command."[14] This means that Heroku also uses LXC as their virtualization engine, which—as discussed at length earlier—is the same technology on which Docker is built.

If you are considering the use of a PaaS provider for your microservices application, then we definitely recommend taking a closer look at Heroku. We have deployed several microservices in multiple technologies (Ruby on Rails, Clojure, and Go) into Heroku's platform, and we loved the simplicity and convenience of the experience.

Trying to describe all the available tooling on top of Docker containers is like trying to shoot at a very fast-moving target. Much work is being dedicated to managing many distributed Docker instances automatically, and even to create entire cloud platforms that work with Docker containers instead of VMs. We will talk a little more about these later when discussing automated scaling options.

Looking at how to distribute the microservices you run across LXCs/Docker containers, there are even fewer reasonable arguments to co-deploy multiple services into the same container. That is the reason why Figure 10-11 illustrates 9 LXC containers running exactly one microservice inside each and every one of them.

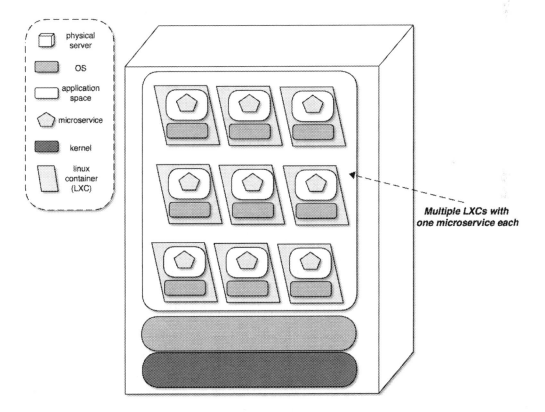

Figure 10-11. *Docker LXCs running on top of a single Linux kernel, with no need for a hypervisor*

Isolating each microservice in its own Docker container is much less resource-intensive than even using one per VM. Following such a "one service per container" mantra enables you to implement all the tenets of deploying microservices listed at the beginning of this chapter, and thereby reap all their benefits.

Note also that nothing keeps you from running LXC containers inside VMs, so if you already have a VM-based infrastructure, you can fairly easily add finer-grained virtualization this way. In fact, AWS offers "Amazon EC2 container service," which is specifically aimed at helping you manage Docker containers running on EC2 instances that are defined by AMIs, and which can be autoscaled to go on- or offline based on load.

Using Serverless Architectures

The newest technology option to arrive on the block for running microservices is something most generally referred to as *serverless architecture*. It can best be described as an additional layer that aims to alleviate you from even thinking about service hosts, so that service development is uncluttered and can be taken to a higher level of abstraction.

When services run serverlessly, there is no longer a need for the developers to operate and maintain the computing resources themselves. The serverless platform where you run your service code will take care of all of these aspects on your behalf. This has the potential to remove a large amount of complexity and operational workload. Automatically scaling up and down, resilience, delivery and deployment, operating system and library updates, setting up monitoring, alarming, and logging capabilities, and so on will now be a responsibility of the platform that provides the serverless computing services.

AUTOSCALING—THE HOLY GRAIL OF INFRASTRUCTURE AUTOMATION

Autoscaling is definitely not a "Day One" issue for getting started with microservices architectures. There are quite a few preconditions that need to be met before you can even start thinking about attempting to take advantage of such a feature.

For one, your organization needs to be set up for speedy and fully automated provisioning of computing resources. This means that your services are either running inside VMs or LXC containers (as provisioning new physical servers—even via automated means—will simply have too much lead time to be useful), or you are running in a public cloud (like AWS or MS Azure) or inside a PaaS (like Heroku).

All major public cloud platforms allow for automated scaling in one way or another. As an example, AWS has long had support for autoscaling (`https://aws.amazon.com/autoscaling/`). When you run your own cloud via Docker containers, there are solutions based on Google's kubernetes (see `http://kubernetes.io/docs/user-guide/horizontal-pod-autoscaling/`).

Next, you will do well to research what exactly the autoscaling parameters and triggers are, and how you can tweak them. Most autoscaling mechanisms built into the platforms we have seen are more reactive than proactive: infrastructure monitoring discovers that CPU load increases, server memory runs low, or that there is a lot more traffic on a particular service, and subsequently spins up new computing power (in the form of a new service instance, for example).

While such after-the-fact smarts certainly help deal with acute resource shortages, getting into situations where the client experience degrades can be entirely avoided by some proactive planning. In our experience, you can learn a lot of useful things from watching your site's traffic patterns, which you can apply to "semi-automatic" scaling: if you see that your customers mostly visit your site during the US time zones' lunch hours, then introduce rules that anticipate this behavior and add computing resources ahead of time, so that the site is ready for the rush hour.

At the time of writing, there are not many providers for serverless platforms. Early providers are Hook. io (`https://hook.io`), Webtask.io (`https://webtask.io/`), and Amazon's AWS Lambda (`https://aws.amazon.com/lambda/`). Amazon offers another complementary service called AWS API Gateway, which can add a layer in front of Lambda functions to aid security, transform request and response messages, and provide options for throttling and auditing.

Moving to a serverless model for running your services also scores very high in checking which of the microservices operational tenets are met. In fact, the only two points we do not see addressed by the currently available options for serverless platforms are *"you build it, you run it"* and *"locality of technology choice."*

It can certainly be argued that the underlying assumptions for the first of these two tenets are no longer valid. The main point of serverless computing is that developers need to be less involved in most of the operational concerns. What remains desirable, though, is that the development team gets notified via alarming if any of the operational metrics of their services start to deviate from normalcy. Amazon's AWS Lambda platform integrates very closely with AWS CloudWatch, so at least this platform has that aspect covered.

Where current platforms are definitely lacking are the technology options they provide out of the box. Webtask.io requires you to write all code in Node.js using JavaScript. AWS Lambda currently only supports JavaScript, JVM-compatible, and Python code. Hook.io is the platform that has the longest list of supported languages.[15] There are also other restrictions on each of the platforms around technology choices; for example, the backing file systems or data store options, and neither of them appears to be set up out-of-the-box to support arbitrary, user-defined replacements.

As mentioned at the beginning of this subsection, serverless applications are a very new and rapidly evolving technology, with proprietary approaches and platforms, which carries a high potential for provider lock-in. There is not much that has been written about the subject, but we are looking forward to reading Obie Fernandez' upcoming book[16] on the subject.

Summary

This concludes our overview of what we consider the most important aspects of deploying and running microservice-based applications.

One of the main points to take away from all this is that automating as much as feasibly possible around building, testing, deploying and releasing is an absolute must if you want to make microservices work for your team.

Introducing continuous integration for each of your services helps to significantly shorten the feedback loop during your development cycle, and the traceability of your large code artifacts, as long as you heed our advice to place each service into a separate code repository and set up CI for each one of them.

Going a step further and adopting continuous delivery from code commit to deploying it on the production hosts is also a practice we highly recommend adopting. Building a delivery pipeline per microservice can be done with the support of a number of existing tools.

---

[15]See the code examples page for a list of languages in which samples are implemented; `https://hook.io/examples`
[16]Obie Fernandez, *Serverless: Patterns of Modern Application Design Using Microservices (Amazon Web Services Edition)*; `https://leanpub.com/serverless`

You can even go so far as to automate the step of releasing new code to customers, but in this case, you have to think about how to do so safely. We explain strategies for implementing safety measures, including the use of a staging environment in which to let your code mature prior to production release, blue-green deployment and canary releasing.

We also discussed the available options for assigning computing resources to your microservices, based on seven tenets we identified as beneficial for deploying microservices. We explained the different levels of virtualization available today, and how their use can support the advantages gained by employing microservices.

In the next chapter, we will place our focus on design and implementation aspects of consumer-facing client applications backed by a microservices architecture.

## PART IV

Putting Everything Together

CHAPTER 11

Polyglot Services

As laid out in Chapters 4 and 5, applications in a service-oriented architecture can profit greatly from using common protocols and data formats (such as JSON over HTTP), and from choosing a single IDL for interapplication communication.

In this chapter, we lay out why applying uniformity of programming languages, data stores, or other technology components across all the services in your microservices application might not be the best choice.

After looking at the various components in which the services in your overall system can change, this chapter discusses the benefits and pitfalls of using differing technologies throughout your service implementations. Next we provide some guidelines for deciding when to become more polyglot in your architecture. Finally, we'll offer some practical tips for the process of introducing technology options to your microservices application.

Dimensions of Change

The majority of services in a microservices environment expose many areas that together make up a multidimensional vector for potential improvements.

Many service applications can be rewritten using different programming languages. Even if they choose to keep the language the same across services (or different versions of the same service), the service owners can use a different set of libraries to rely on. Some companies we know, while keeping the core programming language the same, vary application frameworks between different deployment units.

Another popular change is to examine the use of a different type of data store, such as by switching some portion of the service's persistence layer to use a NoSQL solution in place of an RDBMS.

Introducing a caching layer, for example by adding CDN usage to a publicly exposed service, or by adding Memcached or in-memory caching between the service application code and the data persistence layer, is another adjustment that is often introduced after the initial launch of a microservices application, and it can be applied selectively to a subset of the services an organization has deployed.

Advantages of Using Different Languages and Technologies

Considering the fact that software engineering as a discipline is less than seven decades old, the number of options for technological choices any software developer faces in today's industry landscape is simply staggering.

Let's look at some of the resulting advantages of such advancements in technology diversity, and see why a business would want to operate in a polyglot technology environment.

Specialization

When looking at the various layers of systems that make up the entirety of a modern online application, you will find a large number of different languages and technologies in use.

Looking at the mobile devices landscape, Apple's iOS and Google's Android deliver very specialized operating systems, programming languages, and API frameworks, as well as surrounding tools to build native applications. The main goal of this specialization is to enable developers to use the limited resource of the devices optimally.

Specializing in simple use cases of key-based access, key-value stores can be optimized for much more efficient access to persisted data than any SQL-based database system.

The lingua franca of dynamic web-based clients is JavaScript, mostly because all major browsers support it. But still, even *within* the JavaScript ecosystem, several different frameworks have been able to establish themselves, further specializing for particular use cases. Examples are:

- Google-sponsored Angular.js (`https://angularjs.org`), which is particularly popular for building single-page web applications because it offers synchronized two-way data binding, and alleviates much of the hassle of writing code for DOM manipulation.

- Facebook's React.js (`https://facebook.github.io/react/`), which shines when it comes to highly dynamic web applications, where the concept of working on a virtual DOM results in client-side performance gains.

- Yehuda Katz' MVC framework Ember.js (`http://emberjs.com`), which aims to combine the two-way data-binding and server-side DOM rendering advantages of the previous two frameworks.

The main theme in all of these specializations is optimizing for the requirements of new use cases. The fact that all these technologies exist and continue to thrive is a testament to the fact that they serve a purpose, and any business that wants to build a successful online application is effectively forced into being polyglot already.

By the same token, and as an extension to this point, applying diversity to the languages and frameworks with which the service applications are being built in the back-end can also help with optimization at this layer.

Experimentation

Progress in the computer software and hardware space is still very fast-paced. And even if skeptics are correct that the applicability of Moore's law about transistor density in integrated circuits is about to cease, software system will still see orders of magnitude improvements. Google's company culture asks their employees to apply "10x thinking" when thinking about innovation. Their rationale is:

> *[T]rue innovation happens when you try to improve something by 10 times rather than by 10%.*[1]

Both the development and the use of such quantum leap advances require a great deal of willingness to experiment. Therefore, curiosity remains a key competitive advantage for any software developer, as well as for the businesses that employ software engineers; in our experience, it is usually the most talented people who will be motivated by opportunities to learn new technologies.

---

[1]"Creating a Culture of Innovation: Eight ideas that work at Google", Google for work, `https://apps.google.com/learn-more/creating_a_culture_of_innovation.html`, as of September12, 2016

The good news is that implementing a microservices architecture provides a business with many benefits for experimentation. Because the units of deployment are small applications with very limited concerns, experimentation can happen with a very low impact on the overall business.

Evolution

Businesses can only achieve longevity when they learn how to adapt to an ever-changing environment, and staying agile by quickly adjusting or reversing course is key. Often the result of such environmental changes is that the business needs shift toward lesser, or sometimes even entirely new, use cases.

As an example, we have been part of companies where the initial system was not designed to cater to sophisticated, end user triggered product searches, often including search criteria that are dependent on geolocation data gathered about the customer. This can often be best addressed by researching and introducing specialized technology, such as Apache Lucene (`https://lucene.apache.org`) and Solr (`https://lucene.apache.org/solr`), or Elasticsearch (`https://www.elastic.co/products/elasticsearch`) for the search use cases.

It is also not uncommon that companies become the victim of their own success, having to serve a much larger number of online visitors than initially envisioned. In such a case, evolving the core services of your infrastructure to a language or framework that makes better use of CPU and memory resources, or that can more easily deal with a higher-level concurrency, can often help in addressing the bottleneck before it turns into a case of subpar user experience or bad press.

Navigating the Pitfalls of Being Polyglot

Going from an environment where all your services are using the same technology stack to embracing a more diverse set of tools surely also has some inherent risks that need addressing.

First, you will need to think about the development cycle. Your software engineers will need some time to familiarize themselves with the new language or any other technology that is being investigated. This is not simply restricted to learning the syntax of an unfamiliar language, but also extends to decisions about libraries, frameworks for automated testing or web request handling, and how to automatically install the development environment on an engineer's work computer.

Usually, these bootstrapping decisions are most efficiently made by a very small group of engineers that are passionate to learn about the technology in question. Their findings can then be spread among the rest of the service-owning team in short "brown bag lunch" tech talk sessions.

Similar issues can be encountered in the area of deploying new technologies, especially when you have to work in an environment where host machines are shared between services, and the new technology could potentially impact deployment strategies of existing services.

The cleanest option to address such concerns is generally to avoid co-deploying more than one system, for example, using application containers.[2] Otherwise, we recommend pairing up an application developer with an operations engineer to investigate the cleanest way to deploy the new tools alongside existing technology. That way, initial deployment guidelines for the new language stack, or the like, benefit from input of a larger set of engineering functions in the business.

Once deployment issues are addressed, it is paramount not to forget the requirements for operational support for running new machinery in a production environment. As mentioned for the deployment aspects, having dedicated servers or containers per service will make this task easier, as the newcomer will not be competing for resources with existing services.

---

[2]See Chapter 10 for an in-depth discussion of options for deploying and running microservices.

Another thing that could help during the deployment and operational support research steps is choosing a technology that is significantly similar to other standards you have already chosen. If, for example, your company already supports JVM applications via running JRuby, and you are trying to introduce a new language that is also JVM-based (such as Clojure), then you might find that you will have to address fewer open issues when introducing this new technology.

It is very important to involve all parties that have a stake in supporting the new technology in production in the process of deciding how to initially launch the new tech component in production. If your organization is following the "you built it, you run it" setup where application developer teams entirely support the software they own in all production aspects, then fewer departments need to be part of this decision process. But if you are in the fortunate position to work with a technical operations support team, make sure you involve them in these discussions.

Considering the tail end of a technology's usage life cycle, you should also think about what it will take to retire any system you introduce. For one, this applies on the one hand to technologies you experiment with and find that they do not add enough value to justify the effort of maintaining them. But more generally this also applies to the technology that is superseded by its successfully tested replacement. Make sure to have follow-through on such technology retirements and replacements, or you will run the risk of having too many technologies to support.[3]

A Process for Adopting New Technologies

When adding new technologies to their stack, companies are well advised to come up with a written policy concerning the selection process. The advantage of this lies in the fact that decision making can be based on a published, step-by-step process with clear milestones and measurable criteria for moving forward.

This section lists a few questions to answer during the selection, implementation, and production launch steps.

Document All Findings

We have seen all too often that decisions about adopting or rejecting a certain language or technology tool are made without documenting the results on which the rationale for those decisions is based. The drawbacks of such lack of documentation are at least twofold.

For one, there is a potential for wasted time and effort of a second internal team, which might have started its own investigation process for the same technology, although they could have taken advantage of the results of the previous investigations that were unknown to them.

Second, the business or technological environment in which the company operates might change over time, and those circumstances might invalidate, or at least significantly affect, the findings of a prior investigation of a given technology. If there is no detailed documentation about past technology trials, then the company might miss out on the competitive advantage a previously rejected tool might bring them under the new conditions.

Statement of Motivation and Goals

When documenting your technology trials, we recommend starting out with a section that describes the motivation for the new language or toolset.

Often such sections will list areas where the current tech stack is known to be lacking, or particular aspects that need to be considered with regard to a new technology (for example, maturity, safety, community and tool support, or performance).

---

[3]See notes on a process for evaluating a new technology later in this chapter.

At other times the goal of the experiment might not necessarily be directed at a well-established and recognized problem. The motivation might simply be that the general tech community is praising a new tool or language that can solve problems for which there was no prior awareness inside your company, or where improvements can help the company to be more successful.

A reason for investigating a new language might be that the same language could be used in several layers of your stack, thereby reducing the general skill set required from your developers. We have seen this argument used when companies decide to introduce Node.js (`https://nodejs.org/en/`) to write their back-end services in JavaScript when their browser-based logic is already coded in this language. Similarly, we often hear the argument for adopting ClojureScript (`http://clojurescript.org/`) in the front-end from companies that are invested in Clojure as their service-side language.

Another very prominent reason for testing a new technology is the attempt to speed up the performance of business-critical areas. We know of companies that have discovered that full-text search in their product database became an increasingly important feature for their growing customer base, and investigations needed to be made to replace the initially MySQL-backed search functionality because of performance issues. Similar arguments sometimes lead companies to experiment with migrating a service implementation from one programming language to another one (for example, moving from Ruby to Rust, Go, Elixir, or the like).

In attempts to avoid being a victim of their own success, many companies realize later on in their existence that the technology they chose does not scale well under load, so they will need to research switching to technologies that behave more resource-efficiently under high load.

Do you see the costs of maintaining a particular technology you use skyrocket? Then it might be time to research more stable or more easily extensible alternatives.

If your company has a hard time attracting talented engineers or keeping your most valuable tech personnel engaged and excited, then experimenting with new and exciting technologies to counteract attrition or to increase the recruiting success is surely also a reasonable motivation for experimentation.

Whatever turns out to be the reason behind your research, make sure to explicitly state the areas you will cover in your experimentation, and list the expected outcomes and metrics associated with judging the success of the experiment.

Implementation Planning

Once the groundwork is laid with the description of the goals of the research, the first milestone to pass is to get an official go-ahead from the company's management that the experiment can proceed, and that the metrics and acceptance criteria are sound. We highly recommend getting such buy-in, and officially setting aside time for team members to work on such "new tech" projects. In our experience, these projects will not happen unless they appear on a formal roadmap for company work.

Now it is time for planning the execution. It is always a good idea to publicize the plan to test a new technology internally to the broadest possible group of people.

This can not only help solicit feedback on the strategy and goals, but also aid in finding support and like-minded co-workers who are interested in pairing on the initial implementation.

Make sure to measure and record all data that you laid out in your statement of goals as you go about implementing the new technology in your organization. This documentation will help you and a potential gatekeeper decide if the experiment results meet the acceptance criteria to take things to the next step. And even if the outcome of that analysis is such that a go-ahead cannot be recommended, it is very useful to document just this fact and preserve this knowledge within your organization.

In an ideal scenario, most of this implementation can be performed in a sandbox of staging environment, although we realize that true results—especially where performance is concerned—will only be achieved once the new technology is exposed to production traffic.

Go-Live Criteria

The most important point before adding any new technology to production is to clearly understand the potential impact and failures modes. Hopefully you have had a chance to discover some of these scenarios during a pre-production test in a staging environment.

If you are replacing existing functionality like for like, such that the new technology has to support all the current use cases, then a great help in verifying that the new service behaves as expected will be a suite of black-box tests[4] that you run against both the old and the new system.

To help mitigate the risk involved in such projects you should seriously consider adopting deployment strategies that allow for a fast and easy rollback mechanism (such as blue-green deployments or canary releases, which were explained in the previous chapter).

Aspects that you can never neglect when going to production are logging, monitoring, alarming, and data collection. If you cannot analyze a technology's status messaging, then you will never know if it is in failure mode or what particular problems it might encounter in case of an outage. And if your business prides itself on being data driven, then integrating the newcomer into the data warehouse layer must be a first priority.

It is generally a good guideline to keep the number of languages and other technology options in production as small as possible, but as large as necessary. This reduces maintenance costs and cognitive load for the tech personnel while at the same time providing an environment for staying ahead of the curve and agile.

It is never a good idea to use a technology that only one or two technical people in the company are sufficiently familiar with to support it in a production setting. This means that you should neither adopt a technology where only a small number of developers understand the system, nor migrate away from a technology after there is too little know-how left to grasp what it takes to deprecate it.

One way to avoid this is to focus on hiring polyglot and well-rounded engineers who make a habit of learning the company's infrastructure. Make sure that a significant amount of time during the on-boarding process for new team members is spent learning the ins and outs of all technologies that are in use by your team.

A Case Study: Moving books-service from Rails to Rust

When looking at our example book store business that is running in a microservices environment, we discovered that our most trafficked service is the books-service, which contains all the core product data about the books for sale on the site.

The service has been implemented using the rapid application development framework Ruby on Rails, mostly because the developers were most familiar with this technology, and because it is very convenient and easy to implement a JSON API service in it.

During day-to-day operations the team owning books-service notices that response times start to become affected during peak business times when the largest number of customers browse the product catalog. While there is no immediate urgency to address the issue—that is, no decrease in purchase rates can be correlated to these times of heavy load—the development team is starting to investigate the root cause of the scaling issue.

Analysis of the logs and New Relic APM[5] data for books-service shows that much time is spent in garbage collection of Ruby objects, and—even though the service was implemented as a Rails API-only[6] project—lots of framework code is logged as being busy handling the request and response objects outside the actual application logic.

---

[4]Chapter 9 has more details about such tests, and how to craft them.
[5]This is an application-performance monitoring tool. See `https://newrelic.com/application-monitoring`.
[6]A variant of a standard Ruby on Rails application that tailors the middleware components used to the minimum need for API services. See the respective Rails guide at `http://edgeguides.rubyonrails.org/api_app.html` for more details.

Alice, one of the senior engineers on the books-service team, suggests starting to investigate alternatives, and the team agrees to take over part of her current responsibilities so that she has time to dedicate to this effort.

Thus tasked, she starts out by writing down a problem statement, including all data gathered about the nature of books-service's perceived scaling issues.

After doing some research about more resource-efficient languages and less impactful web frameworks, she comes across the Mozilla Research-sponsored language Rust (https://www.rust-lang.org/), which seems very promising for addressing the perceived performance challenges. Additionally, the language seems to raise a lot of interest in the community, and many of the great engineers in her professional network have started to gravitate toward Rust.

Alice formulates a goal statement of the experimentation to include concrete and measurable gains in performance and reduction in computing resource usage, compared to the current production-deployed version of books-service. She also includes specifics about the expected advantages of using the Rust language for the experiment, quoting some very rudimentary benchmarks she has gathered from credible sources, as well as her own small experiments. As the company is hiring and therefore in competition with many other employers for experienced, high-quality engineers, she also lists the increase in attractiveness to potential engineering candidates caused by using a cutting-edge technology like Rust. Her metric to test this hypothesis is to compare feedback from the engineering team's combined professional network, so she plans to ask all teams to survey their contacts about an increase in interest in a company that uses Rust in its technology stack.

The books-service team meets to discuss Alice's proposed experiment based on the statement of motivation and goals, and unanimous agreement is given to go ahead with the next phase of the experiment. This means that time is officially dedicated in the next two team sprints to work on the first stage of the implementation plan. Alice will pair with Peter, another engineer on her team, on this project, simply to make sure that knowledge is not restricted to a single person, and they agree to schedule regular "brownbag lunch" sessions where they share updates with the rest of the team.

Alice and Peter are also asked to work to identify a contact on the company's technical operations (TechOps) team, in order to share knowledge about potential deployment or operational concerns, as well as solicit suggestions they might have for running Rust in the existing infrastructure.

After learning the basics of the Rust language and identifying potential API frameworks in the language, Alice and Peter decide to use Iron (http://ironframework.io/)—a very lightweight and extensible web framework for Rust. They experimented with several other Rust frameworks, but found that they introduced more latency than Iron, and as performance is one of the main objectives of the experiment, they decide to stick with Iron.

While reimplementing all the features of the existing Ruby version of books-service in Rust, they can rely on an existing, out-of-process black-box test suite, written in Ruby using the Cucumber DSL. Once they get to the point of feature equivalence between the Ruby and Rust versions, they can finally measure response times and resource usage for the Rust service under a simulated large load in the company's staging network environment.

Initial results are very promising, and Alice and Peter write up a page on their internal company Wiki which summarizes the results. They present the results first to their own team, which is impressed with the observed 10x response time improvements in the staging environment.

An official vote is taken and recorded to go ahead and spend time investigating and addressing all the necessary steps that are involved with a "go-live" decision in production. These steps include more training on the technologies in use for developers and TechOps engineers, as well as making sure that the team has visibility into the new service's production behavior by integrating it with the logging and alarming infrastructure. Data warehouse integration of the metrics gathered for business intelligence queries also needs to be addressed before the Rust service can go live.

Once integrating Rust into the company's canary deployment process is addressed by the TechOps department, the team can finally observe the new service under actual production load, and compare it side by side with the existing Ruby version of the service.

Summary

This chapter discussed the implications of being technologically polyglot. After explaining the vectors of change in a microservices architecture where technological diversity can and should be tried, we looked at the opportunities in adopting several competing technologies.

We identified the main potential advantages to be the benefits of specialization, progress achieved by experimentation, and remaining agile by setting yourself up to evolve more quickly with your business requirements.

Next we looked at how to navigate around the potential pitfalls of working in a polyglot technology environment, before shifting our focus to describing a viable process for experimentation with, and adoption of, a new technology in a company's tech stack.

We concluded the chapter with a fictitious case study about replacing a Ruby-on-Rails based microservice in our example bookstore with an equivalent service and APIs implemented in Rust.

The next chapter will go into much more detail about the implementation of the microservices architecture that makes up the sample book store application.

CHAPTER 12

Single-Client Application—Mobile and Web

Your microservice-powered application will ultimately be displayed to actual people using a web browser or mobile devices; we call those *customer facing applications*. In order to function well, those applications need to make calling each service they depend on a trivial task. We know that many developers have been exposed only to the ideas and concepts behind the microservices architecture, and still have very little actual exposure to how all the pieces fit together in practice.

In this chapter, we share our book sample project; it has working code that resembles a real-life scenario, so that you can run all the services in this project and see a web application running. Our project implementation is far from complete, as that's not the goal of this book; we only have enough pieces in place to show how everything connects. We will focus on explaining the main building blocks of a few pages of the sample project, and explain the components that make each part of some pages work. We will show code in Ruby and Rust, which are the two languages we are comfortable with and can fairly easily use to showcase interaction between a web application and a few services. Even if you are not familiar with those languages, we recommend you follow along with this chapter as it will put into practice a lot of the concepts we have described in the book so far.

Application Overview

Before we get started, take a look at the architecture of what we are building in this chapter. We'll be implementing much of the application example described throughout the book in the following services:

- `showcase` is a client-facing web application, built in Ruby on Rails, that will be receiving requests from customers. The source code is available at `https://github.com/microservices-from-day-one/showcase`.

- `books-service` is a service responsible for owning all data associated with books, built in Rust. The source code is available at `https://github.com/microservices-from-day-one/books`.

- `purchases-service` is a service responsible for owning all data associated with shopping carts and purchases, built in Ruby. The source code is available at `https://github.com/microservices-from-day-one/purchases`.

- `reviews-service` is a service responsible for owning all data associated with book reviews, built in Ruby. The source code is available at `https://github.com/microservices-from-day-one/reviews`.

© Cloves Carneiro Jr. and Tim Schmelmer 2016
C. Carneiro Jr. and T. Schmelmer, *Microservices From Day One*, DOI 10.1007/978-1-4842-1937-9_12

The diagram in Figure 12-1 makes it easy to visualize that our customers will be using their browsers to point to the web server that is running the showcase app, which will then make requests to books-service, purchases-service and reviews-service in order to render web pages to our users.

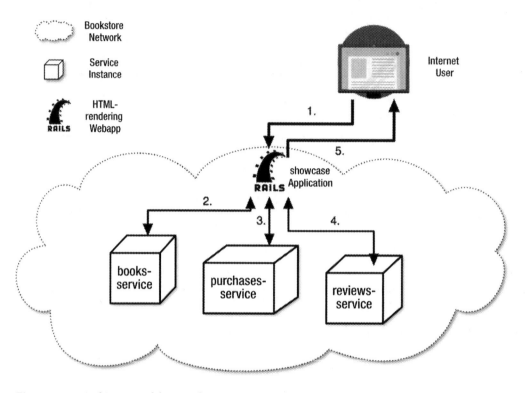

Figure 12-1. *Architecture of the sample project*

▦ **Note**   You can—and should—follow along by loading the code available from the URLs shown. Each service has a Readme file with details on how to set up each application, and we also provide a repository with more documentation at https://github.com/microservices-from-day-one/docs.

It is time to put all that we've talked about in this book together, and demonstrate a working web application in a microservices environment. The sample application for this book is a bookstore, which has a set of fairly standard features that we will describe and dissect in this chapter. We'll talk about each of the application's pages, and will explain all service calls that happen in order to get each page rendered. The sample application is not fully functional, as it would probably require a team of full-time developers to implement and maintain such an application; however, we decided to implement enough functionality that will showcase a lot of the topics covered in this book.

Home Page

The home page for the bookstore is a fairly standard e-commerce landing page, as you can see in Figure 12-2.

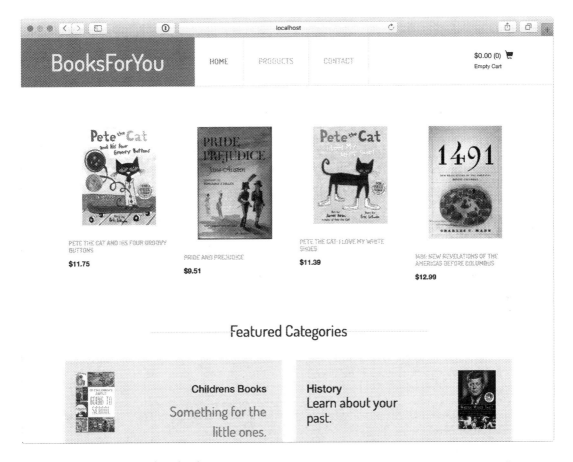

Figure 12-2. *Home page of our bookstore*

Before we go into the details of a few elements of the home page, we want to bring to your attention the client library we are using to connect to our services. You probably remember from Chapters 5 and 6 that we decided to use the JSON API standard to describe all our responses, which would keep our services interfaces and responses similar across the whole system. We build a client library in Ruby—known as a Ruby gem—to interface with our services. The payoff for using a standard starts to appear, as we were able to build our own library on top of an open source JSON API compliant library called `json_api_client` (`https://github.com/chingor13/json_api_client`).

In our client library, named `api_client` and available at `https://github.com/microservices-from-day-one/api-client`, you can see that we have defined one module per service, so we'll have a module called `ApiClient::Books` for `books-service`, another called `ApiClient::Purchases` for `purchases-service`, and so on. Each module is very simple and leverages the `json_api_client` gem; they also define a `Base` class, which is responsible for having code that will be shared by all models. The `Base` class for `ApiClient::Books` is listed here:

```
module ApiClient
  module Books

    class Base < JsonApiClient::Resource
      def self.site
        @site ||= "#{ServiceDiscovery.url_for(:books)}/v1"
      end
    end

  end
end

require 'api_client/books/book'
require 'api_client/books/category'
```

That class is responsible for mainly two things, defining where the endpoint for `books-service` is to be found, as implemented in the `site` class method, and defining a base resource, which inherits from `JsonApiClient::Resource`; therefore all the subclasses of this class don't really need to know that detail of the implementation.

With the `Base` class in the client library explained, we'll now show how a specific resource is defined. Our example is the `ApiClient::Books::Book` class, which represents the book model as served by `books-service`; the class is defined here:

```
module ApiClient
  module Books

    class Book < Base
    end

  end
end
```

As you can see, there is really no code associated with this class; we are able to define a standard resource, which has a set of well-known method available that match to a RESTful set of CRUD endpoints—again, one of the advantages of following a standard. So our client library is, as we expected, a very thin layer that allows client applications to reach the service endpoints we wrote.

Now it's time to look at how some of the elements of this page have come together. An element that is a constant feature in most e-commerce applications is our shopping cart widget, which shows us the current value of the cart, as well as the number of elements in it. All details related to purchases are owned by `purchases-service`, which also owns all cart details. When any user accesses the bookstore, this service tries to find a cart associated with the user, which is saved in the session:

```
def current_cart_id
  if session[:cart_id].nil?
```

```
    cart = ApiClient::Purchases::Cart.create
    session[:cart_id] = cart.cart_id
  end
  session[:cart_id]
end
helper_method :current_cart_id
```

As you can see in this code, the application will load the card_id associated with the user from the session. For new users that do not have an associated cart_id, a new cart will be generated in purchases-service via the ApiClient::Purchases::Cart.create call. Again, we will take a look at the implementation in purchases-service, available at https://github.com/microservices-from-day-one/purchases, which is a Ruby service. In Ruby, we have an open-source gem called jsonapi-resources (https://github.com/cerebris/jsonapi-resources), which is described as "a resource-focused Rails library for developing JSON API compliant servers." By following the JSON API standard, and defining a set of resources that define the models to be exposed in the API, this gem makes it very easy to create JSON API-complaint services. In purchases-service, the Cart resource is defined as follows:

```
module V1
  class CartResource < JSONAPI::Resource
    attributes :cart_id, :expires_at, :total, :items_count
  end
end
```

The cart's endpoints are defined in the V1::CartsController class, defined as:

```
namespace :v1 do
  jsonapi_resources :carts
end
```

in routes.rb and implemented as:

```
module V1
  class CartsController < JSONAPI::ResourceController
  end
end
```

That is all that we need in order to render the shopping cart widget. It currently shows the number of items in the cart and its value as 0; however, that will change when we implement the endpoints and code to add books to the cart.

Now it's time to look into how some of the elements of this page have come together. The main block in the home page displays four featured books that are presented to the user. We will start with a very simple implementation, which is a service call that will return the six most recent books in books-service. The code that makes that service call is

```
def home_products(limit: 8)
  @home_products ||= ApiClient::Books::Book.paginate(page: 1, per_page: limit).to_a
end
```

When this code is executed, the following request comes to books-service:

```
GET http://localhost:5000/v1/books?page%5Bnumber%5D=1&page%5Bsize%5D=6`
```

It returns

```
{
  "data": [
    {
      "attributes": {
        "author": "Mo Willems",
        "cover_image": "https://images-na.ssl-images-amazon.com/images/I/61jurA6wsFL._SX258_
BO1,204,203,200_.jpg",
        "description": "Diva, a small yet brave dog, and Flea, a curious streetwise cat,
develop an unexpected friendship in this unforgettable tale of discovery.",
        "isbn": "978-1484722848",
        "pages": 80,
        "price": 987,
        "slug": "the-story-of-diva-and-flea",
        "title": "The Story of Diva and Flea"
      },
      "id": "2497fe7d-4797-4506-a3cd-85e42d90415b",
      "type": "books"
    },
    {
      "attributes": {
        "author": "Charles C. Mann",
        "cover_image": "https://upload.wikimedia.org/wikipedia/en/b/b7/1491-cover.jpg",
        "description": "In this groundbreaking work of science, history, and archaeology,
Charles C. Mann radically alters our understanding of the Americas before the arrival of
Columbus in 1492.",
        "isbn": "978-1400032051",
        "pages": 541,
        "price": 1299,
        "slug": "1491-new-revelations",
        "title": "1491: New Revelations of the Americas Before Columbus"
      },
      "id": "2d831aba-75bb-48b6-bae6-9f1bb613d29b",
      "type": "books"
    },
    {
      "attributes": {
        "author": "Jane Austen",
        "cover_image": "https://themodernmanuscript.files.wordpress.com/2013/01/pride-and-
prejudice-1946.jpg",
        "description": "Pride and Prejudice is a novel of manners by Jane Austen, first
published in 1813. The story follows the main character, Elizabeth Bennet, as she deals with
issues of manners, upbringing, morality and education.",
        "isbn": "978-1484110980",
        "pages": 279,
        "price": 951,
        "slug": "pride-and-prejudice",
        "title": "Pride and Prejudice"
      },
```

```
      "id": "12892302-7ef4-4023-9999-2b3560a2a4d6",
      "type": "books"
    },
    {
      "attributes": {
        "author": "James Dean ",
        "cover_image": "https://i.harperapps.com/covers/9780062303899/x300.png",
        "description": "Pete the Cat is going scuba diving! Before he hits the water,
        Captain Joe tells him about all the sea creatures he can encounter, and Pete is
        super excited to see a seahorse.",
        "isbn": "978-0062303882",
        "price": 319,
        "slug": "pete-the-cat-scuba-cat",
        "title": "Pete the Cat: Scuba-Cat"
      },
      "id": "8217e21a-97db-4be9-9feb-4cea97a64948",
      "type": "books"
    },
    {
      "attributes": {
        "author": "Eric Litwin",
        "cover_image": "https://i.harperapps.com/covers/9780061906220/x300.png",
        "description": "Pete the Cat goes walking down the street wearing his brand new
        white shoes. Along the way, his shoes change from white to red to blue to brown to
        WET as he steps in piles of strawberries, blueberries, and other big messes.",
        "isbn": "978-0061906237",
        "pages": 40,
        "price": 1139,
        "slug": "pete-the-cat-i-love-my-white-shoes",
        "title": "Pete the Cat: I Love My White Shoes"
      },
      "id": "008672a6-c48c-49b2-98e8-b78914f2fce4",
      "type": "books"
    },
    {
      "attributes": {
        "author": "Eric Litwin",
        "cover_image": "https://i.harperapps.com/covers/9780062110589/x300.png",
        "description": "Pete the Cat is wearing his favorite shirt—the one with the four
        totally groovy buttons. But when one falls off, does Pete cry? Goodness, no! He
        just keeps on singing his song—after all, what could be groovier than three groovy
        buttons?",
        "isbn": "978-0062110589",
        "pages": 40,
        "price": 1175,
        "slug": "pete-the-cat-and-his-four-groovy-buttons",
        "title": "Pete the Cat and His Four Groovy Buttons"
      },
      "id": "20ee1ef4-6000-460a-b715-40da50979fc7",
      "type": "books"
    },
```

191

```
    {
      "attributes": {
        "author": "James Dean",
        "cover_image": "https://i.harperapps.com/covers/9780062304186/x300.png",
        "description": "Pete the Cat takes on the classic favorite children's song \"Five
Little Pumpkins\" in New York Times bestselling author James Dean's Pete the Cat: Five
Little Pumpkins. Join Pete as he rocks out to this cool adaptation of the classic Halloween
song!",
        "isbn": "978-0062304186",
        "pages": 32,
        "price": 791,
        "slug": "pete-the-cat-five-little-pumpkins",
        "title": "Pete the Cat: Five Little Pumpkins"
      },
      "id": "25f2db6f-966a-4c24-9047-1fdfeb43e465",
      "type": "books"
    }
  ]
}
```

With those products retrieved, the code in the template that renders the page will pick four random books out of those six, so that users see different books in subsequent requests:

```
<% for product in home_products(limit: 6).shuffle.first(4) do %>
  <%= render partial: 'home/product', locals: {product: product} %>
<% end %>
```

We've started with a very simple service call; however, as the site develops a wider range of products and starts to collect user behavior data, this is an area that could benefit from the existence of user recommendations, which could be implemented in a recommendations service, and be based on an algorithm that takes into consideration the user's purchase habits, along with the purchase habits of similar users, to maximize sales opportunities.

Featured Categories

In the second half of the home page, we have the Featured Categories block, which is a section used to feature a couple of categories the business is interested in focusing on. In the showcase application, we make a call to the featured_categories endpoint in books-service, available at /v1/categories/featured, which is responsible for knowing the logic behind deciding how a category gets featured; in the browser, that call looks like Figure 12-3.

Featured Categories

Figure 12-3. *Featured categories block in home page*

```
def featured_categories
  @featured_categories ||= ApiClient::Books::Category.featured.first(2)
end
```

The Category resource in the service returns a JSON API-compliant resource, with a response that looks like this:

```
{
  "data": [
    {
      "attributes": {
        "description": "Something for the little ones.",
        "image": "http://sleepingshouldbeeasy.com/wp-content/uploads/2013/01/childrens-
books-about-going-to-school-vertical.jpg",
        "name": "Childrens Books",
        "slug": "children-s-books"
      },
      "id": "20a05be7-3a9b-4ed0-a36b-ed36b0504557",
      "type": "categories"
    },
    {
      "attributes": {
        "description": "Learn about your past.",
        "image": "http://media1.s-nbcnews.com/ij.aspx?404;http://sys06-media.s-nbcnews.
com:80/j/streams/2013/November/131120/2D9747505-Where_Were_You_book_jacket.blocks_desktop_
vertical_tease.jpg",
        "name": "History",
        "slug": "history"
      },
      "id": "cc7f1963-23fc-485c-89ec-d1efb25966d1",
      "type": "categories"
    },
```

```
    {
      "attributes": {
        "description": "It is promise and hope. Titillations and excitations.",
        "image": "https://s-media-cache-ak0.pinimg.com/564x/29/bd/9e/29bd9eafd49a185874e706
fb4f896ba0.jpg",
        "name": "Romance",
        "slug": "romance"
      },
      "id": "c85102c8-3ed2-4af9-be8b-f1008448f6cb",
      "type": "categories"
    }
  ]
}
```

In the service code, the featured endpoint has been implemented as a response that returns categories in random order, so that all categories are featured equally. Of course, in a production setup, we'd want to implement featured_categories based on business logic, probably based on featuring-best selling categories. In the described architecture, changes to the algorithm of how categories become featured are just an implementation detail of books-service and will have zero impact on the rest of the system, given that the API interface remains unchanged. Here's the current implementation of the featured_categories endpoint, implemented in Rust, and as we discussed in Chapter 11.

```
pub fn featured(req: &mut Request) -> IronResult<Response> {
    let pool = req.get::<Read<::AppDb>>().unwrap();
    let conn = pool.get().unwrap();

    let mut categories: Vec<Category> = Vec::new();
    for row in &conn.query("SELECT category_id, name, description, slug, image FROM
categories ORDER BY random()", &[]).unwrap() {
        let category = Category::from_row(row);
        categories.push(category);
    }

    let response = jsonapi::json_collection_wrapped_in("data", categories);
    Ok(Response::with((status::Ok,
                       Header(jsonapi::jsonapi_content_type()),
                       response)))
}
```

One last thing to mention about this element is that it is probably the most "cacheable" element of the home page, meaning that it's very unlikely we will want featured categories to change frequently throughout the day; thus, we can use client-side caching to cache the featured categories block for a specific period of time (usually to be decided by the business), and not even have to make the service call on most requests, which also makes the application more performant and resilient to service failures. In this case, caching the response for 4 hours seems acceptable; so we could surround the client-side code with these lines:

```
<% cache 'featured_categories', expires_in: 4.hours do %>
  <%= render partial: 'home/offers' %>
<% end %>
```

Users Should Never See Internal Errors

Now that you have seen some code, and we have the home page being rendered by loading data from a few services, we'll look into how we want to treat service errors in this user-facing application. We believe strongly that users should never see server errors; developers and designers should think about the user experience to be presented to the user when there's something wrong with the application. Based on the particular use case, treating errors will take a unique shape, as there are cases that you can easily recover from, and others not so much.

The rule of thumb is that you need to catch errors that happen when interacting with the server, give your users a fall-back, and try to degrade gracefully in all areas; but degrading means different things based on the situation. In some cases, you can make it look like there is no error at all, and in others, you still have to display a "something went wrong" message, which is still more user-friendly than a 500 server error.

We will start by looking at the shopping cart widget, which we described a few pages ago, and will see what happens to the application when that service is not available—*down*. To simulate purchases-service being down, we can just Ctrl-C that process and wait until we are sure it's no longer running. After doing that, just refresh your browser, and you will see that the home page greets you with an ugly ConnectionError error (see Figure 12-4).

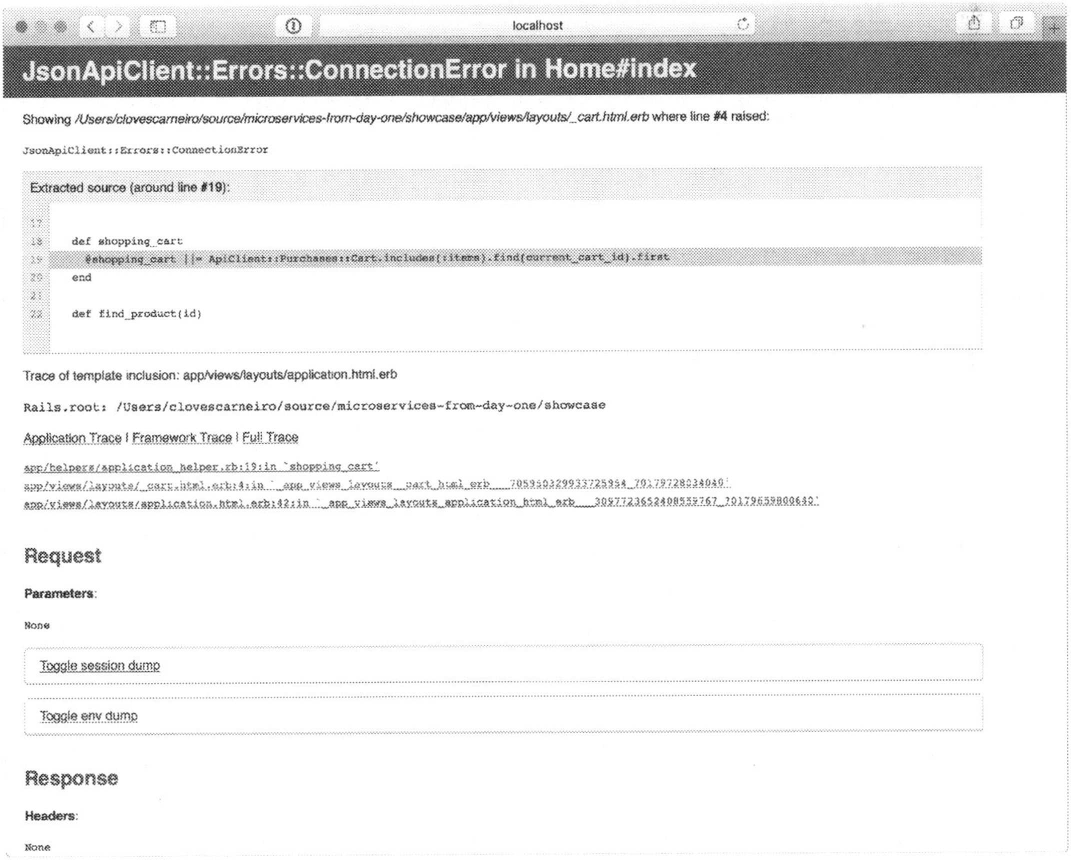

Figure 12-4. *Error when loading the home page when dependencies are not available*

The shopping cart widget gives us an insight into what is currently in the cart, and also works as a link to the cart page. In this case, we could treat that error to make sure that we still render the widget, without the number of items in the cart nor the current cost. That fall-back seems to be acceptable, since it should only happen during down times of that one service. We've changed the helper method that loads the shopping cart object by adding error-handling code, and we also made sure we logged the error that is happening and left a TODO comment inline to alert us that something is wrong. In Chapter 14, we talk about some options for alerting this type of issue. The code ends by returning a nil object:

```ruby
def shopping_cart
  @shopping_cart ||= ApiClient::Purchases::Cart.find(current_cart_id).first
rescue JsonApiClient::Errors::ConnectionError => e
  Rails.logger.error("Error loading shopping_cart: e=#{e.message}")
  # TODO: alert that an error is happening
  nil
end
```

We can check for a nil object in the template that renders the shopping cart information:

```erb
<% if shopping_cart %>
  <div class="total">
    <span class="simpleCart_total"><%= render_price(shopping_cart.total) %></span>
    (<span id="quantity" class="quantity"><%= shopping_cart.items_count %></span>)
  </div>
<% end %>
```

Figures 12-5 and 12-6 are screenshots of the shopping cart widget first when it's working as expected and then under the error case, which may not even be noticeable to the user.

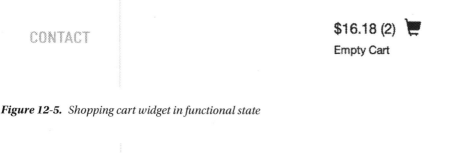

Figure 12-5. *Shopping cart widget in functional state*

Figure 12-6. *Shopping cart widget when purchases-service is down*

We demonstrated an error case that had a simple solution that didn't impact the page at lot; we could easily degrade gracefully. However, there are cases where that is not possible. For example, if the user were in the book detail page, and the `books-service` happened to be nonresponsive, you'd have to return a page with an error message that asks the user to "try again in a few minutes."

Circuit Breakers

In most cases, the type of error handling code we've just explained is enough to help one application handle failure from a downstream dependency; however, in environments with a very high number of requests, it's possible that having a client-facing application keep making requests to a service when it knows it's down isn't a good solution, for two reasons:

- The calling application will be slightly delayed, as it may have to wait for its timeout to realize that a dependency is unavailable, which may slow other systems.

- The struggling server takes longer to respond, or come back to life, if it keeps receiving requests that it cannot handle, compounding the existing problem.

For that type of situation, the calling application should use the circuit breaker pattern we introduced in Chapter 6. It is a mechanism that will make the calling application try to request a resource from a service even when it notices that the service has not been responsive. Circuit breakers are usually set up by defining a failure threshold in the calling application that when met will cause the circuit to "open" for a predetermined period of time, causing the calling application to go into error handling mode without even calling the downstream dependency, because it already knows that it has been struggling to properly serve requests. This spares us from the two unwanted scenarios we described earlier and makes a system even more resilient in the face of an abnormal situation.

Book Detail Page

The next page we will look at is the book detail page, shown in Figure 12-7, which is probably the most important page in the application; it's where users will make a purchase decision. Here is some of the information a user would expect to see on the book page:

- bibliographic information such as title, author, cover image, description, ISBN, price, page count and publisher name

- reviews of books

  - other people's review,

  - ability to review yourself

- add to a wish list

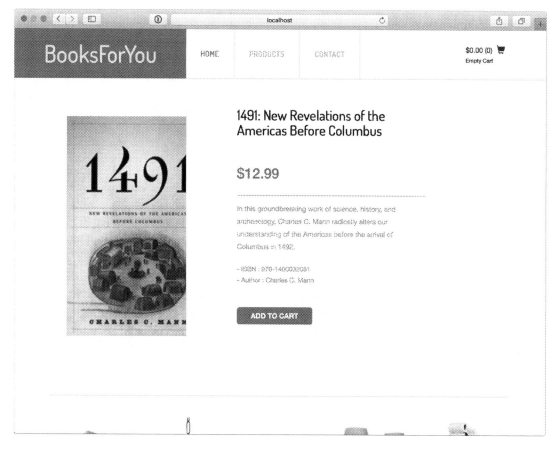

Figure 12-7. *Screenshot of book detail page*

The initial set of attributes we need to load are what we could call book metadata, and are owned by `books-service`; the client helper will load data from that service, by using the book "slug," which is a unique SEO-friendly string used in the book URL, such as `http://localhost:5004/products/pete-the-cat-i-love-my-white-shoes`.

```
def book_details
  @book ||= ApiClient::Books::Book.where(slug: params[:id]).first
end
```

The code above will make this service call:

```
GET http://localhost:5000/v1/books?filter%5Bslug%5D=pete-the-cat-i-love-my-white-shoes
```

The call in turn returns:

```
{
  "data": [
    {
      "attributes": {
        "author": "Eric Litwin",
        "cover_image": "https://i.harperapps.com/covers/9780061906220/x300.png",
        "description": "Pete the Cat goes walking down the street wearing his brand new
white shoes. Along the way, his shoes change from white to red to blue to brown to WET as he
steps in piles of strawberries, blueberries, and other big messes.",
        "isbn": "978-0061906237",
        "price": 1139,
        "slug": "pete-the-cat-i-love-my-white-shoes",
        "title": "Pete the Cat: I Love My White Shoes"
      },
      "id": "008672a6-c48c-49b2-98e8-b78914f2fce4",
      "type": "books"
    }
  ]
}
```

As mentioned previously, our ApiClient library knows the JSON API standard well, and transforms that response into an object we can easily use in the template code, such as this:

```
<div class="single-para ">
  <h4><%= book_details.title %></h4>
  <h5 class="item_price"><%= render_price(book_details.price) %></h5>
  <p class="para"><%= book_details.description %></p>
  <div class="prdt-info-grid">
    <ul>
      <li>- ISBN : <%= book_details.isbn %></li>
      <li>- Author : <%= book_details.author %></li>
    </ul>
  </div>
</div>
```

We hope this is starting to feel easier to follow; we'll follow exactly the same pattern to make service calls to load review information from reviews-service, which follows the same pattern of loading the book data.

The last element we'll talk about in the book detail page is the "related books" block, shown in Figure 12-8, which is a set of links to books that are somehow related to the book featured in this page. Much like the home page's Featured Books block, this is an element that will benefit from having its own endpoint, so that the business can tweak the rules for selecting those elements without that affecting any work on the front-end client application. The first step in implementing this is to define an endpoint in books-service that asks for books related to a specific book. We settle for an endpoint in the following format:

```
GET /v1/books/2d831aba-75bb-48b6-bae6-9f1bb613d29b/related
```

Reviews

No reviews for this book yet.

ADD TO CART

Pete the Cat and His Four
Groovy Buttons
$11.75

The Story of Diva and Flea
$9.87

Pete the Cat: Five Little
Pumpkins
$7.91

Pete the Cat I Love My
White Shoes
$11.39

Pete the Cat: Scuba-Cat
$3.19

Figure 12-8. *The related books block in the book detail page*

In this example, the UUID (2d831aba-75bb-48b6-bae6-9f1bb613d29b) is the ID of the book for which we want to receive "related books." For the sake of this example, we decided on using a very straightforward implementation that loads five random books that are not the book_id passed in the URL. Here's the implementation in Rust:

```
pub fn related(req: &mut Request) -> IronResult<Response> {
    let book_id = iron_helpers::extract_param_from_path(req, "book_id");
    let book_uuid = Uuid::parse_str(&book_id).unwrap();

    let pool = req.get::<Read<::AppDb>>().unwrap();
    let conn = pool.get().unwrap();

    let sql = "SELECT book_id, title, author, description, isbn, price, pages, \
        slug, cover_image FROM books WHERE book_id != $1 ORDER BY random() LIMIT 5";

    let mut books: Vec<Book> = Vec::new();
    for row in &conn.query(&sql, &[&book_uuid]).unwrap() {
        let book = Book::from_row(row);
        books.push(book);
    }

    let response = jsonapi::json_collection_wrapped_in("data", books);
    Ok(Response::with((status::Ok,
                      Header(jsonapi::jsonapi_content_type()),
                      response)))
}
```

When called, the preceding returns the following response:

```
{
  "data": [
```

```
{
  "attributes": {
    "author": "James Dean",
    "cover_image": "https://i.harperapps.com/covers/9780062304186/x300.png",
    "description": "Pete the Cat takes on the classic favorite children's song \"Five
Little Pumpkins\" in New York Times bestselling author James Dean's Pete the Cat:
Five Little Pumpkins. Join Pete as he rocks out to this cool adaptation of the
classic Halloween song!",
    "isbn": "978-0062304186",
    "pages": 100,
    "price": 791,
    "slug": "pete-the-cat-five-little-pumpkins",
    "title": "Pete the Cat: Five Little Pumpkins"
  },
  "id": "25f2db6f-966a-4c24-9047-1fdfeb43e465",
  "type": "books"
},
{
  "attributes": {
    "author": "Eric Litwin",
    "cover_image": "https://i.harperapps.com/covers/9780062110589/x300.png",
    "description": "Pete the Cat is wearing his favorite shirt—the one with the four
totally groovy buttons. But when one falls off, does Pete cry? Goodness, no! He
just keeps on singing his song—after all, what could be groovier than three groovy
buttons?",
    "isbn": "978-0062110589",
    "pages": 100,
    "price": 1175,
    "slug": "pete-the-cat-and-his-four-groovy-buttons",
    "title": "Pete the Cat and His Four Groovy Buttons"
  },
  "id": "20ee1ef4-6000-460a-b715-40da50979fc7",
  "type": "books"
},
{
  "attributes": {
    "author": "Charles C. Mann",
    "cover_image": "https://upload.wikimedia.org/wikipedia/en/b/b7/1491-cover.jpg",
    "description": "In this groundbreaking work of science, history, and archaeology,
Charles C. Mann radically alters our understanding of the Americas before the
arrival of Columbus in 1492.",
    "isbn": "978-1400032051",
    "pages": 100,
    "price": 1299,
    "slug": "1491-new-revelations",
    "title": "1491: New Revelations of the Americas Before Columbus"
  },
  "id": "2d831aba-75bb-48b6-bae6-9f1bb613d29b",
  "type": "books"
```

```json
    },
    {
      "attributes": {
        "author": "Eric Litwin",
        "cover_image": "https://i.harperapps.com/covers/9780061906220/x300.png",
        "description": "Pete the Cat goes walking down the street wearing his brand new
        white shoes. Along the way, his shoes change from white to red to blue to brown to
        WET as he steps in piles of strawberries, blueberries, and other big messes.",
        "isbn": "978-0061906237",
        "pages": 100,
        "price": 1139,
        "slug": "pete-the-cat-i-love-my-white-shoes",
        "title": "Pete the Cat: I Love My White Shoes"
      },
      "id": "008672a6-c48c-49b2-98e8-b78914f2fce4",
      "type": "books"
    },
    {
      "attributes": {
        "author": "Mo Willems",
        "cover_image": "https://images-na.ssl-images-amazon.com/images/I/61jurA6wsFL._SX258_
        BO1,204,203,200_.jpg",
        "description": "Diva, a small yet brave dog, and Flea, a curious streetwise cat,
        develop an unexpected friendship in this unforgettable tale of discovery.",
        "isbn": "978-1484722848",
        "pages": 100,
        "price": 987,
        "slug": "the-story-of-diva-and-flea",
        "title": "The Story of Diva and Flea"
      },
      "id": "2497fe7d-4797-4506-a3cd-85e42d90415b",
      "type": "books"
    }
  ]
}
```

With everything implemented server-side, we have to make a tweak to the api_client library so that we can make calls to that endpoint. The json_api_client gem makes it ridiculously easy to give ourselves access to that endpoint; we just need to define a custom_endpoint in the Book class:

```ruby
module ApiClient
  module Books

    class Book < Base
      custom_endpoint :related, on: :member, request_method: :get
    end

  end
end
```

Turning our attention back to the front-end application, we render those five related books in a separate template, known as a *partial*, called related:

```
<%= render "related", books: book_details.related %>
```

The partial looks like this:

```
<% for book in books do %>
  <div class="col-md-2 btm-grid">
    <a href="<%= book_path(book.slug) %>">
      <%= image_tag book.cover_image, alt: book.title, style: "width: 120px" %>
      <h4><%= book.title %></h4>
      <span><%= render_price(book.price) %></span>
    </a>
  </div>
<% end %>
```

The Shopping Cart Page

We've talked about the shopping cart widget, available in all pages in the application, but now let's turn our attention to the shopping cart page, shown in Figure 12-9, which is where the user is taken when clicking in the shopping cart widget. As expected, the shopping cart detail page has not only the summary about

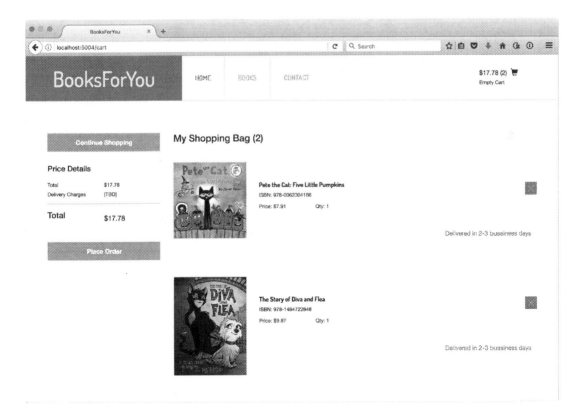

Figure 12-9. Shopping cart page

number of items and total price in the cart, but also information about each of the items the user has added to the cart. In our example, we have two books in the shopping cart.

In purchases-service, shopping carts are modeled as multiple entities. A Cart is the shopping cart main model, it has attributes such as items_count, total, user_id, and expires_at, and an Item has attributes such as item_id, quantity, and price. In order to display the shopping cart details, we need to have access to each line item in the cart; this is unlike the shopping cart widget, which only needed basic cart information. We've decided to use a single endpoint to return cart information, but return a richer response. This is what we have referred to as different representations of the same data in responses.

The following service call:

```
GET http://localhost:5001/v1/carts/35c082ba-b974-4d78-9526-4fc6ed7b54a2
```

returns this:

```
{
  "data": {
    "id": "35c082ba-b974-4d78-9526-4fc6ed7b54a2",
    "type": "carts",
    "links": {
      "self": "http://localhost:5001/v1/carts/35c082ba-b974-4d78-9526-4fc6ed7b54a2"
    },
    "attributes": {
      "cart_id": "35c082ba-b974-4d78-9526-4fc6ed7b54a2",
      "expires_at": "2016-10-23T01:54:29.408Z",
      "total": 1618,
      "items_count": 2
    },
    "relationships": {
      "items": {
        "links": {
          "self": "http://localhost:5001/v1/carts/35c082ba-b974-4d78-9526-4fc6ed7b54a2/
          relationships/items",
          "related": "http://localhost:5001/v1/carts/35c082ba-b974-4d78-9526-4fc6ed7b54a2/
          items"
        }
      }
    }
  }
}
```

For the cart page, we pass an extra parameter, include=items, to that same API call; it looks like this:

```
GET localhost:5001/v1/carts/35c082ba-b974-4d78-9526-4fc6ed7b54a2?include=items
```

It returns

```
{
  "data": {
    "id": "35c082ba-b974-4d78-9526-4fc6ed7b54a2",
    "type": "carts",
    "links": {
```

```
      "self": "http://localhost:5001/v1/carts/35c082ba-b974-4d78-9526-4fc6ed7b54a2"
    },
    "attributes": {
      "cart_id": "35c082ba-b974-4d78-9526-4fc6ed7b54a2",
      "expires_at": "2016-10-23T01:54:29.408Z",
      "total": 1618,
      "items_count": 2
    },
    "relationships": {
      "items": {
        "links": {
          "self": "http://localhost:5001/v1/carts/35c082ba-b974-4d78-9526-4fc6ed7b54a2/
          relationships/items",
          "related": "http://localhost:5001/v1/carts/35c082ba-b974-4d78-9526-4fc6ed7b54a2/
          items"
        },
        "data": [
          {
            "type": "items",
            "id": "2d831aba-75bb-48b6-bae6-9f1bb613d29b"
          },
          {
            "type": "items",
            "id": "8217e21a-97db-4be9-9feb-4cea97a64948"
          }
        ]
      }
    }
  },
  "included": [
    {
      "id": "2d831aba-75bb-48b6-bae6-9f1bb613d29b",
      "type": "items",
      "links": {
        "self": "http://localhost:5001/v1/items/2d831aba-75bb-48b6-bae6-9f1bb613d29b"
      },
      "attributes": {
        "item_id": "2d831aba-75bb-48b6-bae6-9f1bb613d29b",
        "quantity": 1,
        "price": 1299
      }
    },
    {
      "id": "8217e21a-97db-4be9-9feb-4cea97a64948",
      "type": "items",
      "links": {
```

```
      "self": "http://localhost:5001/v1/items/8217e21a-97db-4be9-9feb-4cea97a64948"
    },
    "attributes": {
      "item_id": "8217e21a-97db-4be9-9feb-4cea97a64948",
      "quantity": 1,
      "price": 319
    }
  }
 ]
}
```

As you can see, the second response is much richer; it contains information about the two items currently included in the cart, so we'll definitely use that in our cart page. The main advantage of this approach is that we can use the same endpoint in both use cases—cart widget and cart page—but still have a faster response time in the case where we need less data, avoiding sending unnecessary data over the wire and making fewer database calls to provide a response in the service, thus improving overall system performance.

Back to the showcase application, where we define a new helper method to load that information.

An interesting feature supported by the JSON API specification is called *sparse fieldsets* (http://jsonapi.org/format/#fetching-sparse-fieldsets), which allow a client to request that an endpoint return only specific fields in the response on a per-type basis by including a fields parameter. Sparse fieldsets can be useful in responses that may return a large number of attributes by default, where clients may gain performance by specifying only the attributes they are interested in. For example, if we had code that needed only the current value in dollars of a cart, we could use the client gem to load only that attribute by calling ApiClient::Purchases::Cart.select(:total).find(..), which would make the following service call:

GET http://localhost:5001/v1/carts/35c082ba-b974-4d78-9526-4fc6ed7b54a2?fields[carts]=total

and would generate this response:

```
{
  "data": {
    "id": "35c082ba-b974-4d78-9526-4fc6ed7b54a2",
    "type": "carts",
    "links": {
      "self": "http://localhost:5001/v1/carts/35c082ba-b974-4d78-9526-4fc6ed7b54a2"
    },
    "attributes": {
      "total": 1618
    }
  }
}
```

Exercises for You

As we mentioned at the beginning of the chapter, we've just scratched the surface of functionality that can be built for our bookstore, and we have some ideas about what could be done next. We'll list a couple of services that you could spend some time implementing, if that sounds like something interesting to you. One of the great things about it is that you can use whatever programming language/environment you're most comfortable with.

An obviously missing piece is a user service, responsible for storing and managing data associated with the users of the bookstore. A user should be able to, among many things, register an account and log in, save books to a wish list, "like" book categories, see his or her own—and others'—wish lists, and follow other users. Based on those quick requirements, some of the endpoints we would want to see implemented are:

- User CRUD
  - name, email, password (hash), ID, books_in_wishlist, categories
- Add liked category: `[user_token, category_id]` -> `[user_id, category_id]`
- Remove liked category: `[user_token, category_id]` -> 204
- Get all liked categories: `[user_token]` -> `[category_id1, category_id2, …]`
- Add to wish list: `[user_token, book_id]` -> `[user_id, book_id]`
- Remove from wish list: `[user_token, book_id]` -> 204
- Get all books on wish list: `[user_token]` -> `[book_id1, book_id2, …]`
- Follow a user: `[user_token, user_id]` -> `[user_id, user_id]`
- Unfollow a user: `[user_token, user_id]` -> 204
- Get users I followed: `[user_token]` -> `[user1, user2, ...]`
- Get users that follow me: `[user_token]` -> `[user1, user2, ...]`

We also mentioned that the home page would eventually evolve and benefit a lot from showing books that match the logged-in user; a recommendations service would be a very welcome addition to our microservices architecture. That service would probably feed from user-service, since it will have quite a bit of information about users, as well as purchases-service, which has data about what books have been purchased, or are currently in the cart. To make its API very simple, the service could have a single endpoint that, given a user_id, returns a book_id list as recommendations.

Service Orchestration

You probably have noticed that a lot of the service-related code in the showcase front-end application is actually simple, because it has to make fairly simple service calls in many places; you can imagine that this can get complicated, and some service calls depend on the results of other calls, which can introduce complexities at the front-end layer that may be better suited elsewhere. To help simplify some of that complexity, we recommend using a Back-end for Front-end (BFF) service, briefly introduced in Chapter 7, which would be a service that knows exactly what data the front-end needs to render its pages and would be responsible for fetching that data from many different clients. A practical example of that is the home page, which makes multiple service calls to many services. The code in showcase could be simplified if it could

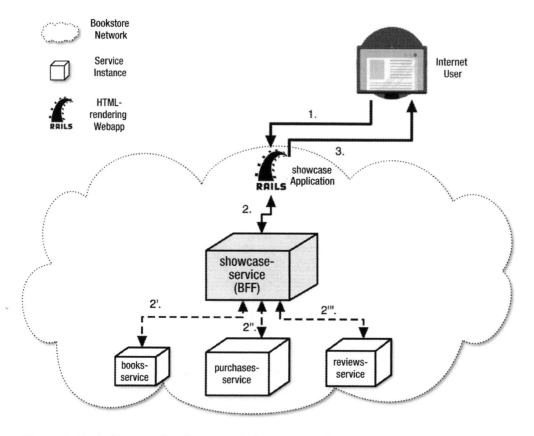

Figure 12-10. *Architecture of application with* showcase-service *in place*

make a call to a showcase-service, which would be responsible for orchestrating calls to multiple services, and properly deal with error conditions there. Figure 12-10 diagrams this approach.

We have described most of the service interactions of this chapter with the web front-end in mind, but most applications have multiple client-facing applications from the start nowadays, which would be mobile iOS and Android applications. In the case of mobile applications, we really recommend the use of a BFF— let's call it mobile-service, because your product and service will evolve; and unlike a web application that has only one version deployed at any time, you will always have a population of users who will not upgrade your application to the latest and will get stuck making calls to APIs that you may want to change, and even deprecate.

Performance Considerations

We have deliberately mentioned performance in this chapter only briefly; we touched on some aspects that will make your application faster, such as sparse fieldsets and using a cache to reduce the number of service calls. We believe that all services should be fairly fast, and that performance will only be a serious problem when you start having slow service responses; so we recommend that you keep an eye on each service's response times to easily identify which service is slow so that you can fix it. A microservices architecture is not an excuse for having poor performance. We believe that it is actually the opposite; if you have very specific performance requirements, you can build services that will be responsible for reaching those numbers. We will go into detail about monitoring in the next chapter, so you can find out which dependencies are slow or slower, and how to get alerted.

A very efficient technique for speeding up calls to distributed services is to make parallel service calls whenever possible. For example, we know that on the book page, we'd need to make calls to load the book details, the list of categories, and the shopping cart; we could make those three service calls at the same time, and our application's overall response time would benefit as a whole. Some programming languages make it easy—or hard—to work with threads, so your programming environment of choice may make this trivial—or not.

Summary

In this chapter, we dove into our sample project; that is, a bookstore with a client-facing web application that makes requests to a set of four services in order to display book information, and has a simple but working shopping cart. We went into detail showing code in multiple layers to give you a sense of how all the pieces fit together, and left a set of possible enhancements as exercises for the more adventurous. We hope we gave you some extra reasons to choose a standard for your APIs, as we've demonstrated a few nifty features included in the JSON API specification.

In the next chapter, we will describe the what and how of service monitoring, to help you figure out when your services are misbehaving.

CHAPTER 13

Monitoring Your Services

As you've seen throughout this book, embracing a microservices architecture will mean that your production environment has a large number of deployable units, which you will be ultimately responsible for making sure are functioning as expected, based on your requirements. As with any type of software, you will want to know when issues are happening, ideally before they start to affect your company's business metrics, such as user visits, signups, or sales. In some cases, it could take hours—or days—to find out that one small piece of software is malfunctioning, and you don't want to discover production issues after your users do.

It is extremely important that you set up a well-tuned monitoring toolset to alarm you and your team when services are misbehaving. You should spend a significant amount of time thinking about failures modes, and make it easy to integrate new services into your monitoring and alarming system.

Monitor All Services

We start this section with a rule: "Every single service in your environment needs to be monitored; no exceptions. Yes, even that one service that was built months ago, and only get 10 requests per day."

The only things we can monitor are the ones we measure. In general, this is an area where you should err on the side of collecting more metrics than you are actually using; it's much better than the alternative.

Some of the tools we have recently used for monitoring are these:

- **StatsD:** A network daemon that listens and collects statistics and sends aggregates to many pluggable back-end services. It allows for very fast metric collection in a simple way. You can tell StatsD to count or time any metric you're interested in, and it will save that data for you.

- **Graphite:** Graphite is a visualization tool for statistics configured from various sources. You can create customizable reports and dashboards, and it is one of the preferred front-ends for StatsD. Graphite is where you go to see and analyze—hopefully pretty—graphs, based on the data you push to it. Our former colleague Matt Aimonetti has a very thorough blog post about the subject, titled "Practical Guide to StatsD/Graphite Monitoring" (https://matt.aimonetti.net/posts/2013/06/26/practical-guide-to-graphite-monitoring/).

- **New Relic APM:** Application monitoring in one place allows you to see your application performance trends at a glance. You need an application-monitoring platform that is closely tied to your programming environment and can help with finding the root cause of slowdowns/outages. Among many things, tools like New Relic APM help pinpoint parts of the code that are slow, database queries that are not optimized, and endpoints that are returning errors.

© Cloves Carneiro Jr. and Tim Schmelmer 2016
C. Carneiro Jr. and T. Schmelmer, *Microservices From Day One*, DOI 10.1007/978-1-4842-1937-9_13

- **PagerDuty:** PagerDuty's incident resolution platform sits between your monitoring tools and your on-call responders to make sure your incidents are resolved quickly and efficiently. PagerDuty is the tool that notifies individuals/teams when an error condition has arisen; it allows teams to setup rotations, and notifies its users via a large set of media, such as email, SMS, or phone calls.

Some monitoring tools have a narrow responsibility, and only help with collecting metrics; other tools are more comprehensive, and can also be used for logging and/or alarming, which we will cover later in this chapter.

What Do You Need to Monitor?

We want services that are available, aka "up and running." The first thing you should make sure is that your services are indeed reachable from their clients, be they inside or outside your network. A simple way to monitor that a service is available is to hit a health-check endpoint, which is usually responsible for hitting whatever data store it uses and replying with a simple response.

We want services that are efficient and respond to requests in a correct and timely fashion. In this case, "correct" means that service responses look like what you have promised to the outside world in all cases. We touched on how to validate that service responses do abide by their contract in Chapter 9. It's hard to define the exact meaning of "timely fashion," but it's imperative that it's something that will not hurt your end-user experience.

In a 2006 talk at Stanford University, Greg Linden, from Amazon, said that "every 100 ms delay costs 1% of sales" on the eCommerce juggernaut's site,[1] which can also be read as "you sell more by being fast." In reality, end-users want an experience that is fast, and a UI that is snappy; it's known that site speed even affects how Google ranks search results (`https://googlewebmastercentral.blogspot.com/2010/04/using-site-speed-in-web-search-ranking.html`), so being performance-oriented in a good thing. As your company grows, we recommend having a small team that specializes in fixing performance issues, so that you end up with fast services and have a set of performance-oriented principles specific to your environment.

Focus on Perceived Performance

We recommend special attention to *perceived* performance in your monitoring. Perceived performance is a measure of how quick a user thinks an action is. The usual example of perceived performance is that a user can think that a web site is fast because of how it renders a page, or how soon he can interact with the site; the real important metric is user perception. Another type of perceived performance metric is how fast clients of your service think you are; a classic example is of one client that claims that a service is responding in 150msec, while the service maintainers claims that the exact request renders a response in 20msec. it's possible that both are right! By monitoring perceived performance, you can see such discrepancies in performance numbers that can lead you to investigate and find that, for example:

- There is too much latency in the network call between clients and servers.

- Or communication is happening using SSL connections inside a private subnet.

- Or the client library used for accessing the service has a performance bottleneck caused by an inefficient JSON/XML parser.

---

[1]"Make Data Useful," Greg Linden, November 29, 2006; Presentation at Stanford University; `https://docs.google.com/viewer?a=v&pid=sites&srcid=ZGVmYXVsdGRvbWFpbnxnbGluZGVufGd4OjVmZDIzMWMzMGI4MDc3OWM`

The bottom line is that being able to see that perceived performance is slower than expected will lead you to spend time investigating the reason for such disparity. However, don't go crazy and make one single data service endpoint extremely fast; it could be that saving 20 msec of response time—which can be an impressive and fun accomplishment—isn't helping your overall perceived performance if your web site that renders that data is extremely slow because of other web assets, such as JavaScript and CSS So you should know what battles are worth getting into.

Adhere to SLAs

Define service-level agreements (SLAs) for every single service endpoint in your environment.

> *A service-level agreement (SLA) is a part of a standardized service contract where a service is formally defined. Particular aspects of the service – scope, quality, responsibilities – are agreed between the service provider and the service user.* [2]

In practical terms, an SLA for a specific endpoint will list some of the following service expectations:

- Throughput for the endpoint
- Number of concurrent clients
- Average response time
- 90th percentile response time
- 95th percentile response time
- Uptime, availability, and any other nonfunctional requirements

After you have SLAs in places for all your services, you can start to leverage that data in many ways:

- If you're building a new service that will have four downstream dependencies you need to call sequentially, and each of those dependencies has an average response time of 100msec, then it's unlikely that the new service can deliver requests averaging less than 400msec of response time; you can derive SLAs based on your dependencies.

- If you're designing a service that needs to deliver response times much faster than your SLAs currently guarantee, you know that you may need to introduce new components to your infrastructure to hit the performance numbers you are aiming for.

One advantage of having SLAs is that they will help you set up your alarming because you will have data points for what is acceptable and what isn't. More importantly, they help to set expectations for the clients of a service, as well as for the service owners' level of support.

Business Metrics Are Important

There is a tendency among software professionals to focus on technical metrics, which is not a bad thing; but every organization needs to keep an eye on important business metrics, as it allows the organization to also find out about issues that went otherwise unnoticed.

---

[2] "Service-level agreement," Wikipedia, referenced on August 27, 2016. https://en.wikipedia.org/wiki/Service-level_agreement

An example of an error condition that can happen in any web application is having a login page that no longer works because of a JavaScript issue, or even a missing Login button. From a systems perspective, all involved systems—web application, authentication and authorization service—could be working as expected, and are looking functional in all their own monitoring graphs; however, there's a clear issue happening. If you have a business metric called "sign-ins," you can set that up to alarm after there are no sign-ins for a specified time, alerting you that something is not working as expected even when all services are working properly.

AN IMPORTANT BUSINESS METRIC

The most famous business metric at Amazon is the order rate of the retail site. Amazon has good enough tracking about its order rate—orders per second—that it predicts for any point in time that the order rate has to be within a calculated threshold; it will alarm—and wake up—developers in many teams when the order rate drops below the threshold. Whenever that happens, it is expected that specific teams have had their own alarms go off to help pinpoint where in the order processing chain a failure may be happening.

Examples of failures that would make the order rate drop significantly could be issues in the services that authenticate users or in the payment processing service. While the order rate alarms will certainly fire in these situations, it should certainly be the responsibility of the teams owning the primary (authentication or payments processing) services to be alerted of issues in their systems long before sales on the site are affected.

Identifying Requests

Your toolset has to make sure that a globally unique ID identifies each request so that you can track requests as they travel in your infrastructure; we recommend you always use UUIDs. We'll call those "request IDs" for now; they need to have the following characteristics:

- Unique across all applications and services
- Easy to create, forward, and log
- Easy to trace

Some modern web application frameworks already generate unique request IDs per end-user request; thus, you have to make sure that, once generated, the request ID is forwarded to all underlying services so that one of them can load all the internal requests generated by a specific request. Having such a tool will help you pinpoint issues when nobody is sure what system is failing; you should be able to trace a request through all your system easily. You also need to make sure you can attach that request ID to requests you make to external APIs, so that those are also traceable during debugging.

For example, a request that goes from our bookstore sample project for order processing will pass through the web application, the books service, and then to purchase/payment services, and will likely be forwarded to one external API for payment processing; there are quite a few players involved in making sure that the purchase experience goes smoothly, and the last thing you want to do is to make guesses when orders are not functional.

Logging All Requests

Having a unique and traceable request ID is only the first half of being able to investigate issues in a distributed environment. You also need to make sure every single request in your environment is saved to a log file, and that each one of those log files is easily accessible. Using the right tools and defining a common log format can help with this effort.

Logging Tools

As you set up your infrastructure, it's probably easy to look at raw log files using simple command-line tools like grep; but, as your infrastructure grows, you should use a more sophisticated tool for log inspection. Here are some tools you can use to search your log files:

- **Splunk:** Splunk captures, indexes, and correlates data (usually logs) in a searchable repository from which it can generate graphs, reports, alerts, dashboards and visualizations.

- **Logstash:** A modern tool for managing events and logs, with an ElasticSearch back-end which allows a high degree of searching and filtering.

- **Kibana:** A modern, beautiful visualization tool that works seamlessly with Logstash and ElasticSearch. It features a no-code setup, real-time analytics, and much more.

- **Amazon CloudWatch Logs:** CloudWatch Logs can be used to monitor your logs for specific phrases, values, or patterns. For example, you could set an alarm on the number of errors that occur in your system logs or view graphs of web request latencies from your application logs.

We've discussed in previous chapters that in a distributed environment, it's crucial to write code that properly deals with downstream dependencies being unavailable or timing out. It's important that code handling error conditions writes to logs for every single error encountered, whether a timeout or a service error. Once you have log entries that indicate that a service is down, you can use log analysis tools to alarm based on log entries; many tools on the market, including the ones listed above, support that.

Defining a Uniform Log Format

The data you include in your log files should follow a uniform format to allow easy parsing by your tools. You should also have standards for what you decide to log; ideally, each request should have at least two entries in your log format, the first when a request reaches a service, and another after a request is being processed. You can also log more data, especially when this extra data may become valuable information for debugging purposes.

To illustrate this further, let's look at a few log entries that were generated by a single request to our product catalog service:

```
I, [2015-12-28T01:31:14.322076 #24041]  INFO -- : Started request_method="GET"
request_url="/offers/deal-1542454.json" request_time="2015-12-28 01:31:14 +0000"
request_ip="172.17.4.48" HTTP_CLIENT_IP="172.17.4.93" HTTP_X_FORWARDED_FOR="172.17.1.102,
172.17.4.93" HTTP_USER_AGENT="Ruby/ls-catalog/v6.2.1" HTTP_X_LIVINGSOCIAL_API_CLIENT_
NAME="mobile_production" HTTP_IMPRINTID="e9f8bb4a-41e0-4d87-982b-78f1f3eb3668"
HTTP_TRUE_CLIENT_IP="172.17.4.93" HTTP_X_REQUEST_START="t=1451266274269000"
representation="deal_large"process_pid=24041 request_id=e9f8bb4a-41e0-4d87-982b-
78f1f3eb3668
```

```
I, [2015-12-28T01:31:14.325896 #24041]  INFO -- : method=GET path=/offers/deal-1542454.json
format=json controller=offers action=show status=200 duration=5.39 view=0.13
db=0.64 time="2015-12-28 01:31:14 +0000" client_name=mobile_production process_pid=24041
request_id=e9f8bb4a-41e0-4d87-982b-78f1f3eb3668
I, [2015-12-28T01:31:14.326133 #24041]  INFO -- : debug_value="something important"
process_pid=24041 request_id=e9f8bb4a-41e0-4d87-982b-78f1f3eb3668
```

First, note that all three log entries here share the same process ID (24041), which indicates that they were produced by the same application service process. Next, you can see that the request_id UUID values also match on all entries, which denotes that all three log messages were produced during the processing of the same client request cycle. All three messages also carry increasing microsecond-based timestamps (2015-12-28T01:31:14.322076, and so on), which proves that they were processed in the order they are listed in the log file.

The main difference between the three messages is the event that generated them: the first message logs the arrival of a request (alongside many interesting properties of the requesting client), and the second message provides info at the end of the request cycle (including response codes and processing time), while the final message simply logs additional debugging information.

Note that all information is given in a key=value format, which makes automated post-processing of this information with log analysis tools much simpler.

Reading Metrics

Now that you are measuring as many metrics as possible, you have to be aware of how you view and interpret those numbers. We've all read our share of dubious statistics-based articles in our social network feed; I'm sorry to say that the metrics we collect do sometimes tell a similar story.

Averages Lie

A common mistake that is made is to look at—and rely on—average response times for monitoring overall service performance. Average response time is a "convenience metric" that gauges overall response time as if it were very linear. Averages can convey a wrong one-dimensional number that doesn't really take into account outliers, and they only paint an accurate picture of overall system health if your response times follow a normal distribution, which is rarely the case with services.

AVERAGES HIDE OUTLIERS

The main user-facing web application at LivingSocial receives up to 20K requests per minute during peak time, showing average response time for all requests and endpoints usually below 200msec, which seems to be decent performance for most cases. However, when you look at some endpoints, it's easy to find that endpoints with low usage average terrible response times, sometimes above 2 seconds, just at the web server layer. It's almost impossible for a terribly implemented endpoint to make a dent in overall average response time in such an environment. Some monitoring tools default to showing overall response time, which doesn't really tie into any single change that gets deployed, making it really easy to hide endpoints with suboptimal performance.

An Endpoint Tells Many Stories

Another mistake we have seen often is to judge an endpoint's performance by averaging all requests to that endpoint in one single metric. This particularly applies to endpoints that perform some sort of search, and possibly return a variable number of records, based on an API input. It's possible that one caller of an endpoint usually requests 100 records to be returned; so, if you have endpoints whose performance can vary greatly based on caller parameters, it may make sense to have metrics based on those parameters.

In general, developers should default to looking at data for the 95th or 99th percentile, which will give you numbers for the worst 5% or 1% of your responses, which is where performance is at its worst and where gains can be made most consistently.

A major advantage of looking at the 95th or 99th percentile is that you will be able to recognize potential performance problems before they happen system-wide. If you have an issue with a downstream dependency that is causing your average response time to degrade, then it's usually too late to prevent some sort of service degradation or even an outage; however, if you start getting alerted as soon as a small percentage of requests goes above your SLA threshold, then you're more likely to solve that issue before it causes serious damage.

Look into Your Slowest Responses

Even when services are functioning well, and have response times you are proud of, you can still learn about how your services work, and find potential performance issues by paying attention to your slowest responses. A very slow response can showcase a lot of potential issues:

- Possible database contention at specific times of the day may cause a slow response due to a slower than usual query.

- Excessive object allocations may make garbage collection kick in at unexpected times.

- There may be new data access or creation patterns that your service was not designed for (for example, because of a change in business strategy that exposes the service to clients with very different data access patterns).

- There may be a slow response from a downstream dependency, which could itself need to be fixed. Remember that a service response can't possibly be faster than its dependencies.

Sometimes you can see that a specific use case of your service can't possibly be efficient within the constraints of your current design; it may require extra joins or do a lot of in-memory calculation, among other things. A really slow service response could be a "design smell"; it may show that a specific use case would be better served by a new endpoint, or even a dedicated service altogether.

FIXING PERFORMANCE WITH SLOW REQUESTS

In a well-performing service we run at LivingSocial, we were seeing occasional responses taking above 1 second to respond. That service had one client—out of 20+—that needed a response with hundreds and sometimes thousands of objects in its body. We knew that those requests were supposed to be slow most of the time, and never questioned the slowness. The requests happened in a cron job, so they impacted nobody; but they kept appearing in our "slowest responses" report, so we decided to take a quick look into them one day. To our surprise, 80% of the processing time for those responses was happening building the JSON string to be returned as a response, which was a bit of a surprise because we were expecting to see most of the time spent in the database. That service used a series of JSON templates based on a templating language we had assumed was fast enough for our use cases; however, that high number made us look into its performance in more detail. After some experimentation, we decided to get rid of that templating language and used a much simpler solution that saved us 15–30% in performance in all requests, even the ones that were already fast enough.

Adjusting Alarms

At this point, you have started to collect metrics about your services and hosts, and have defined a set of SLAs that you need to deliver on. It's time you start to send alarms to your team when something goes wrong. Most modern alarming tools allow their users to pick their preferred method of paging, whether it's email, SMS, or phone call, so make sure you use a flexible tool. You can issue alarms under many circumstances:

- Whenever an error happens (any response with a 500 status)

- Response time exceeds the SLAs, or even better, response time is getting close to exceeding your SLAs

- While still meeting its SLAs, a service sees a significant change in response time (for example, more than 1 standard deviation over the past 5 minutes)

- One of the business metrics is beyond its acceptable threshold

After you start sending out alarms, someone will have to wake up and fix slow or broken services or hosts. In a well-run microservices architecture, an alarm will notify a developer—or ops person—who will log into their terminal and start to look into the reported incident. Being notified of a live issue is stressful enough that you want to make sure that:

- You alarm for a good reason. If you alarm—and wake people up—too often, you will create an army of co-workers who will learn to ignore those alarms.

- Thresholds are easily configurable. If you just alarmed someone for a questionable reason, make sure the alarm can be tweaked so that it's only happening when attention is really required. A team should define threshold for alarming based on the SLAs of the services they support, and tweak those SLAs according to how their service is performing.

- Alarms should help with resolution. As a company grows, the number of services grows with it, and you reach a point where not all developers know all services really well. Add a link to an operations manual that is kept up to date, as part of the alarm text, and to an operations dashboard that helps with investigating root cause of issues, and you will make everyone's life much easier. An efficient operations manual should include details about the failing service, links to dashboard/graphs that may help with solving the issue, and description of the possible cases that can lead to failure, along with the preferred solution.

Setting up alarming in a distributed environment is an art, and it will take many tries and constant tweaks to reach a point where a team is confident that a system is always up and performing as expected.

Summary

In this chapter we first looked at tools and guidelines to monitor the important parts of your microservices infrastructure. We clarified that the useful monitoring focuses on performance as it is perceived by the service client, supporting the adherence to published SLAs and measurement of business metrics.

Next, we examined analysis tools and important properties of service logs, explaining the importance of unified, machine-readable formatting to help monitoring and log-based alarming.

We gave tips about correctly interpreting the metrics, explaining the problems with relying on averages and why it is wise to start any investigations by looking at the slowest service responses.

Finally, we laid out guidelines for adjusting the sensitivity for alarms generated from monitoring information.

The next and final chapter examines tools and processes to help with achieving excellence in supporting and maintaining your services through their lifespan.

■ ■ ■ ■

## CHAPTER 14

Operational Excellence with Microservices

Successfully developed and launched software spends the vast majority of its lifecycle in a state where it needs maintenance and support. In an environment where the number of services can easily outnumber the number of developers in your engineering organization, it is business-critical that operational support runs efficiently and effectively, without impacting the productivity and retention of your engineering staff.

This chapter will look at the processes and some of the available tools to help with achieving excellence in supporting your services. We will intersperse the discussion and recommendations with examples to underline the lessons learned from our experience of being on-call for many years.

What is Operational Support?

Let's first define what we understand by operational support.

To us these are all activities that are aimed at supporting the functioning of an already launched service or feature according to the expectations—explicitly and implicitly stated—of the clients.

Implicitly stated expectations are requirements that are common sense, but were not explicitly stated in any specifications of the service or feature. If, for example, a newly introduced API functions as designed, but it causes the service to degrade in stability, responsiveness, or correctness of other APIs or features, or it results in scaling issues under increased load, then these issues should be accounted for as operational support.

The activities included in operational support work can be rather wide-ranging. They include not just root cause analysis for, and fixing of, obvious bugs and errors reported by automated monitoring or client reports, but also general maintenance work related to library or service framework upgrades, adding missing documentation, proactive searching for potential security bugs or edge cases that have not been accounted for, and answering technical questions by the client team.

Embracing Ownership

One of the major advantages that many developers (ourselves included) report getting out of working in a well-functioning microservices environment is that they feel empowered by the level of autonomy given to them. The *"you build it, you run it"* approach leads to encouraging the team to feel like true owners of their domain, and hence also feel more like they own an actual part in the business as a whole. And along with the feeling of true ownership comes a feeling of responsibility that needs embracing; your new-found autonomy means that the buck stops with you, as well.

© Cloves Carneiro Jr. and Tim Schmelmer 2016
C. Carneiro Jr. and T. Schmelmer, *Microservices From Day One*, DOI 10.1007/978-1-4842-1937-9_14

Customers First

The first rule of business you should embrace is that if you don't add value for your customers, then your business is doomed to failure. The best teams have it engrained in their culture to settle situations of disagreement and conflict asking themselves this question:

What is the best thing to do for our customers?

If you have this mindset, then not only will decisions be easier to make, but you will also elevate the discussion of disagreements to a level where the egos of the people on your team are easier to extract from making business-savvy decisions. The focus will be on designing services for usability and solving real problems and thereby adding maximum business value.

Is the Customer Always Right?

Note that we intentionally did *not* phrase the question as "What does the customers say they want?" The question we did ask, about what is best for the customer, means that you should make sure you understand what the customer is trying to achieve, balancing the mission and architectural constraints of the services you own against the requests.

As an example, if a client team asked the books-service team to vend all books sold in the US, sorted by revenue in the shop, then the owners of the books-service should figure out whether such an API can be reasonably exposed in an efficient manner. At the very least, the service team should try to understand the constraints in which they can operate. Will the API really need to vend *all* books in the US? What would the client do with this data? Can the information be paged? Is there room for staleness in the revenue numbers by which to sort, or in the list of books? What is the anticipated call volume?

Only then can the service team make educated decisions about how best to serve the needs of this particular client, and also implement such an API without impacting other clients and overall system stability and responsiveness.

Operational Support Benefits Customer Trust

Many companies spent a lot of money on acquiring new customers. But how much budget does your business dedicate to keeping the customers you have happy and engaged?

A big factor in repeat business from your clients is how well you manage to establish and maintain their trust. But customer trust is hard to earn, and it is easily lost when you disappoint the clients' expectations. That is exactly where operational support comes in: it is all about making sure that your service maintains client expectations. Therefore, investing in operational support is an investment in customer trust.

Making sure all systems are operational is not just contributing in the obvious and direct way, for example, by enabling your customers to make purchases on your site, or to sign up for your services. It is also an investment in keeping current customers' trust that the site will be up, running, and behaving as they expect when they visit it.

It is much harder to regain a customer's trust after it was lost due to a bad experience, and the money and time you've spent on acquiring the client in the first place is wasted. When a judgment call needs to be made between allocating developers to implementing new features and fixing already launched functionality, then a monetary value needs to be attached to the estimated loss of customer trust incurred per day of broken functionality, and it needs to be factored into the prioritization process.

For that reason, in the majority of successful businesses we have worked for, addressing operational issues always outranked new projects or feature work. When an outage arises and is noticed in a service that has launched, then this underlying issue should best be seen as a use case that was missed during development. It is just seen as though the launched feature is not entirely finished and hence needs fixing first before any new functionality is released.

No Code without an Owning Team

There should be absolutely no line of code (or whatever unit of software is run in the infrastructure) for which it is unclear who owns the maintenance and support issues.

Another very important point in this context is that software ownership is never assigned to a single person. Every service is owned by a team of people, and they share all ownership privileges and responsibilities. That does not mean that you cannot have subject matter experts in your team; in fact, you probably want to encourage developers to dive as deeply as they would like into the services they own.

It just means that shared ownership reduces the risk for the team, and the company as a whole, that all expert knowledge about a service in your system would depart with the single owner. Sharing ownership and knowledge in a team also sets up the team to support several services via an on-call rotation, the details of which we will discuss later in this chapter.

Any team can of course own several services, and in a microservices environment where the number of deployment units is often a multiple of the number of team members this is in fact the only practical approach.[1] Therefore make sure that the team knows and documents exactly at each point in time which services, applications, libraries, and/or third-party software packages they own and maintain.

Keeping such complete and up-to-date mappings of software-to-team can be implemented and enforced in different ways. Your code control system could make sure that code repositories need to be owned by an existing team, and your deployment infrastructure scripts could check that an ownership field is present and validate its value with an up-to-date list of teams. To advertise the team-to-software details, you could introduce a simple, well-known engineering-wide documentation page, or a web UI on top of an ownership database, or even an actual service discovery registry in your microservices infrastructure.

The most important part is that maintaining such a mapping is universally accepted as part of your engineering team culture. Such acceptance and visibility needs to go so far that plans for engineering-internal team reorganizations always include a line item that makes sure that, after the reorganization, all software systems have a new owning team. If reorganizations do not include reassigning the services owned by disbanded teams, then you will end up with unowned but live systems, which therefore will become unsupported and hence are an accident waiting to happen.

Finally, avoid set-ups where some software is tagged to be owned by multiple teams. We have never seen such cross-team ownership arrangements work out well, as in practice such shared responsibility leads to confusion and often ultimately leads to no team feeling responsible for services that are officially of shared ownership.

Boosting Team Cohesion

Working on operational support for the services they own as a team is essential for embracing true ownership as part of the team's culture. In a "you build it, you run it" environment, the team soon realizes that the systems they create spend the vast majority of their lifecycle in production and needing operational support; implementing and launching services is only a minute episode in the existence of a successful software application.

Organizing all the team's activities and practices around making the software it owns easy and efficient to maintain becomes an objective that is in the team's self-interest. This way, the team's interests are well aligned with the clients' interests, and—by extension—those of the entire business.

---

[1] While it is very hard to give meaningful guidance about optimal team sizes or the best number of services per team developer, in our experience the sweet spot most successful microservices companies choose is between 5 and 8 developers per team. If automation is advanced in an organization, then the ratio of microservices per team member (or developer) does not have a clear upper bound. Running multiple services per developer is definitely possible if development and deployment processes are streamlined.

Another team-internal practice that helps team cohesion and the happiness of engaged and curious developers is to rotate team members through the feature development projects for all the software owned by the team. As mentioned above, there surely are advantages of having subject matter experts for each service, but allowing them to work on other services owned by the team can be a cost-effective risk reduction strategy.

The team will be able to shake the dangerous reliance on individual "heroes," thereby mitigating the risk of time-intensive research and coming up-to-speed of other team members when the hero leaves the team. In short: the real heroes share their special powers to enable others to rely less and less on them.

When team members start working on services they previously did not engage with, there is great potential for cross-pollination: they see how things are done in a different code base, and so might recognize patterns that can be applied to the service in which they usually work. Conversely, having a new set of eyes on an existing service might contribute ideas about how to handle tricky problems or inelegant solutions in an improved way.

An advantage of rotating team members during feature development that applies directly to the team's operational support efforts is that all team members become more familiar with the entire set of services the team owns. As a consequence, they usually also become more comfortable with being on-call for the full set of systems owned.

Our final advice regarding ownership and team cohesion is to avoid placing developers in a position where they straddle multiple teams at the same time.

This does not mean that we advise against loaning team members out to other teams; loaning is especially useful when a project in the developer's home team is blocked by missing functionalities in a service dependency that is owned by a team is not staffed to dedicate time to implementing such feature.

In our experience it is simply not advisable to expect the developer who is on loan to another team in such situations to still fulfill responsibilities on the home team. When someone is on loan, she will be truly and fully embedded in the team to which she is on loan. This way, the loaned-out developer has enough time to focus on the task and give the members of her temporary team time to gain confidence that the code contributed by the embedded person can be maintained and supported by the receiving team.

What It Means to Be On-Call

In order for a team to implement operational support effectively and efficiently for the systems it owns, a (set of) developer team member(s) need(s) to be nominated and act as the point person(s) for addressing any and all support issues.

This role is usually referred to as being *on call*, and this section will explain the responsibilities and privileges of the person filling it. We will lay out an etiquette and code of conduct to be followed by the on-call person herself, as well as by the rest of the team and the organization in which they work.

While many of the points mentioned in the next section are applicable regardless of the architecture that is chosen for the overall business application, we will conclude this section by touching on some points that are particularly important to on-calls supporting microservices architectures.

Defining the Role and Process for Being On-Call

The most succinct, to-the-point definition of the role of an on-call developer comes from a presentation our former colleague Jon Daniel delivered at the 2015 DevOpsDays in Pittsburgh:[2]

> *The on-call's role is to react to failure and prevent catastrophe.*

---

[2]Jon Daniel, "Ethical and Sustainable On-Call," August 13 2015, DevOpsDays Pittsburgh; An overview of Jon's inspirational talk, including slides and a link to a video recording of the talk, can be found on his personal blog at: `https://chronicbuildfailure.co/ethical-and-sustainable-on-call-c0075e03a7b`

This accurately summarizes the priorities of the person in charge of supporting a team's production-deployed systems. First and foremost, the on-call person needs to make sure that new and current failure situations are addressed as they are ongoing, all with the overarching goal of preventing even greater impact through a potential total outage.

Issue Receipt and Triage

The ways production issues are reported or noticed can differ greatly. Some are manually generated bug reports from colleagues. Others are created automatically, via integration of your monitoring and alarming systems with your ticketing system. Where such integration is lacking,[3] the on-call will have to manually create issues for tracking when aberrations become obvious from monitoring or alarming. Sometimes issues that are reported to the on-call are mere hunches about potentially faulty behavior, or requests for an in-depth analysis of the expected behavior under a given set of circumstances regarding one of the systems owned by the team.

In all such cases, the first step for an on-call is to make sure a support ticket[4] for the issue exists; and if that is not the case, to create a ticket herself. It is essential that the team has a template for trouble tickets, with fields for minimally required information, such as "expected behavior," "observed behavior," "steps to reproduce the issue," and so on. This helps to cut down on avoidable back-and-forth communication attempting to clarify information the on-call needs to track down the issue, thereby leading to faster resolution of the problem.

Once a ticket is created, it needs to be triaged based on the severity of its impact, and prioritized in relation to other unresolved production issues. For that it is important that the team think about generalized rules for severity and priority assessment. We will discuss an example for such rules in the subsection "Defining and Advertising Team Policy" later in this chapter.

Note that in organizations where development happens against services that are deployed to a shared sandbox fabric, it is usually the policy that the team's on-call is also responsible for the proper functioning of the sandbox instance of the team's services. While it is of course a serious impediment for the organization if the development efforts for teams that depend on the affected sandbox instances are impeded, the on-call generally applies a lower priority to such issues than is applied to problems surfacing in production.

Deciding What Work to Pick Up

Once the issues are properly triaged, the on-call will always pick the top priority-item on the list to work on and resolve. If the on-call person ever gets into a situation where all trouble tickets are resolved, then most teams all have a backlog of items that serve operational improvements. Examples of such operational improvement backlogs are tasks to address missing documentation for some of the systems owned by the team, or to add additional metrics to the team's monitoring dashboard, or to fine-tune alarming rules. It is often also very useful to update the Standard Operating Procedure (SOP) documentation for the team's services when new approaches to address recurring issues are discovered during the on-call's current duty. Often, the on-call will also be tasked with writing or following up on post-mortems for outages in which her team has stakes or was directly involved[5].

If the on-call still has spare cycles left to invest, they can often best be used to try to anticipate errors, hunt for issues that could arise in edge cases, delete unused code, or generally "kick the tires" of the application in use.

---

[3]Automatic ticket creation is hard to get right, as often this leads to many duplicated or similar trouble tickets that are rooted in the same underlying issue. An on-call person will then spend a lot of time on de-duplication and other unnecessary ticket management tasks.

[4]We will discuss properties of useful trouble ticketing system later in this chapter.

[5]We will talk in more detail in later subsections about dashboards, SOPs, and post-mortems.

Whatever the on-call person chooses to spend her time with, she should decidedly try to steer clear of signing up for feature development or necessary technical improvement work that is tracked in the team's sprint. In our experience, counting on the on-call to contribute to the team's project work will lead to suffering: the team cannot rely on the on-call person's availability for working on features, so they might over-promise features to representatives of the business-focused departments, which will lose trust in the team's ability to deliver on their promises. At the same time, the on-call person—feeling pressured to deliver features—runs the danger of dropping the ball on critical operational issues.

As a corollary, this means that the number of members in an on-call rotation (usually, the team size) should be large enough to support a dedicated on-call person, which in our experience means that it should include around five to eight developers.

On-Call People Increase Team Efficiency

If this approach of dedicating a person to operational issues meets resistance in your organization, then the arguments raised usually amount to not being able to afford a dedicated on-call person, given other business pressures. Our advice in such a situation is to raise awareness of the costs of neglecting operational emergencies. It is not a question *if* outages will happen, but only when they will hit you, and if you can afford to not be prepared and—as a consequence—lose business or customer trust.

Try to compare the decision to save on operational support to an "unhedged call option" for stocks, rather than using the usual metaphor of "technical debt"[6]: unhedged calls can cost an unpredictable amount of money should they be exercised, whereas debt is predictable and can be managed.

Another part of the on-call role is to defend the rest of the team from interruptions. By being dedicated to all interrupt-driven issues and distractions, the on-call person shields the rest of the team from being disrupted, thereby guarding their focus.

Very conclusive arguments can be made that dedicating a single person to working on all the unpredictable, highly disruptive and stressful tasks increase the team's overall productivity. Again, disruptions are a fact of life with technology, and even more so in an environment of distributed systems. Acknowledging this reality and preparing for the inevitable outage is a smart decision for every business to make.

The acting on-call person will act as the single point of contact for all operational and technical inquiry issues. Any other developer on the team should *only* be contacted and interrupted by the on-call person, and only if she deems it necessary (in cases where an urgent technical issues requires the knowledge or advice of another team member).

A Responsibility to Rest

In order to be successful in the role of acting as the team's firewall, it is the responsibility for the on-call person to be alert and focused while dealing with operational problems. In most around-the-clock businesses, on-call people will need to be able to tend to problems as they arise, any time of the day or night. For that reason, they usually carry a pager or similar device, on which they can be made aware of urgent issues 24 hours a day.

In order for the on-call person to stay awake at the wheel, she cannot be allowed to be sleep-deprived and worn out for longer than is required to take care of high-severity operational problems. As a result, it should be expected that the on-call person is entirely autonomous regarding her time management. In short, if the on-call person feels worn out and tired after a night of dealing with outages, then they should

---

[6]See Steve Freeman's blog post "Bad code isn't Technical Debt, it's an unhedged Call Option" (July 23 2010) for a more detailed explanation of this argument: http://higherorderlogic.com/2010/07/bad-code-isnt-technical-debt-its-an-unhedged-call-option/

feel obligated to sleep and relax during times with less trouble. During such times, the on-call should notify the secondary on-call person (whose role and responsibilities we will explain a little later) that he should step in when any urgent issues need addressing.

The On-Call Person in Relation to the Team

As laid out above, on-call duty play an important part in a development team that is also concerned with the operational aspects of the software they deliver. That is why investing thought into how to set up on-call duty for the team is valuable.

While being on-call means that you get exposure to a broad range of operational aspects of all services owned by the team, it can also be very distracting and stressful. So, in order to prevent developer burnout, make sure to establish a rotational assignment for on-call duty within your team. We have seen weekly rotations work best in practice, as shorter rotations impact effectiveness on follow-through of ongoing issues, while longer rotations easily can lead to loss of focus and fatigue.

It is important for team morale to include all team members in the rotation schedule. Make sure to respect the schedule and raise the expectation that it is important to integrate into planning. For example, make sure that, if your time-off overlaps with your on-call rotation slot, you trade slots with another team member before leaving.

Note that we also recommend including new team members and junior engineers into the rotation schedule as soon as possible. While it is natural that there are justified concerns from both the new or inexperienced team members and the more experienced ones that operational issues may not be addressed appropriately, new team members can always shadow the on-call person, or be a secondary on-call—a concept we explain more later. We have found this to be an excellent way to familiarize new team members quickly in a hands-on setting with the breadth of the systems that the team owns.

Another good tip we have is to make the on-call rotation overlap for an hour or so. This way, the previous on-call has time to walk through any operational issues still in flight, and the next on-call person is sure to hit the ground running.

While it is certainly true that the on-call people act as a protector of the team's productivity by being a single point of contact for all interruptions, they should definitely not hesitate to escalate issues to team members when they feel stuck or in need of assistance. They need to be made comfortable to use their best judgement about when investing more time to understand the issue has diminishing returns given the severity of the issue and the expected contribution from another team member who is considered the expert in the area affected by an issue at hand. Operational issues are another realm where pig-headed attempts at heroism are unwarranted, as they might hurt the business. It is much better to admit defeat early and learn from pairing with the expert on resolving the issue.

Asking team members for input is especially important during the triage phase. You want to make sure that the impact and severity assessment of an unfamiliar issue is correct. In teams with a dedicated Technical Project Manager (TPM), the on-call person can often direct questions about prioritization of work relating to operational issues to the TPM, in case there are competing high-severity issues to be addressed.

We have seen that it usually takes at most one full rotation of on-call duty through the team until the benefits become very obvious for everyone involved. Especially the team members that are alleviated from distractions by the on-call person come to really appreciate the role she takes on. They soon start to develop the necessary empathy for the person currently on call, and they will even start to excuse grumpiness and irritability caused by constant interruptions and operating in fire-fighting mode. Everyone knows that they will be on-call sooner or later, as well, and that they can expect empathy, as well.

ADVANTAGES OF A SECONDARY ON-CALL

Some teams set up on-call rotations with two developers, one acting as the *primary* on-call, and another the *secondary* on-call. While assigning two people to operational emergencies might seem uneconomical to many businesses at first, there are quite a few advantages to take into account when considering the cost-benefit ratio.

For one, the secondary on-call can often be used as a very effective on-boarding tool for new team members who might still need training. The services that their new team owns are still unfamiliar to them and researching and fixing bugs can often be a very practical and manageable way to get initial exposure.

Additionally, when secondary and primary on-call decide to pair on resolving operational issues, then the benefits are not perceived only by the secondary; many times just having four eyes and two brains dig into an issue leads to faster resolution or at least validation of trains of thought or design decisions.

The biggest benefit of identifying a secondary on-call person is most likely that he can act as a "human fail-over" for the primary. If you can set up your alarming system to escalate to the secondary on-call any critical items not acknowledged by the primary within, let's say, 15 minutes, then your business has implemented better risk mitigation for situations in which the primary on-call is unavailable (for example, when the pager fails to catch the primary on-call's attention).

As a practical tip, teams we were part of in the past have set up their on-call rotation schedules such that the secondary on-calls transition to being primary immediately following their secondary shift. This helps continuity and efficiency for situations in which addressing on-going operational issues span more than one on-call shift.

We have found having a secondary on-call person especially useful during a team's "tuning phase," during which not all services and applications have documented Standard Operating Procedures. Secondary on-calls can use their time taking down, and later publishing, notes about recurring tasks that the primary on-call performs to address operational tasks in the services owned by their team.

Secondary on-calls are also much more likely not to be fully occupied with operational work, so they *can* dedicate some of their time to feature development and other sprint goals. We still recommend officially not counting on contributions of secondary on-calls; under-committing and then over-delivering is still a better outcome than the alternative.

Being On-Call in a Microservices Environment

While it does not diminish their validity or importance in a microservices setting, any of the previous points about operational support apply more generally than just to microservices. This subsection addresses the finer points that are more directly focused on microservices.

Because of the extremely distributed nature of a microservices application, it is especially necessary to identify and document the list of all direct service dependencies. Outages of each of these dependencies not only need to be mitigated in the code, but they also need to be tracked, and potentially alarmed on, by teams owning dependent services.

For that reason, it is very handy for the team's on-call to have access to the on-call logs and ticket list for all services that the team's systems depend upon. Additionally, try to set up direct communication channels between team on-calls for related inquiries (for example, support chat rooms for well-known operations).

In the case of more widespread and impactful outages, it is advisable to spin up dedicated "war rooms," which can be used to coordinate efforts to resolve ongoing cross-team issues. Note that such war rooms should not be abused to ask for extensive or repeated status updates; while an issue is still "hot," no focus should be diverted from resolving it first. Status updates should be performed by the on-call person in charge, recorded alongside the ticket inside the ticketing system, and at a prenegotiated frequency (such as every 15 minutes, or even better, based on the issue's severity).

Another great trait for an on-call person to have is to be very suspicious and follow hunches. If the metrics graphs on the team's services dashboard just simply don't look right, or if a seemingly transient issue remains unexplained, then an on-call person is more often than not well advised to investigate such oddities; more than once in our careers have we seen "icebergs of problems" hiding beneath seemingly small irregularities, so resist the temptation to sweep issues under the rug.

In a good microservices architecture, failures are kept from propagating by introducing expectations for acceptable response times, error counts, or other sensible business metrics (like sales per hour, and so on.). A team's on-call person should be particularly wary of adapting alarm thresholds. Make sure to discuss any adaptations of alarming limits with the rest of the team and other potential stakeholders in your business. If your monitoring detects increased failures in services on which you depend, make sure you pass these issues on to the teams that own the dependencies. Insisting on having SLAs, and on adhering to them, is in everyone's interest, as ultimately they benefit the consumers of your business's application.

Tracking and Scheduling Operations Support Work

Even when microservices teams dedicate a (set of) developer(s) to operations support tasks, it is often unrealistic for all operational tasks to be resolved as part of an on-call duty; keeping the service up and running, or responding in adherence to its SLAs, simply outranks issues like version upgrades of frameworks used in the services.

A Lightweight Process Proposal

Whenever an operational issue arises that is estimated to take more time than a given low threshold (such as 15 minutes), a trouble ticket should be created. This guarantees visibility and traceability of operational support efforts. This means that reports can be run to identify the services that generate the most operational workload. Such visibility gives the team great input for prioritization efforts: a maintenance-intensive service can often easily justify refactoring work to fix the underlying issues that cause the frequent production issues.

Sometimes, when a team inherits a service that they did not develop themselves (for example, as a result of company department reorganization), they have a hard time answering requests or researching issues that relate to the correctness or expectations concerning the inherited service's behavior. Such situations should be taken seriously, and often the creation of a "research and document" ticket is appropriate.

When the tickets generated outnumber the tickets resolved during any given on-call rotation shift, the operational workload is carried forward. In that case, it is important that you have a trouble ticketing system in which to track all backlogged operational tasks. The tickets in the backlog need to be tagged with an assessed impact severity level (based on team or company policy).[7] Work on the tickets is generally guided by the SLAs associated with the tickets, but for tickets with similar resolution deadlines and severity, prioritization is handled ad hoc with input from other team members.

---

[7]The "Defining and advertising team policy" section later in this chapter lays out points to address in a policy for severity assessment and issue prioritization.

An important role in this could fall to a Technical Project Manager (TPM). A TPM is a person who acts as the interface between the business departments and the engineering team. The TPM is usually a very technically proficient person (such as a former software developer), who has acquired management skills and is also well informed about the business's current priorities and future direction. Both the technical and business skills are needed to coordinate the development team's day-to-day work priorities. The TPM should not just be aware of the team's project work, but should also have enough information to help clarify an on-call person's questions regarding the prioritization of trouble tickets.

In order to schedule work effectively in a microservices development team, it will help to have a tool in which all tasks currently workable by the team are visible. Such an overall team work items board should identify tasks in progress, as well as backlogged, ordered by priority, and it should include both project work *and* operational tasks. If your team implements agile software development principles, then such an overall work items backlog can be very useful during sprint planning. For example, we have worked in teams that decided to have an "all hands on deck" sprint dedicated to clearing out a backlog of important operational issues, after explaining the impact of addressing long-standing operational problems to the TPM, who then in turn successfully communicated to the business stakeholders that project work would temporarily be put on hold.

Under ordinary circumstances, though, all work items in the operational backlog should only be handled by the people on call. As mentioned before, this is important for shielding the rest of the team from distractions, so they can be more focused when contributing feature work. While on-calls should the only people allowed to contact the rest of the team for help with operational issues, they should still use this tool wisely to respect the team's overall productivity.

Features to Look for When Picking a Trouble Ticket System

When choosing the right toolset for managing operational support it is important to understand the use cases you envision your organization to have. Once you understand your needs, you can research the features of existing trouble ticket systems that cover your use cases directly, or at least allow for customization. Following are the features we find most important when working with trouble ticketing systems in a microservices organization:

- **Company-wide use:** Make sure the entire company has access to the list of operational issues, past and ongoing, so that research about outages can be performed without unnecessarily contacting and distracting on-calls. On a related note, we recommend *not* to expose the internal trouble ticket communications directly to external customers, as you do not want to burden the fire-fighting on-call people with public relations concerns, or matters of inadvertently exposing classified information or hints about security vulnerabilities.

- **Tracking by severity:** A view of the list of issues, with the ability to sort and filter by a user-assigned severity, is essential. The on-call person can use this view to guide her decisions about which issue to work on next, while (internal) customers can understand the severity attached to an issue they are following, and how much workload is placed on the team's on-call.

- **Tracking by SLA:** Trouble ticket systems need a way to attach expected and agreed-upon deadlines for their resolution. It would be great to make these fields mandatory and potentially even prepopulated based on the ticket's impact severity. This way, the team can communicate a date to the customers which they can use for their own planning purposes. Additionally, on-call people should be able to sort tickets by proximity to their respective deadlines, so that they can make sure to meet the issue's resolution timeline based on the team's published operational SLAs.

- **Help in identifying issue owner:** In an environment with hundreds of services and multiple teams, it is often not self-evident which team's on-call person should investigate an issue. The trouble ticket tool should be set up to guide the person filing the ticket in identifying the right team that can resolve the cause of the problem. As a corollary, the ticket system should allow for reassignment of issues, in case it was previously misassigned.

- **Ticket history and searchability:** Trouble tickets should never be deleted, even when they are closed or resolved. This helps in being able to search the ticket database during issue analysis and severity assessment. Also, all changes to a ticket's properties, as well as comments, status updates, changes in assignee or impact severity, and the like, should be logged in an audit trail entry, alongside a timestamp and handle of the acting user. This will help in later reviewing the exact timeline as part of a potentially triggered post-mortem (discussed later in this section).

- **Relating tickets:** It should be possible to relate tickets to each other. In particular, it should be able to tag a given ticket as being blocked due to another, related ticket. The team's on-call should be notified once the blocking ticket is resolved, so that she can make a decision about continuing work on the now unblocked task. To take this feature further, all internal customers should be able to subscribe to filterable status changes (like comments or updated severity), so that they don't need to waste time actively checking status.

- **Integration with on-call scheduling tool:** In order to correctly notify the team's current on-call person of new tickets, and all other ticket-related communications, the trouble ticket system should be able to find out which (set of) developer(s) to notify. If your team runs on-call duty via a rotation schedule, then you want to be sure that changes in the rotation are automatically picked up by the trouble ticket system, to avoid delay and confusion in tending to operational issues. Often, the tool that is used to administer the on-call rotation schedule is also in charge of alerting the on-call of high severity issues, and escalating to a potential secondary on-call person, or the team's manager. In that case, the trouble ticket system needs to be able to notify the on-call rotation system that new high-severity tickets have been filed, or that they are past their SLA date.

- **Integration with project work tracker:** We advise that each team have easy access to, and visibility into, *all* work that the team needs to handle. Having an integration point that relates trouble tickets to tasks inside the project work tracking tool helps to address these needs.

- **Integration with post-mortems:** We will explain the detailed contents and processes behind post-mortems later, but for now let's focus on the fact that outages of a certain severity trigger deeper research into possible actions to take to prevent similar outages from reoccurring. The action items identified in a post-mortem should manifest themselves in trouble tickets with the appropriate owner, severity, and SLA, and status updates need to be visible in the post-mortem tracking tool.

- **Reporting capabilities:** Many teams try to improve on dealing with operational workload, and you cannot improve in areas for which you have no metrics and measurements. Reports about new vs. resolved tickets per month, adherence to SLAs, and the services and features that are the heaviest contributors to operational issues are just some immediately obvious examples of reports your team would want to run. Many successful businesses (including Amazon.com) have very high visibility of trouble ticket reports, and the senior leadership level focuses on keeping operational churn low.

Analyzing all available trouble ticket systems is definitely not in the scope of this book, as the range of available features in each of them varies significantly. However, Wikipedia has an excellent overview and comparison page for issue tracking systems,[8] which not only lists most of systems, but also tries to show an updated feature matrix.

While we have worked with a fair number of trouble ticket systems over the course of our work experience, we have not come to find a tool that we could unequivocally recommend. That said, we have worked in organizations that have successfully employed and customized Atlassian's JIRA and BMC's Remedy to handle operational issues satisfying the majority of the use cases we've discussed.

Dashboards to Support Operations

Another essential tool for on-call duty is a set of dashboards that graph the behavior of the systems owned by, or of interest to, the on-call's team.

A service owning team should try to include metrics in dashboards that are based on at least two sources: data collected on the service-side, and data as seen from the service clients' perspective.

Good candidates for inclusion in a dashboard that focuses on service-side metrics are, for example:

- **Endpoint response times:** Add graphs per service API endpoint that track the API's response time as measured in the service application. Make sure to monitor not just average response times, but also the times in which 95%, 99%, or even 99.9% of all requests are processed.

- **Response times per client:** Draw the same response times per service API endpoint broken down by the client applications. As before, make sure to visualize not just average values, but also the outliers.

- **Call volume by endpoint:** Seeing the call frequencies for each API endpoint is very useful as a way to detect peak times, and to relate potentially longer response times to a root cause.

- **Call volume by client:** Displaying the API calls on a per-client basis is useful for analyzing sudden drops or surges, as they might indicate a client-side outage or unintended change in behavior. This is also very useful for verifying intended behavior in call patterns, for example, when a migration from a deprecated API to a new service API has been deployed and needs confirmation of having taken effect.

- **Error responses per code:** Seeing the number of error responses returned by a client can give you indications about bad data or other service-side outages.

- **Error responses per client:** If one particular client is affected by most error responses, then it is easier to pinpoint the client in which logic has changed causing bad requests, or requests for data that causes service-side data processing problems.

- **Messages consumed and published:** If your service relies on consuming or publishing messages on an internal message bus, then visualizing metrics about the frequency of messages consumed or published on each of the relevant topics is useful information to observe.

---

[8]"Comparison of issue-tracking systems" Wikipedia. https://en.wikipedia.org/wiki/Comparison_of_issue-tracking_systems

- **Business metrics:** Tracking business metrics around purchase rates, number of new customers, number of comments or reviews, and so on gives very expressive feedback and can help uncover problems that remain undetected when simply tracking the proper functioning of the technology involved. They can also help track down the root cause for changes in other metrics (like call volumes or service response times), or provide good indications for when planned outages or feature launches can be least impactful or risky (for example, to launch changes to the comment-service between 2AM and 4AM Eastern time because business metrics show that this is the period when the fewest customers post comments on the site).

Figure 14-1 shows operational metrics for an internal service in LivingSocial's infrastructure. The metrics shown are extracted from service-side logs, aggregated and graphed using Splunk's operational intelligence and log management tool.

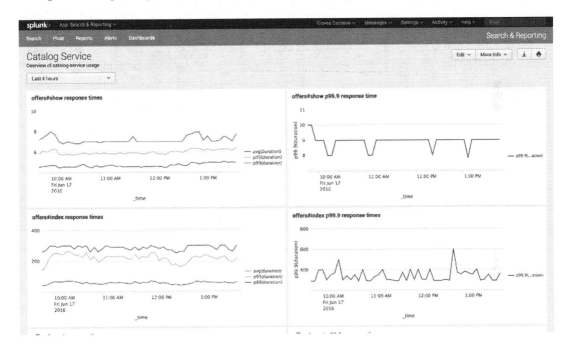

Figure 14-1. *Splunk dashboard showing service-side log-based real-time metrics*

Client-side metrics that can help track down issues with a service can include:

- **Client-side error code data:** Tracking success and failure rates of requests to the service inside a particular client can be used to alert a team to outages in a dependency, or indicate that a client-side library update did not go as expected.

- **Client-side performance data:** The service performance data that matters the most is how it is perceived inside the client. Clients care deeply about the SLAs of their service dependencies, as their own responsiveness often is directly tied to their dependencies being performant.

- **Object deserialization costs:** Wrapping code that turns the wire format of transmitted data back into programming language objects might indicate that perceived service slowness is in fact more accurately rooted in slow deserialization in the client, which might be fixed by requesting smaller response objects from the service.

- **Timeouts:** While dependency timeouts should not lead to cascading issues, they are a welcome indicator for why the clients' own functionality might degrade.

- **Circuit breaker status:** Getting an overview of all open circuits for a client can help to identify which circuit settings might be overly stringent, or which dependency teams should be consulted about SLA improvements.

The graphs shown in Figure 14-2 are part of a dashboard that displays operational data collected in the client library of the internal service shown in Figures 14-1. The data was collected using StatsD (`https://github.com/etsy/statsd`), and the dashboard tool Grafana (`http://grafana.org/`).

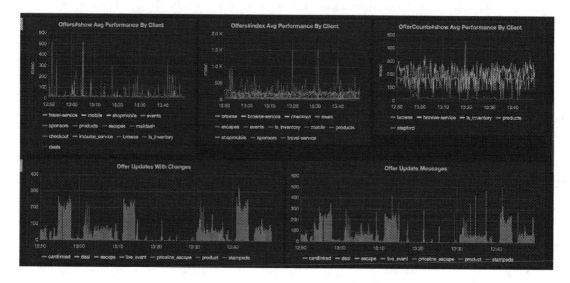

Figure 14-2. *Grafana dashboard for client-side metrics based on StatsD held data*

One reason for the usefulness of dashboards is that automated alarms to alert the team of exceptional behaviors are great when they work, but monitoring and alarming automation is never complete. Human intelligence often notices trends earlier and more reliably than algorithms do, and therefore can aid in detecting holes in alarming.

Some teams even go so far as to display the most important dashboards on large screens visible from their work and break room areas. The rationale for featuring these live metrics so prominently is that the cost involved is a good investment in raising awareness of how the system dashboards look under normal circumstances. Humans are incredibly efficient at pattern matching even when subconsciously observing visual clues, and we have seen engineers infer operational aberrations on numerous occasions simply by looking at out-of-the-ordinary patterns in graphs they regularly observe. As mentioned above, being suspicious and not shrugging of irregularities is an essential trait of someone taking on-call duty seriously.

Outage Etiquette

No matter how good your development and test processes are, outages *will* happen. The real question will be how quickly your team will be able to recover from the failure of a launched system. This section covers tuning your process for dealing with outages and working preparedness for these cases into your team's routines.

Every Pager Alarm is a Failure

An organization is well advised to consider every occasion when a pager goes off—and a person is potentially woken up—as a failure whose root cause needs fixing. An intrusive alert should not happen unless it is unavoidable because the underlying problem has not been identified and addressed.

If you start seeing every instance of a pager alerting as an exception to root out, then you do not run the danger of simply accepting it as a fact of life as an on-call. You will start to see delaying the true resolution as the only unacceptable course of action. Sweeping the issue under the rug via some rationalization you or someone else comes up with cannot be acceptable.

The very least you should do is to analyze whether the problem is truly worth alarming someone about, and you should not take the research lightly. If you and the team determine that the problem was *not* truly worth waking up someone, then you need to find ways to make the alarming rules smarter to improve on discerning between relatively benign issues and issues that cause a pager to alert.

If you do *not* address such "false positives" in your alarming, you will see that fatigue and indifference to alarms will set in, and truly impactful exceptions run the danger of being ignored. Additionally, having overly sensitive alerting rules that require your person on call to investigate in a very stressful and disruptive setting will burn out your developers, and you will see increased levels of attrition.

If your company implements a policy that humans can manually trigger pager alerts—for example, when they have reason to believe they noticed a significant outage that has not yet been brought to anyone's attention—then you need to set clear expectations about which class of issues are "pageable." Therefore, a team—or even better, company—policy for operational support and SLAs is essential to implement. We will discuss the contents of such a policy later in this chapter. It should be made clear that, for example, requests for information regarding behavior of a system or the existence of, or implementation request for, a given feature are not acceptable reasons to page an engineer.

On the other hand, engineers need to keep a professional attitude when being paged by a colleague, irrespective of the time of day or night the pager rings. Ask the reporter for enough details needed to investigate and reproduce the issue. It is very reasonable to require that a ticket exist for any issue that is worth being paged about, so make sure you insist on recording all information as comments in the trouble ticket. If the issue is serious enough, based on criteria also defined in your operational SLA policy, then such information will be essential when you have to create a post-mortem.

Playbooks for Operational Support

Imagine you are the team's on-call person, and your pager wakes you up at 3:00 AM. You are trying to adjust, wake up and not well enough rested to have all your mental capacity.

We have seen many teams address this problem by writing down *Standard Operating Procedures* (SOPs) in the form of step-by-step recipes, useful links, checks to perform or investigations to start. These are meant to be very explicit and easy to follow, so they can be consulted by an on-call person who is new, stressed out, or otherwise not in the best state of mind to analyze the root cause of an outage.

Here are a few things we encourage including in SOP playbooks:

- **Links to operational dashboards**: Quick access to an overview page for all operationally relevant metrics is very useful for analyze root causes of issues.

- **Links to access and error logs:** Looking at error traces and client access patterns is often invaluable when trying deal with an outage.

- **Contact information for owner team:** Links to communication channels (such as a Slack channel) where to discuss outages, contact information for subject matter experts.

- **Architectural overview:** Adding overview diagrams for the service's architecture and its main component and dependencies helps tremendously when attempting to reason about the cause for an outage, or where to best place a patch.

- **If-then scenarios:** This section lists known issues or previously experienced outages that could recur, keyed by how such issues usually manifest themselves, plus a checklist for verifying that the issue is encountered, and steps for fixing or mitigating. This is especially useful if it includes listing investigative steps for researching business alarms.

- **List of service dependencies:** In a massively distributed microservices environment it is unfortunately rather common that an on-call person receives an alarm that is caused by degradation of a service dependency. While circuit breakers should prevent cascading failures, it is still essential that the dependent team know about the situation. Links to trouble ticket boards of all service dependencies and the contact details for all service dependencies' on-call people should be easily found.

- **Health-check URLs:** Verifying that an issue is no longer present, or helping to reproduce an exception, include URLs or cURL statements for every feature or API endpoint in your service application.

- **Production server access details:** Sometimes problems can only be tracked down or reproduced by having direct access to the production hosts, where data or server condition can be checked or a service console needs to be opened. This also includes access to time-based jobs (such as `crontasks`) and their logs.

- **FAQs:** Answering often-asked questions about the way some functionality works can be made much more efficient when listing them in an easy to find section on the SOP page. Also, such a section can list recipes for common administrative tasks, for example, modifying data not exposed by an API, running diagnostics queries on a secondary database, or whitelisting new client applications.

Note that such playbooks are only useful if they are followed often, and maintained and updated when found outdated, incorrect, or lacking. Whenever you find them in such a state, either directly update, or add to them as part of following these instructions, or create a support ticket to take care of it in the near future.

What to Do When the Pager Goes Off

In a team that takes addressing and fixing operational issues seriously, no two outages are exactly the same, simply because the previous outage was fixed in a way that will not allow it to recur. It is still worth providing some general proven rules and behavioral patterns that are appropriate when being alerted about an urgent production issue.

First and foremost, there is no use in falling prey to the temptation of panicking. Being informed by a very loud alert about an impactful outage certainly gets your blood flowing, but that should only go so far as making you aware that your undivided attention is needed to investigate the issue. Dealing with production system failures needs to take the highest precedence for you *and* the rest of your team, so if you feel like you are stuck or ineffective in fixing the issue, then this is an "all hands on deck" situation, and the entire rest of your team can be pulled in to help.

Next, make sure that you acknowledge the alarm, so and others do not get unnecessarily alerted. Getting alerted over and over is just annoying and distracting, and consequently counterproductive to quick resolution of the problem at hand. In many pager-duty support systems, tickets escalate automatically when not acknowledged, so be respectful of other people on the escalation path.

Once you have acknowledged the alert, create a trouble ticket (unless it already exists) and do *just* as much research as it takes to be reasonably confident you know enough to either fix the root cause, or improve the situation significantly. If you find a quick route to improve conditions, then take it! This often buys you time to work on a more complicated fix in a less impactful setting.

If you are in the unfortunate position that you get woken up by an alarm, then feel free to patch as little as necessary to address the immediate problem, but *do* make sure to work on a more permanent fix once you are fully rested.

While you research root cause and potential fixes, take a small amount of time to update the trouble ticket whenever there is news to share. Do not feel obligated to answer questions about status or progress while you work on researching or otherwise addressing an issue. If the inquiries become distracting, inform the person inquiring politely that answering questions distracts you from resolving the issue. Most teams make it a point in their team policy for operation support to mention intervals in which an in-progress trouble ticket of a particular severity is updated. Try your best to adhere to such a published SLA, but favor acting on fixing the issue over updating the ticket.

If, on the other hand, you need help or information from other on-call people or other team members, do not hesitate to reach out to them. Unless they themselves are busy dealing with issues of the same or higher operational severity, they should make every effort to help you.

It is also important that in your role as on-call person you refrain from passing blame while an issue is being actively worked. The time to assess what went wrong and how it can be prevented from recurring is *after* the issue is no longer causing production issues. A post-mortem, which is discussed in the next section, is the best place for such analysis.

Supporting Tools

There are quite a lot of choices for tool support for the above-mentioned measures to establish a well-functioning operational emergency protocol.

SOP pages and playbooks should first and foremost be easily found. If your company has not already launched an internal tool to enable teams to self-publish documentation, then it is definitely worth evaluating tools like Atlassian's *Confluence* (https://www.atlassian.com/software/confluence) or a self-hosted Wiki (see http://www.wikimatrix.org/ for a site that lets you compare features of Wiki implementations).

As far as incident management and escalation tools go, we have personally had experiences with *PagerDuty* (in use at LivingSocial) and a heavily customized version of BMC's *Remedy* (in use at Amazon.com). Other alternatives include *VictorOps* (https://victorops.com/), *OpsGenie* (https://www.opsgenie.com/), and the open-source tool Openduty (https://github.com/ustream/openduty).

The main features we have found indispensable for such a tool to be effective are:

- An ability to acknowledge an incident and hence stop further alerting for it

- Being able to de-duplicate incidents, so that no more than one alarm is generated for the same issue

- The ability to integrate with a trouble ticket system for automatic ticket creation and relation

- The ability to maintain an on-call rotation schedule that allows correctly routing alarms to team members based on the current rotation shift

Another valuable feature, albeit in the nice-to-have category, is to offer integration points to group communication tools like email, Slack, or Campfire to alert all stakeholders of incident status.

How to Learn from Outages:—Post-Mortems

The best engineering organizations strive to achieve operational excellence by learning from past outages. A post-mortem can be a powerful instrument to achieve this goal.

Post-mortems—originally used in the context of medical examinations otherwise known as autopsies—generally refer to the process of assessing successes and failures of a task or process after its conclusion. In the realm of on-call duty and operational excellence, their main purpose and value is to help with identifying lessons learned from an incident with a large impact.

When Is a Post-Mortem the Right Tool?

Good indicators for the usefulness of a post-mortem are that:

- The issue that occurred, or could have occurred, is severe.

- The occurrence of the issue appears preventable at first sight.

- The root cause for the (near-)outage appears to need more research.

- The issue analysis is worth sharing with a wider audience or preserving for posterity.

We recommend creating a post-mortem for every high-impact incident of a severity level that is negotiated within the engineering organization. As a rough guideline, you should discuss the value of creating a post-mortem each time your team's on-call person gets paged, or *should* have been paged.

Additionally, it should be acceptable for anyone in the company to call for creation of a post-mortem, if she can argue that there is enough value to the business to outweigh the costs of going through the motions of a full post-mortem.

■ **Note** Try to make sure that post-mortems are not understood as punitive in your organization. It needs to be made clear that the reason for the effort involved is the chance to improve on what you do, and to prevent further operational issues.

Structural Elements of a Post-Mortem

While there is no globally accepted table of contents for a post-mortem, we strongly advise that your engineering organization adopt a template that is shared across all teams. The following list outlines such a template, listing the contents we suggest discussing as part of every post-mortem:

- **Action summary:** This lead-in contains a very brief, "executive summary" description of the outage that was dealt with and the actions that were taken to address the issue.

- **Business impact:** A very succinct, to-the-point synopsis of the loss to the business is mentioned in here, with calculations that are as accurate as currently possible. The loss could be in various areas, for example, negative revenue impact, exposure of sensitive data, or loss of customer trust.

- **Actors:** This section should include all people involved in causing or fixing the issue discussed.

- **Turn of events:** A post-mortem should lay out a detailed and accurate timeline of all relevant events, starting from the initiation of the outage (such as the deployment of unsafe code artifacts), all the way to the (potentially temporary) resolution of the underlying issue. All significant actions and findings should be included and attributed.

- **Successes:** In this part, the author of the post-mortem lists actions and practices that contributed to lessening the impact of the outage.

- **Root cause analysis:** This section starts out with a more in-depth technical explanation of the cause of the issue and continues by analyzing the actions and circumstances that contributed to causing the outage. We highly recommend using the *"Five Whys"* technique to aid in these efforts (see the accompanying sidebar).

- **Lessons learned:** Areas for improvements are identified and listed in this part, and they should be based on the results of the root cause analysis.

- **Action items:** The points listed in this section are concrete, actionable improvements. They should directly relate to the cause(s) of the outage, and they should explain how they help to fix the identified root of the problem.

THE FIVE WHYS[9]

The Five Whys symbolize a strategy for identifying the true cause-and-effect relationships at the heart of a problem, in an attempt to be sure which steps to take to truly fix the issue. At each stage of the ever-deeper drilling chain of questions about causality, the current level asks "Why?" referring to the cause of the previous step; that is, each stage forms the basis of the next step. The significance of the *Five* in the technique's name comes from the experience that—for the majority of problems initially researched—asking "Why?" down to the fifth level typically reveals the end of the causality chain.

Example of a *Five Whys* analysis:

What happened? The laptop computer did not start up.

1. *Why* (did the laptop fail to start up)? The battery is dead.

2. *Why* (is the battery dead)? The charger for the computer is not functioning.

3. *Why* (is the charger not working)? The power cable has broken.

4. *Why* (is the power cable broken)? The power cable was often rolled up, and hence friction caused it to disintegrate.

5. *Why* (was there a lot of friction)? The charger has a design that exposes sharp edges close to where the cable is meant to be fastened.

First used within the Toyota Motor Corporation, the *Five Whys* has been adopted by technology and engineering companies like Amazon.com. Its power lies in its simplicity and straightforwardness when trying to determine the true causes of problems.

---

[9]See "5 Whys," on Wikipedia, for more details about the origin and history of this technique. https://en.wikipedia.org/wiki/5_Whys

Post-Mortem Ownership

Every post-mortem has exactly one owner. The owner is *not* necessarily the same person or team who will work on addressing all action items identified as part of the post-mortem. Usually this role is filled by the author of the post-mortem, but often we seen the author's manager take on ownership of all post-mortems authored by his team.

The owner of the post-mortem is tasked with helping to identify and track all resulting action items. She creates trouble tickets for each of them, each of which has a deadline and a ticket owner (or owning team) associated with it.

The owner will chase all tickets to completion by the assigned teams, and then she will resolve the post-mortem itself. She will also notify all parties involved of the resolution, and will make sure that the finished document is stored in a searchable repository, so that the knowledge gained is usable in the resolution of future issues.

While this process of following up and coordinating post-mortem action item resolutions can be time-consuming, it is nevertheless of utmost importance to make the process useful; if follow-through is not taken seriously, then the post-mortem process is mostly ineffective and should most likely be dropped entirely, as it will then only incur costs for very little value in return.

Defining and Advertising Team Policy

A lot of what makes an organization achieve efficiency and excellence in operational matters is rooted in the quality of the processes and policies they apply to support the systems they own. This section will lay out which points should be addressed in a policy for operational excellence, and we will give examples of policy points we have seen work well in practice.

Impact Severity and SLAs

In order to improve focus and enable the on-call person to make decisions about which operational issue to work on at any given point in time, it helps to categorize trouble tickets by level of severity.

To do that, define a handful of distinct levels of severity and classify each of them with its level of impact. Additionally, assign a priority level to each severity level, so that client expectations can be set about the on-call person's attention to incidents in each severity category. For clarity, it usually also helps to add examples of outage situations that would fall into the specified severity and impact levels.

Figure 14-3 shows an example of how such incident severity, impact, and priority levels could be defined.

Severity level	Example	Impact	Example	Priority
1 - Business critical	• books.com down • 10% order drop over 5 minutes	Critical	• Loss of customer trust • Loss of revenue	High
2 - System/service critical	• Login not working	Major	• Loss of customer trust	High
3 - Group productivity impaired	• Blocked by external ticket • Missing product ownership	Moderate	• Delayed resolution • Delayed feature	Medium
4 - Individual productivity impaired	• Missing system permissions	Minor	• Team still functional	Medium
5 - No immediate impact to productivity	• Feature request	Cosmetic	• Customers not negatively impacted	Low

Figure 14-3. Definitions for issue impact and severity, with examples and priority levels

Once you have defined the severities, your customers need to know what level of service they can expect from your team. As a customer-focused team, you should set expectations for, and facilitate, communication with your customers. SLAs are an essential tool to achieve such customer focus, and they will also let you know when your on-call process is working and, more importantly, when it is not.

An example for a team SLA, based on incident severities, is shown in Figure 14-4.

Severity level	First contact	Update	Resolution
1 - Business critical	30 minutes	Hourly	1 Day
2 - System/service critical	30 minutes	Hourly	1 Day
3 - Group productivity impaired	24 hours	Daily	3 Days
4 - Individual productivity impaired	24 hours	Daily	1 Week
5 - No immediate impact to productivity	72 hours	Weekly	1 Month

Figure 14-4. SLA for first contact, updates, and resolution of incidents by severity level

The meaning of *first contact* in the SLA definition is the most important part of the issue lifecycle, next to resolution. This initial contact informs the client that the issue has been acknowledged. Without such an entry in your SLA, the wait time can be frustrating for your clients. With a defined SLA, it becomes clear when follow-up will be warranted. In addition to reducing client uncertainty, the SLA reduces unnecessary and inefficient back-and-forth, allowing the on-call person more time to focus on issue resolution.

Similar arguments hold for the *update* SLAs. Sometimes, resolving a trouble ticket can take the on-call person several days. Updating a ticket that is in progress serves a similar purpose to the first contact, as each update shows the client that their issue has not been abandoned. Updates that simply state that the efforts continue to be blocked still demonstrate strong ownership. By keeping your customers abreast of progress, anxiety and uncertainty is reduced.

Also advertise which type of incidents you consider worthy of analyzing in a post-mortem. You can use the severity level as an indicator (for example, all incidents of severity 1 and 2 trigger post-mortems), or you could take the stance that they apply mainly to more systemic issues that need to be addressed. As we have shown earlier in this chapter, a post-mortem is an effective tool to address process failures for systemic issues.

Publishing an SLA for issue *resolution* is the most important step for your clients, as it sets expectations they can rely on. If this underlying problem is blocking work on the client side, this expectation can help your customers identify risks in their own roadmaps.

While it is first and foremost the team's responsibility to set the SLAs and severities, the results need to be acceptable to the clients and other stakeholders in your company. Deciding whether an SLA or a severity judgement needs to be adapted is up to negotiations between your team and the internal customers, but it is very important to publish your policy up front.

Share the Steps of Your Process

Publishing the details of how your team goes about processing your operational issues helps clients to understand each phase involved in resolving an incident.

A sample list of steps could be as follows:

- **Generation:** When an operational issue for one of the systems owned by the team arises, a trouble ticket will be created and assigned to the correct on-call person. Make sure to advertise how to find the correct group in the trouble ticket system so that the ticket does not get misassigned and therefore might linger longer than needed.

- **Triage:** The team's current on-call person will investigate the issue to a level where he can assess its severity, and an appropriate label (such as SEV-3) will be added to the ticket.

- **Processing:** The on-call person is in charge of deciding which issues take priority, and hence will be worked at any given point in time. Decision guidelines for the on-call are based on issue severity and published SLAs, along with feedback from other team members and other engineers. All communication about a ticket's cause, technical details, and status will be captured in ticket comments. This mainly serves historical and documentation purposes. External inquiries about status should be kept to a minimum in order to avoid distracting the on-call from actually working on the issue's resolution. In return, the on-call aims to update ongoing issues based on the published SLAs, so that ticket stakeholders can be kept abreast of developments.

- **Resolution:** The team will strive to adhere to the published resolution SLAs, and it will alert stakeholders with as much advance notice as possible about any risks that could cause such deadlines to slip. Issues of severity 1 and 2 should automatically result in a post-mortem.

Finally, it is within each team's ability to customize its on-call policy, but strive to streamline the policies, process and SLAs across the entire company. This will help internal clients to have confidence that their issues will be addressed, that no time is lost trying to contact owners, and they can set their *own* customers' expectations correctly based on a generally accepted the process.

Summary

This chapter focused on all aspects of what it means to be part of a team that works under the "you build it, you run it" premise. After defining what operational support means, we explained what comes along with the obligations of true ownership for microservices.

Next we looked at the role of being on call for the services owned by your team. We discussed responsibilities for the on-call person, in relation to the rest of the team, as well as when serving client teams that rely on the software you own.

We also gave tips for how to organize and prioritize operational workload compared to the project work requests handled in a microservices team, and we discussed important features for tools that are meant to support the team's efforts to track both types of work.

After a brief examination of operational dashboards, we gave an overview of a practical approach to handling system outages when being the on-call person in charge.

We showed the importance of learning from outages, and walked through the process of analyzing such incidents using post-mortems.

We concluded this chapter by discussing the topic of defining and sharing a policy of how your team handles operational ticket work, and how to best set client expectations using SLAs and incident severity definitions.

Index

© Cloves Carneiro Jr. and Tim Schmelmer 2016

C. Carneiro Jr. and T. Schmelmer, *Microservices From Day One*, DOI 10.1007/978-1-4842-1937-9

Get the eBook for only $4.99!

Why limit yourself?

Now you can take the weightless companion with you wherever you go and access your content on your PC, phone, tablet, or reader.

Since you've purchased this print book, we are happy to offer you the eBook for just $4.99.

Convenient and fully searchable, the PDF version enables you to easily find and copy code—or perform examples by quickly toggling between instructions and applications.

To learn more, go to http://www.apress.com/us/shop/companion or contact support@apress.com.

Printed in the United States
By Bookmasters